The Changing Shape
of Metropolitan America:

DECONCENTRATION SINCE 1920

The Changing Shape of Metropolitan America:

DECONCENTRATION SINCE 1920

By AMOS H. HAWLEY

The Free Press, Glencoe, Illinois

FOREWORD

This monograph is the second report in a series dealing with patterns of growth and change in metropolitan areas of the United States, It was begun as a part of the Scripps Foundation's program of research in the field of population distribution, the funds for which were provided by the Rockefeller Foundation. A four year contract granted the Scripps Foundation For Research in Population Problems by the Housing and Home Finance Agency made it possible to greatly enlarge the scope and increase the detail of the work for the study. Hence the Housing and Home Finance Agency shares its financial sponsorship with the Rockefeller Foundation.

The first report, prepared by Dr. Donald J. Bogue, bears the title *Population Growth in Standard Metropolitan Areas, 1900-1950, with an Explanatory Analysis of Urbanized Areas.* In his study Dr. Bogue analyzed growth trends in metropolitan areas which in each census year, beginning with 1900, conformed to the 1950 definition of Standard Metropolitan Area. He observed the effects of size, regional location, and other factors on differential growth as between central cities and metropolitan rings. This study complements Dr. Bogue's in that it also treats population redistribution within metropolitan areas for the period 1900 to 1950. It differs, however, in giving close attention to the relation of population change to distance from central cities and in the selection of independent variables analyzed. These and other monographs to follow in this series are intended to provide a fuller knowledge of the patterns of and factors associated with metropolitan development than has been available heretofore.

The author wishes to express his indebtedness to Dr. Warren Thompson and Dr. Donald J. Bogue for their assistance in the preparation of this monograph. Mr. Howard Brunsman, Dr. Henry Shryock, and their colleagues in the Population Division, U. S. Bureau of the Census, gave substantial aid to the research on numerous occasions.

Sarah Jacobson, Thelma Batten, Lois Pratt, Leo Schnore, and Maria Cohn performed the statistical operations required. Marian Rickel typed the manuscript. All offered many helpful suggestions for improving the monograph.

Amos H. Hawley
Ann Arbor, Michigan
October, 1955

CONTENTS

CHAPTER I

INTRODUCTION

Few phenomena are more representative of the trend of modern society with its increasing emphasis on large-scale organization than is the emergence and rapid development of the metropolitan community during the past fifty odd years. Following quickly upon reductions of the time and cost involved in local movements, which resulted from the introduction of the motor vehicle and the hard-surfaced road, improvements in the transmission of electric power, the telephone, the radio and more recently television, the urban community burst its narrow bounds and expanded over the surrounding country.[1] In contrast to the compact city of the nineteenth century the radial scope of which seldom exceeded ten miles, the expanded or metropolitan community embraces in a single organization the cities, villages and other minor civil divisions lying within a radial distance of thirty-five miles or more from a central or core city. This new type of unit has assumed a dominant position in the urban settlement pattern of the United States.

The growth of metropolitan population has been one of the most conspicuous features of population movement in the United States during the first half of the twentieth century. In every decade since metropolitan areas[2] were first identified and reported separately in census volumes the part of the population so classified has maintained a higher growth rate than has any other part of the nation's population. As may be observed in Table 1, the rate of metropolitan population growth exceeded, in almost every decade, the rate of total population growth by 50 percent or more, and it exceeded the growth rate of population residing outside of metropolitan areas by 100 to 300 per cent. Thus, in contrast to the 40 per cent of the total population that was classified as urban in 1900, the 168 metropolitan areas in 1950 contained 56 per cent of the nation's population, or about 86 million people. The United States population is living, to an increasing extent, in community aggregates of unprecendented size.

TABLE 1. PER CENT CHANGE OF POPULATION IN THE UNITED STATES, IN METROPOLITAN AREAS, AND IN AREA OUTSIDE OF METROPOLITAN AREAS, 1900-1950

Type of place	1940-1950[a]	1930-1940[b]	1920-1930[b]	1910-1920[b]	1900-1910[b]
Total United States population	14.5	7.2	16.1	14.9	21.0
All metropolitan areas reported	22.0	8.1	28.3	26.9	34.6
Central cities	13.9	5.1	22.3	25.2	33.6
Satellite areas	35.6	15.1	44.0	32.0	38.2
Area outside metropolitan areas	6.1	6.5	7.9	9.6	16.4
Number of metropolitan areas	168	140	97	58	44

[a] Seventeenth Census of the United States.

[b] W. S. Thompson, The Growth of Metropolitan Districts in the United States: 1900-1940. (Washington, D. C., U. S. Government Printing Office, 1947).

Just as interesting, however, is the fact of differential growth, or population redistribution, within metropolitan areas. It is to be noted in Table 1 that the ratio of central city growth to satellite growth has tended to become progressively smaller. High growth rates, in other words, have shifted from the centers to the outlying parts of metropolitan areas. Consequently the proportion of metropolitan population occupying satellite area has increased steadily from 23 per cent, in the 44 districts reported in 1910, to 42 per cent in the 168 areas of 1950. Table 2 describes that trend.

TABLE 2. PER CENT DISTRIBUTION OF POPULATION IN METROPOLITAN AREAS, BY TYPE OF PLACE, 1910-1950

Type of place	1950[a]	1940[b]	1930[b]	1920[b]	1910[b]
Metropolitan areas	100.0	100.0	100.0	100.0	100.0
Central cities	58.4	68.0	69.1	74.4	76.7
Satellite areas	41.6	32.0	30.9	25.6	23.3
Number of metropolitan areas	168	140	97	58	44

[a] Seventeenth Census of the United States.

[b] W. S. Thompson, op. cit.

The enlarged scale of community size presents many problems most of which seem to arise from the dislocations and stresses incident to unequal rates of change. Urban expansion has involved both (1) a release of industry, residence, and related activities from close confinement in a comparatively small area and (2) a reorientation of the activities of the population occupying areas recently brought within daily access of the central city. Apparently such changes encounter a relatively slight inertia, for they began immediately and their effects have accumulated rapidly. Quite different has been the experience with the capital equipment of urban living, with forms of local government, and with other institutional systems. These have been slow to adapt to the altered situation, tending rather to persist in their early patterns. Hence large sections of metropolitan areas have lacked adequate roads, public water and sewage facilities, and buildings to house community service; the multiplicities of government units have preserved administrative confusion and revenue inequities; and welfare and many other institutions have made only belated attempts to serve the more widely scattered populations. The disparity between the actual scope of the metropolitan community and the development of its service structure constitutes a problem of major importance. But a proper measure of its magnitude as well as decisions concerning how the problem should be treated require more detailed knowledge of the trends and patterns of redistributions within metropolitan areas than has been available to date.

In this study attention is directed to the analysis of population redistribution within metropolitan areas. Although population redistribution is but one phase of the general movement that is involved in the maturation of metropolitan communities, it is more readily accessible to observation than are many other relocation tendencies. Population change, moreover, is one of the most precise indicators of social change.

Metropolitan population redistribution has been treated broadly in various reports.[3] Here, however, the amount and rate of redistribution will be examined with special reference to distance from central city. The growth of metropolitan organization, it has been pointed out, has resulted from the conquest of distance as a barrier to community size. It was noted also that the reduction of the limiting effects of distance has made possible an extension of the radius of community area from about ten to approximately thirty-five miles. Those radii are approximate maximum distances that can be travelled in an hour's time with the transportation facilities available in the respective periods. It is helpful to think of distance as a friction, which, though it can be reduced by technological improvements, may never be eliminated. The friction mounts with additions to distance, assuming a given transportation technology; that is, the time and energy that must be expended to pass over space increase as the space to be overcome is lengthened. Hence the familiar gradient pattern observed in the spatial distributions of community components. Thus it might be expected that the gradients plotted for the distributions of metropolitan population at successive intervals from a selected date, 1900 for example, would tend to grow longer and flatter. But space is not the only source of friction. The time and energy consumed in moving from point to point may be increased over what would be required on an unobstructed plane by obstacles of various kinds, such as hills, rivers and other topographic features. Urban communities develop a unique friction known as traffic density or congestion. The efficiency of modern forms of transportation and communication may be, in fact are, reduced well below their potentials by traffic density. A friction of this kind may operate as both a propulsive factor, encouraging the deconcentration of dense aggregates, and a limiting factor on the linear extent of deconcentration. In any event, there is no simple way of anticipating a priori the emerging pattern of population distribution in metropolitan areas.

The distance involved in the deconcentration of metropolitan population impinges upon the economics of metropolitan development at many points. It describes the areas of shifting housing demand, it affects the feasibility of extending municipal utilities to unserviced localities, and it indicates the dimensions of the changing market for services of all kinds, to mention but a few examples. Intelligent planning of metropolitan communities, therefore, demands as full a knowledge of the scope of population redistribution as can be obtained.

The Problem and the Data

Specifically, this monograph analyzes population redistribution trends in the United States, from 1900 through 1950, by distance from central city, by type of satellite unit, and by selected characteristics of areas, for all metropolitan areas identified in the census of 1950 and for which comparable data for two or more census years are available. The characteristics employed as independent variables include: size of central city; growth rate of central city; proximity of central cities to one another; geographic location of central city; amount of manufacturing employment in area; industrial relocation trend; and regional location.

All data employed in the investigation of the problem as stated are taken from official publications of the Bureau of the Census. The population data are derived from the Series 1 tables which show total population figures for states and minor civil divisions. The location of areas and the delimitation of zones are based on the State and Minor Civil Division maps prepared by the Geography Division of the Bureau of the Census. Various other Bureau of the Census publications, particularly the Census of Manufactures, are used for the classifications of metropolitan areas.

The Definition of Metropolitan Area

Two definitions of metropolitan area are employed in the analysis, one termed the Standard Metropolitan Area and the second described as the Extended Metropolitan Area. The former represents a new concept of metropolitan area introduced into the Census of Population in 1950. It replaces the older Metropolitan District term which had been in use from 1910 through 1940. The latter, that is, the Extended Metropolitan Area, was developed for purposes of the present study and for reasons to be discussed in later paragraphs.

The definition of the Standard Metropolitan Area is stated as follows:

A standard metropolitan area contained at least one city of 50,000 or more in 1950, and each city of this size is included in one standard metropolitan area.....When two cities of 50,000 or more are within 20 miles of one another they have ordinarily been included in the same standard metropolitan area. .....In general, each standard metropolitan area comprises the county containing the city and any other contiguous counties which are deemed to be closely economically integrated with that city.

Contiguous counties are included in a standard metropolitan area when they qualify on two types of criteria. One type is concerned with the character of the county as a place of work for nonagricultural workers and with the density of population, The other type is concerned with the extent to which contiguous counties are socially and economically integrated with the central city. Specifically, these criteria are:

1. The county must have
   a. 10,000 nonagricultural workers, or
   b. 10 percent of the nonagricultural workers in the standard metropolitan area, or
   c. At least half of its population residing in contiguous minor civil divisions with a population density of 150 or more per square mile.
2. Nonagricultural workers must constitute at least two-thirds of the total employed labor force of the county.

3. There must be evidence of social and economic integration
of the county with the central city as indicated by such
criteria as the following:

   a. 15 percent or more of the workers residing in the
contiguous county work in the county containing the
largest city in the standard metropolitan area, or

   b. 25 percent or more of the persons working in the
contiguous county reside in the county containing the
largest city in the standard metropolitan area, or

   c. An average of four or more telephone calls per sub-
scriber per month from the contiguous county to the
county containing the largest city in the standard
metropolitan area.

In New England, where the city and town rather than the county
were used to define standard metropolitan areas, the first and second
criteria set forth above could not be applied. In their place, a
population density criterion of 150 or more persons per square mile,
or 100 or more persons per square mile where strong integration was
evident, has been used.[4]

On the basis of this definition, 168 Standard Metropolitan Areas in
continental United States have been identified.

On the supposition that the scope of the Standard Metropolitan Area
may not be adequate to encompass the full range of metropolitan influence,
and as a test of that probability, the concept of the Extended Metropolitan
Area is also used. This is an area having the same central city as the
Standard Metropolitan Area, and includes all counties, or, in New England,
all minor civil divisions, with centers within 35 miles of the inner core of
the central city. There are thus as many Extended Metropolitan Areas as
Standard Metropolitan Areas. Beyond its use as a test of the adequacy of
the Standard Metropolitan Area concept, the Extended Metropolitan Area
has independent value in description of the scope of metropolitan influence. The mass of detail involved in duplicating all tabulations for both
concepts, however, would soon become so great as to invite confusion.
Hence the analysis of Extended Metropolitan Areas is carried only into
Chapter III.

The locations of the central cities of the 168 metropolitan areas are
shown in Fig. 1.

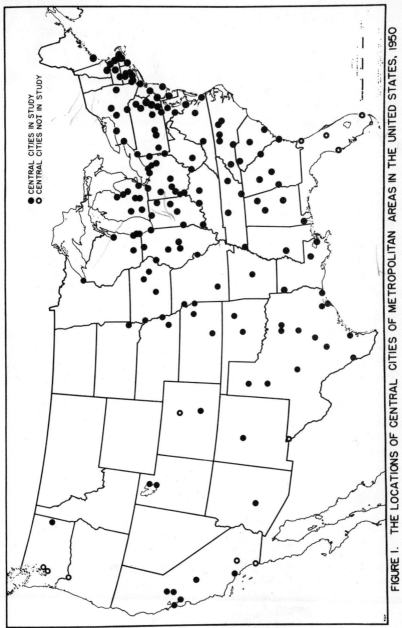

FIGURE I.   THE LOCATIONS OF CENTRAL CITIES OF METROPOLITAN AREAS IN THE UNITED STATES, 1950

Number of Metropolitan Areas in Study

The definitions stated above are applied uniformly in all decades, though many of the areas were not identified as metropolitan in earlier years and many could not have qualified as metropolitan even on the basis of the liberal census definitions of 1940 and 1950. Nevertheless, it has not been possible to include all 168 areas; in fact, the number of areas in the study differ from one decade to the next in the following manner:

Decade	Number
1940-50	143
1930-40	157
1920-30	155
1910-20	153
1900-10	148

Several circumstances are responsible for this. For example, since Oklahoma, New Mexico, and Arizona were not organized as states until after 1900, no data for minor civil divisions are available until later censuses A more important factor affecting the number of metropolitan areas in the study, however, is the practice in some States of frequent redistricting of minor civil divisions, thus eliminating any possibility of comparability between succeeding census years. For this reason eleven metropolitan areas are completely excluded from this study. Some metropolitan areas, notably Los Angeles, are included for only the latter part of the 50-year period because of extensive redistricting in earlier years. On the other hand, fourteen areas, which are included from 1900 to 1940, are omitted for the 1940-50 decade. The metropolitan areas in the study, together with selected characteristics of the areas, are shown in Appendix Table 1.

The Measurement of Distance

Distance from the central city is measured from the approximate site of the city hall of the central city and is expressed in 5-mile intervals. Where two or more central cities are recognized by the Bureau of the Census, the city hall location of the largest city is used as the center. In the few instances in which the companion central cities are of about equal size a point midway between them is selected as the center.

In many metropolitan areas it is possible to identify eight distance zones, beginning with 0-5 miles and ending with 35 miles and over. The exceptions occur where metropolitan areas are surrounded by other metropolitan areas whose centers are less than 75 miles distant and by coastal waters less than 35 miles distant. The New Britain-Bristol metropolitan area, for example, has but a 15-mile radius. Similar limitations of territory occur in other New England metropolitan areas.[5] It should be noted also that, as a result of proximity of central cities as well as of bodies of water, the concentric zones are rarely full circles. Fig. 2, which shows the metropolitan areas and their respective distance zones in northeastern Ohio, illustrates the interruption of zones. As a result of these two kinds of limitations the amount of land area in each distance zone is less than is to be expected in fully circular belts. Thus, as may be observed in Table 3, the proportion of the expected square miles of area contained in each zone declines rapidly with distance. Even the 0-5 mile zone contains no more than four-fifths of the land area expected, a consequence of the location of many central cities on water edges. The greater inclusiveness of the Extended Metropolitan area is apparent.

TABLE 3. EXPECTED AND ACTUAL NUMBER OF SQUARE MILES IN 157 METROPOLITAN AREAS, BY DISTANCE ZONES, 1940

Distance zone	Expected number of square miles	Actual number of square miles		Proportion that actual is of expected	
		Standard Metropolitan Areas	Extended Metropolitan Areas	Standard Metropolitan Areas	Extended Metropolitan Areas
Central cities	4,944	4,944	4,944	100	100
0 - 5 miles	7,691	6,007	6,158	78	80
5 - 10 "	37,052	26,761	30,174	72	81
10 - 15 "	61,701	33,848	50,900	55	82
15 - 20 "	86,350	28,552	63,755	33	74
20 - 25 "	110,999	26,263	77,375	24	70
25 - 30 "	135,648	12,413	71,338	9	53
30 - 35 "	160,297	7,854	ᴜ,832	5	39
35 miles and over	184,946	22,132	92,934	12	50
Total	789,628	168,774	460,410	21	58

Two distance zones require special com   0-5 mile zone is defined to include only that part of the area   mile radius that lies outside the incorporated boundaries of   v. Hence in the

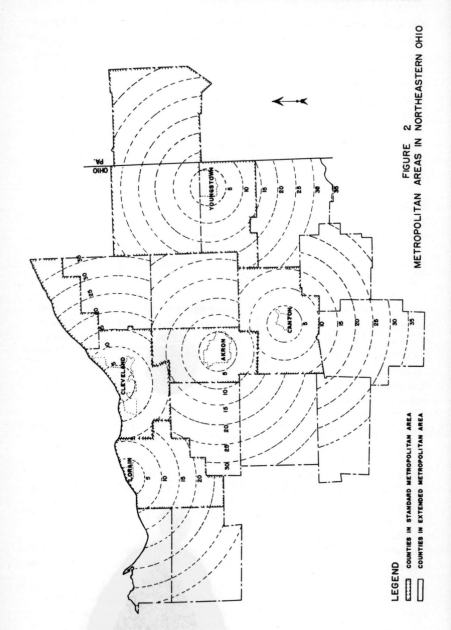

LEGEND

COUNTIES IN STANDARD METROPOLITAN AREA

COUNTIES IN EXTENDED METROPOLITAN AREA

FIGURE 2

METROPOLITAN AREAS IN NORTHEASTERN OHIO

Cleveland area, shown in Fig. 2, the 0-5 mile zone contains but .7 square mile in contrast to an average of 48.9 square miles. An even more extreme case is that of the Chicago area in which the central city occupies all of the area within 5 miles of the city hall and, as does the city of Cleveland, extends into the 5-10 mile zone. Thus the 0-5 mile zones differ in area with variations in the amounts of area contained in central cities. The 35 mile and over zone is of irregular size by virtue of its being an open-ended class. It comprises the parts, that lie more than 35 miles from central cities, of all counties that (a) are included in Standard Metropolitan Areas and (b) are included in Extended Metropolitan Areas, i.e., the centers of which are within 35 miles of central cities.

The area and population of each distance zone are the same as those in the minor civil divisions, e.g., incorporated places, townships, towns, precincts, etc., the centers of which are within the specified distance from the core of the central city. Consequently, the area and the population attributed to each zone differ from what they would be if it were possible to apply a rigorous mileage measure. Such errors, however, tend to cancel one another in averages for a number of metropolitan areas.

The preservation of comparability of distance zones from one census year to another is complicated by numerous minor civil division boundary changes resulting from annexations, consolidations, and redistrictings. Reference has been made already to the effects of broad scale changes of boundaries on the number of metropolitan areas that lend themselves to a given definition. There are also many occasional changes which in general present a less serious problem, for the information required in the making of adjustments is frequently available.

The corrections for boundary changes result in two tabulations of population by distance zones for each decade: one for the end of the decade which states the population distribution as enumerated in the census of that year, and one for the beginning of the decade which states the distribution of population of the preceding census year as it would have been if minor civil division boundaries had been as they were at the end of that decade. Appendix Table 2 shows the total populations for the beginning and the end of each decade for all of both Standard and Extended Metropolitan Areas. Caution should be observed in the use of these absolute numbers. Because the number of areas changes in each successive decade, figures for total populations are comparable only as between the beginning and the end of a given decade.

CHAPTER II

POPULATION REDISTRIBUTION WITHIN ALL METROPOLITAN AREAS

Central Cities and Satellite Areas

The general tendency has been for the rate of growth of metropolitan population to decline through the 50 years since 1900. As may be observed in Table 4, the trend has followed the same pattern, though at different levels, in both Standard and Extended Metropolitan Areas. In both classes of areas the trend has been erratic, reflecting the influences of a number of historic events on population growth and distribution.

A more consistent trend, noticeable in Table 4 and shown graphically in Fig. 3, may be described as a shift of high growth rates from central cities to those parts of metropolitan areas not included in central cities, commonly referred to as satellite areas. The deconcentration movement is not conspicuous, however, until after 1920. The sharp reductions in growth rates in 1910-20 below those of 1900-10 doubtlessly are a consequence of the curtailment of foreign immigration incident to World War I. Although foreign immigration was not resumed on its former scale in the 1920-30 decade, the continued decline of central city growth rates was brought about by the preemptive increase of satellite rates. Again in 1930-40 metropolitan rates of increase were depressed by a failure of migration, though this time it was a failure of rural to urban migration which after 1920 had replaced foreign migration as a source of urban population growth. The absence of job opportunities in urban areas during the 1930's removed a primary incentive to urbanward migration. But depression conditions appear to have provoked an acceleration of the centrifugal[1] movement to satellite areas, for the difference between central city and satellite growth rates widened during 1930-40. And in the 1940-50 decade an equivalent difference remained despite the resumption of relatively rapid increase of metropolitan population. Deconcentration was more pronounced in Standard than in Extended Metropolitan Areas.

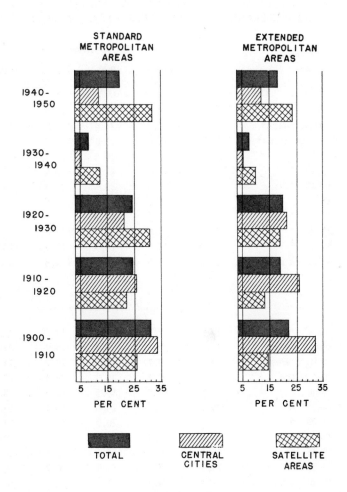

FIGURE 3

PER CENT CHANGE OF POPULATION IN METROPOLITAN AREAS, 1900-1950

TABLE 4. PER CENT CHANGE OF POPULATION IN STANDARD AND EXTENDED METROPOLITAN AREAS, BY TYPE OF PLACE AND DISTANCE FROM CENTRAL CITY, 1900-1950

Distance zone	Standard Metropolitan Areas				
	1940-50	1930-40	1920-30	1910-20	1900-10
All area*	19.7	8.0	24.9	24.5	29.4
Central cities*	11.8	5.1	21.4	25.9	31.5
Satellite areas*	31.6	12.6	31.0	22.2	26.0
0-5 miles	23.6	10.4	26.3	29.3	27.9
5-10 "	36.3	15.0	41.2	23.4	29.4
10-15 "	32.2	11.6	25.4	20.3	24.9
15-20 "	32.9	13.4	32.7	21.8	22.9
20-25 "	30.6	13.5	34.9	20.8	24.1
25-30 "	23.2	9.6	24.2	19.0	23.7
30-35 "	36.8	11.0	17.5	15.6	14.2
35 miles and over	27.2	9.5	18.7	9.3	25.2

	Extended Metropolitan Areas				
All area	17.7	7.4	20.1	19.1	21.9
Central cities	11.8	5.1	21.4	25.9	31.5
Satellite areas	23.2	9.7	18.9	13.2	14.7
0-5 miles	23.6	10.4	26.3	29.3	27.9
5-10 "	35.8	14.7	39.5	22.5	27.9
10-15 "	29.9	10.8	21.6	16.9	19.8
15-20 "	24.5	10.2	20.0	12.2	13.1
20-25 "	18.5	8.9	14.1	8.2	10.0
25-30 "	12.6	6.7	8.1	7.3	8.2
30-35 "	11.9	5.7	7.0	6.7	6.0
35 miles and over	9.4	4.4	5.5	4.3	8.1

*The differences between the figures in these rows and those reported by Donald J. Bogue in *Population Growth in Standard Metropolitan Areas, 1900-1950* (Washington: U. S. Government Printing Office, 1953) are due to (1) Bogue's inclusion of all metropolitan areas in contrast to the use in this study of only those for which comparable data could be assembled for the 50-year period, and (2) his substitution of county equivalents for New England metropolitan areas instead of using the town based areas as defined by the Bureau of the Census.

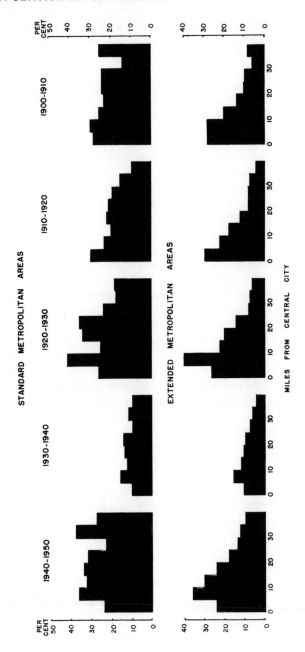

FIGURE 4

PER CENT CHANGE OF POPULATION IN METROPOLITAN AREAS, BY DISTANCE FROM CENTRAL CITIES,

1900 - 1950

The patterns of growth by distance zones, shown in Table 4 and Fig. 4, differ as between the two types of metropolitan areas. In the Standard Metropolitan Areas, growth rates show no consistent variation with distance from central cities. In the Extended Metropolitan Areas, on the other hand, there is a rather uniform gradient, i.e., growth rates decline with distance. The latter, which are considerably larger than the Standard Metropolitan Areas, permit a fuller expression of the effect of distance on metropolitan influence. Stated differently, the definition of the Standard Metropolitan Area tends to select the most rapidly growing portion of each distance zone.

Over the fifty year period high growth rates have moved outward. In 1900-10 the most rapidly growing parts of metropolitan areas were the central cities. In the next decade maximum growth rates occurred in the 0-5 mile zones. Peak rates of growth shifted to the 5-10 mile zones in 1920-30, where they remained through the last two decades. In the meantime population growth was accelerating in many of the more distant zones. But this is more adequately· demonstrated in a later connection. The declining rates of increases in the 0-5 mile zones cannot be attributed to the absorption of progressively larger proportions of the land and population of those zones by central cities, for boundaries have been held constant within each decade. It seems likely that the circumstances which have depressed population growth in central cities have operated also on their immediately adjacent areas. Changes in the 35 mile and over zones suggest an interesting possibility. It seems likely that population changes in areas beyond 35 miles of central cities in the early decades may have occured independently of events in the interiors of metropolitan areas. The distant areas may have remained in relative isolation from the influences of central cities until substantial improvements of highway transportation accumulated in subsequent decades.

Some of the variations in rates of population change from decade to decade undoubtedly result from variations in the growth rates of the total national population. If the rates of change in metropolitan areas are expressed in relative terms, as in Fig. 5, that source of disturbance is removed. Thus it may be observed that the ratios for central cities increased from 1900 to 1920 and then declined through the remainder of the period, falling below unity after 1930. The centrifugal movements of highest rates of change, noted above, is again apparent.

In the Standard Metropolitan Areas, growth rates in the satellite areas fall below those for the nation as a whole only in the earlies decades, and then only in the area beyond 30 miles from central cities. The ratios for

each distance zone beyond 5 miles from central cities tend to increase in each succeeding decade, though the 1930-40 decade remains an exception in all but the zones 30 miles or more from central cities.

Growth rate ratios in the Extended Metropolitan Areas display a somewhat more consistent tendency to increase in succeeding decades. Of greater importance, however, is the evidence of the changing scope of metropolitan influence as shown in the second panel of Fig. 5. In 1900-10 metropolitan growth rates exceeded that of the total United States population only within a radius of 10 miles of central cities. In zones beyond that distance growth rates were less than the national average. During the next four decades approximately 15 miles were added to the radius within which higher than expected growth rates occurred. Thus it appears that, measured on this basis, the radius of metropolitan influence has moved from 10 to 25 or 30 miles in the 50 year period.

A comparison of the rates of change in distance zones with those of central cities, as shown in Fig. 6, reveals the growing importance of the satellite area even more clearly. In 1900-10 the population of central cities increased more rapidly than that of any distance zone. In the next decade, 1910-20, the 0-5 mile zones alone had higher rates of increase than did central cities. As may be observed, the distributions of the ratios for the two types of metropolitan areas are quite similar for 1900-10 and 1910-20. After 1920 their distributions differ markedly. During 1920-30 the area within which the growth rate ratios exceeded unity reach to 30 miles in Standard Metropolitan Areas and to 15 miles in Extended Metropolitan Areas. In the two decades following 1930 the ratios were considerably higher than in preceding decades and the distances over which ratios greater than 1.0 obtained were increased, especially in Extended Metropolitan Areas. It is noteworthy that in the latter class of areas, satellite growth was more concentrated in 1940-50 than in 1930-40. The curve for 1930-40 rises above that for 1940-50 beyond the 20 mile zone. In other words, in the decade of slowest metropolitan growth, the depression years of 1930 to 1940, the relative rates of growth of satellite areas were exceeded only by those of the 1940-50 decade.

The centrifugal tendency in population redistribution within metropolitan areas is also reflected in the manner in which the amounts of change in each decade are distributed over the total area, as shown in Table 5. The proportion of all increase that occurred in central cities declined from three-fifths or more to one third in the five decades, and, of course, a complementary increase took place in satellite areas. While in 1900-10 and 1910-20 three-fifths to two-thirds of all growth occurred within the bounds of central cities, in 1930-40 and 1940-50 a 10-mile radius was required to

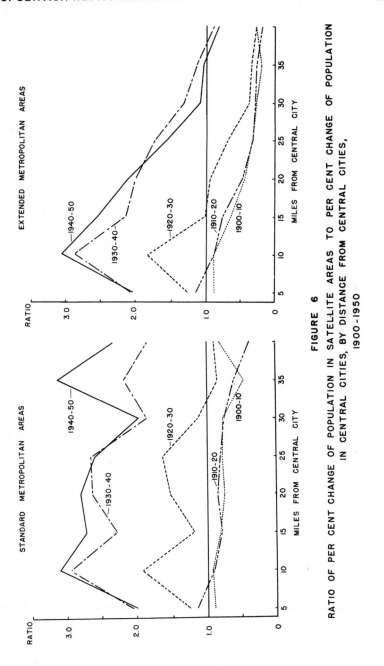

FIGURE 6

RATIO OF PER CENT CHANGE OF POPULATION IN SATELLITE AREAS TO PER CENT CHANGE OF POPULATION IN CENTRAL CITIES, BY DISTANCE FROM CENTRAL CITIES, 1900-1950

TABLE 5. PER CENT DISTRIBUTION OF AMOUNT OF POPULATION CHANGE IN STANDARD AND EXTENDED METROPOLITAN AREAS, BY DISTANCE ZONE, 1900-1950

Metropolitan Area and distance zone	Per cent distribution					Cumulative per cent distribution				
	1940-50	1930-40	1920-30	1910-20	1900-10	1940-50	1930-40	1920-30	1910-20	1900-10
Standard Metropolitan Areas	100.0	100.0	100.0	100.0	100.0					
Central cities	35.8	39.5	54.8	66.4	65.9	35.8	39.5	54.8	66.4	65.9
0-5 miles	7.5	8.0	6.5	7.2	6.0	43.3	47.5	61.3	73.6	71.9
5-10 "	22.6	21.6	16.6	10.0	10.6	65.9	69.1	77.9	83.6	82.5
10-15 "	14.4	12.3	8.6	7.2	7.8	80.3	81.4	86.5	90.8	90.3
15-20 "	8.7	8.3	5.9	4.1	3.7	89.0	89.7	92.4	94.9	94.0
20-25 "	5.0	5.0	4.0	2.4	2.4	94.0	94.7	96.4	97.3	96.4
25-30 "	2.2	2.2	1.7	1.4	1.6	96.2	96.9	98.1	98.7	98.0
30-35 "	1.8	1.3	.7	.6	.5	98.0	98.2	98.8	99.3	98.5
35 miles and over	2.0	1.8	1.2	.7	1.5	100.0	100.0	100.0	100.0	100.0
Extended Metropolitan Areas	100.0	100.0	100.0	100.0	100.0					
Central cities	32.2	34.2	52.0	62.5	61.2	32.2	34.2	52.0	62.5	61.2
0-5 miles	6.9	7.0	6.3	6.9	5.6	39.1	41.2	58.3	69.4	66.8
5-10 "	20.9	19.1	16.0	9.6	10.1	60.0	60.3	74.3	79.0	76.9
10-15 "	14.5	12.0	8.7	7.3	7.6	74.5	72.3	83.0	86.3	84.5
15-20 "	9.8	9.4	6.7	4.6	4.6	84.3	81.7	89.7	90.9	89.1
20-25 "	6.3	7.0	4.4	3.0	3.5	90.6	88.7	94.1	93.9	92.6
25-30 "	4.0	5.0	2.5	2.6	2.9	94.6	93.7	96.6	96.5	95.5
30-35 "	2.9	3.4	1.8	2.0	1.8	97.5	97.1	98.4	98.5	97.3
35 miles and over	2.5	2.9	1.6	1.5	2.7	100.0	100.0	100.0	100.0	100.0

contain a like amount of the total increments. The minimum area required to account for 90 per cent of all growth, however, changed very little for Standard Metropolitan Areas, shifting from an area with a radius of 20 miles to one with a radius of less than 25 miles. In the Extended Metropolitan Areas the radius of the area within which 90 per cent of the growth occurred varied from less than 25 to less than 30 miles. In other words, it appears that the centrifugal tendency, so far as amounts of growth are concerned, operated primarily within rather short distances. Of interest in this connection is the fact that that tendency was actually reversed in both classes of metropolitan areas, in 1910-20. Some evidence of reversal is also noticeable in the Extended Metropolitan Areas after 1940.

The effect of differential growth rates, of course, is to change the pattern of population distribution within metropolitan areas. As may be observed in Table 6, redistribution in Standard Metropolitan Areas moved toward increased concentration through the first 20 years of the 50 year period. After 1920 the prevailing movement was toward dispersion. But the shift in the direction of redistribution after 1920 applies only to the area within a 15 mile radius. Dispersion did not begin to operate in the more distant zones until after 1930.

The proportion of the total population found in central cities, when Extended Metropolitan Areas are employed as units of observation, increased to 1930, 10 years beyond the peak for central cities of Standard Metropolitan Areas. The distribution of population over the several distance zones of the satellite areas was fairly uniform in 1900. From that date to 1950 the prevailing tendency has been toward concentration, particularly within the 25-mile boundary. Thus, if increases in the population in the satellite area be regarded as indicating metropolitan influence, it would seem that the scope of metropolitan areas does not extend beyond 25 miles from the centers of central cities. On this basis it may be argued that, in 1900, metropolitan areas had not in fact emerged, and that their development involved, first, a growth of central cities and immediately adjacent areas, and subsequently, the growth of population in more remote areas within the 25-mile radius.

Although the difference in population distribution between the beginning and the end of the 50-year span is considerable, the amount of change from one census year to the next is fairly small. This is evident in Table 5. It is shown more clearly, however, by a summation of the positive or negative percentage point differences between the percentage distributions of two consecutive census years. The coefficient of redistribution[2], as that summation has been designated, indicates the proportion of the population that would have to be redistributed to make the distribution at the end

TABLE 6. PER CENT DISTRIBUTION OF POPULATION IN STANDARD AND EXTENDED METROPOLITAN AREAS, BY DISTANCE ZONES, 1900-1950

Type of metropolitan area and distance zone	Per cent distribution						Cumulative per cent distribution					
	1950	1940	1930	1920	1910	1900	1950	1940	1930	1920	1910	1900
Standard Metropolitan Areas	100.0	100.0	100.0	100.0	100.0	100.0						
Central cities	55.9	59.9	61.7	63.7	62.8	61.4	55.9	59.9	61.7	63.7	62.8	61.4
0-5 miles	6.5	6.3	6.1	6.2	6.1	6.3	62.4	66.2	67.8	69.9	68.9	67.7
5-10 "	14.0	12.3	11.5	10.0	10.4	10.6	76.4	78.5	79.3	79.9	79.3	78.3
10-15 "	9.8	8.9	8.5	8.4	8.7	9.1	86.2	87.4	87.8	88.3	88.0	87.4
15-20 "	5.7	5.1	5.0	4.5	4.6	4.8	91.9	92.5	92.8	92.8	92.6	92.2
20-25 "	3.5	3.2	3.0	2.8	2.8	2.9	95.4	95.7	95.8	95.6	95.4	95.1
25-30 "	1.9	1.8	1.8	1.8	1.8	2.0	97.3	97.5	97.6	97.4	97.2	97.1
30-35 "	1.1	1.0	.9	.9	1.0	1.1	98.4	98.5	98.5	98.3	98.2	98.2
35 miles and over	1.6	1.5	1.5	1.7	1.8	1.8	100.0	100.0	100.0	100.0	100.0	100.0
Extended Metropolitan Areas	100.0	100.0	100.0	100.0	100.0	100.0						
Central cities	45.9	48.3	49.6	48.9	46.0	42.4	45.9	48.3	49.6	48.9	46.0	42.4
0-5 miles	5.4	5.1	4.9	4.7	4.4	4.4	51.3	53.4	54.5	53.6	50.4	46.8
5-10 "	11.9	10.3	9.6	8.1	8.1	7.9	63.2	63.7	64.1	61.7	58.5	54.7
10-15 "	9.5	8.6	8.2	8.1	8.2	8.4	72.7	72.3	72.3	69.8	66.7	63.1
15-20 "	7.4	7.0	6.9	6.8	7.2	7.7	80.1	79.3	79.2	76.6	73.9	70.8
20-25 "	6.1	6.1	5.9	6.3	6.9	7.6	86.2	85.4	85.1	82.9	80.8	78.4
25-30 "	5.3	5.5	5.5	6.2	6.8	7.6	91.5	90.9	90.6	89.1	87.6	86.0
30-35 "	4.1	4.4	4.5	5.1	5.8	6.6	95.6	95.3	95.1	94.2	93.4	92.6
35 miles and over	4.4	4.7	4.9	5.8	6.6	7.4	100.0	100.0	100.0	100.0	100.0	100.0

of a decade identical to that of the beginning of the decade. Trends in
the rates of redistribution as measured by the coefficient of redistribution
are shown in Fig. 7 for both Standard and Extended Metropolitan areas.
The rate of redistribution in Standard Metropolitan Areas has accelerated
over the 50-year period, though that trend was offset in 1910-20 and again
in 1930-40. Contrariwise, the trend in the rate of redistribution within
Extended Metropolitan Areas moved steadily downward to 1940, and it is
of interest to note that the rate for 1930-40 fits the trend established in
the preceding decades. After 1940 the rate increased abruptly.

Size and Type of Satellite Place

In view of the increasing importance of the satellite area as a location of residence of metropolitan population, it is desirable to know the
trends of redistribution among the different sizes and types of places
comprising satellite areas. Two classifications are used in the following
analysis: incorporated and unincorporated. Incorporated places are not to
be confused with urban places; they include all localities listed in census
reports as having a distinct political identity, and they exclude all special
rule urban places and other unincorporated concentrations of population.

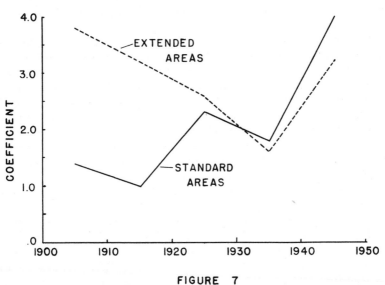

FIGURE 7

COEFFICIENTS OF REDISTRIBUTION, 1900-1950

The latter, despite their greater similarity to urban rather than to rural areas, lack the distinctness required for tracing them through five decades of change. Unincorporated places are included in all unincorporated area.

All satellite incorporated places with populations of 1,000 or more have experienced declining rates of growth, as may be seen in Table 7. The largest and most consistent declines have occurred in places of 25,000 or more population. In cities and towns with less than 5,000 population the rates of increase rose to 1930 and then subsided. Only in unincorporated area was there a constant trend of increase in growth rates. At the end of the 50 years the rate in unincorporated areas within Standard Metropolitan Areas was 160 per cent larger than that at the beginning of the period, while in Extended Metropolitan Areas the difference amounted to 260 per cent. Thus the increased rates of change in all satellite area, in 1940-50 over 1920-30, were entirely a function of rate increases in un-incorporated area. The same statement cannot be made, however, of the rate changes from 1900-10 to 1920-30, since incorporated places of less than 5,000 population also increased their growth rates during those decades.

A second aspect of change concerns the relationship of growth rate to size of satellite place. In 1900-10, growth rates varied directly with size of place, particularly in Extended Metropolitan Areas. By 1930-40 that pattern of association had been reversed, -- rates varied inversely with size of place.

Some insight into the basis of growth in satellite places may be gained from the data, in Table 7, showing the average number of incorporated places per metropolitan area. The two decades of slowest growth rates, 1910-20 and 1930-40, correspond to the periods in which the smallest changes in number of satellite places took place. On the other hand, the decades of highest growth rates are those in which the frequencies of incorporation were highest. It is probably unnecessary to point out that rate of population growth and rate of incorporation are, rather than cause and effect, doubtlessly companion effects of another factor or factors. The declines in the numbers of places of less than 1,000 population are due both to the growth into larger size classes and to the frequent annexation or disincorporation of such places.

The growth rates of all incorporated satellite population shown in Table 8 have declined and increased again in succeeding decades, following the pattern of all satellite population (see Table 4). A line drawn through the decades 1900-10, 1920-30, and 1940-50, however, describes a general tendency toward decline in all distance zones. The diminishing importance of incorporated areas in the growth of all satellite population

TABLE 7. RATE OF CHANGE IN SATELLITE AREA AND AVERAGE NUMBER OF INCORPORATED SATELLITE PLACES PER METROPOLITAN AREA, BY TYPE OF METROPOLITAN AREA AND SIZE AND TYPE OF SATELLITE PLACE, 1900-1950

Type of metropolitan area and size[a] and type of satellite place	Rate of Change					Average number of places per metropolitan area					
	1940-1950	1930-1940	1920-1930	1910-1920	1900-1910	1950	1940	1930	1920	1910	1900
Standard Metropolitan Areas	31.6	12.6	31.0	22.2	26.0	17.9	15.5	16.0	14.7	13.4	10.2
50,000 and over	10.8	1.2	13.1	17.5	35.5	.4	.3	.3	.2	.1	.1
25,000 - 50,000	12.0	2.7	31.2	21.9	37.1	.6	.4	.4	.3	.2	.1
10,000 - 25,000	19.4	7.9	30.0	34.1	32.4	1.7	1.2	1.2	.8	.6	.5
5,000 - 10,000	29.3	9.2	39.0	27.0	43.1	2.4	1.7	1.5	1.3	.9	.6
2,500 - 5,000	35.9	10.7	44.3	38.8	42.2	2.4	2.1	2.3	2.2	1.5	1.0
1,000 - 2,500	31.7	14.7	52.6	31.2	37.6	4.3	3.6	3.5	3.3	3.2	2.3
Under 1,000	32.2	14.0	36.3	21.5	30.6	6.1	6.2	6.8	6.6	6.9	5.6
Unincorporated area	47.6	21.8	31.5	17.3	18.0						
Extended Metropolitan Areas	23.2	9.7	18.9	13.2	14.7	40.4	37.2	37.0	33.8	33.2	28.0
50,000 and over	10.8	1.2	13.1	17.5	35.5	.4	.3	.3	.2	.1	.1
25,000 - 50,000	12.2	2.9	24.7	19.4	32.8	.8	.7	.6	.4	.3	.2
10,000 - 25,000	17.6	7.6	20.9	25.1	23.5	2.5	2.1	2.0	1.4	1.2	.9
5,000 - 10,000	23.3	8.0	27.8	21.3	31.0	3.5	2.9	2.6	2.1	1.8	1.4
2,500 - 5,000	27.7	10.2	29.6	28.6	27.0	4.3	3.8	3.8	3.6	3.1	2.7
1,000 - 2,500	23.3	10.1	29.7	18.6	21.5	9.7	7.8	7.6	7.5	7.2	6.2
Under 1,000	18.6	8.5	15.9	11.2	19.5	19.2	19.6	20.1	19.6	19.5	16.5
Unincorporated area	28.7	13.4	15.3	7.5	7.9						

[a] Places classified by size as of beginning of decade.

TABLE 8. RATES OF POPULATION CHANGE IN INCORPORATED PLACES AND AVERAGE NUMBER OF INCORPORATED PLACES PER METROPOLITAN AREA, BY TYPE OF METROPOLITAN AREA, AND DISTANCE ZONE, 1900-1950

Type of metropolitan area and distance zone	Rate of Change					Average number of places per metropolitan area					
	1940-50	1930-40	1920-30	1910-20	1900-10	1950	1940	1930	1920	1910	1900
Standard Metropolitan Areas	19.4	6.0	30.6	26.7	36.5	17.9	15.5	16.0	14.7	13.4	10.2
0-5 miles	7.6	2.7	20.4	25.4	31.4	1.8	1.5	1.6	1.4	1.4	1.1
5-10 "	19.9	6.4	37.9	27.6	42.0	4.0	3.3	3.4	3.0	2.7	2.1
10-15 "	24.8	5.4	26.7	26.8	36.5	4.1	3.5	3.6	3.3	2.9	2.3
15-20 "	27.4	10.5	45.9	32.7	38.4	3.0	2.7	2.8	2.6	2.4	1.6
20-25 "	14.3	8.4	32.1	26.3	41.5	1.9	1.7	1.7	1.6	1.5	1.1
25-30 "	17.9	5.4	27.6	28.5	29.5	1.2	1.2	1.2	1.1	1.0	.8
30-35 "	27.6	4.4	26.3	22.6	30.2	.7	.6	.6	.6	.6	.5
35 miles and over	16.1	4.1	16.0	11.7	28.2	1.2	1.0	1.1	1.1	.9	.7
Extended Metropolitan Areas	17.7	6.1	22.8	20.8	26.6	40.4	37.2	37.0	33.8	33.2	28.0
0-5 miles	11.6	2.6	20.7	24.0	31.1	1.9	1.8	1.7	1.5	1.5	1.2
5-10 "	19.5	6.5	36.4	26.8	38.4	4.4	4.0	3.8	3.2	3.0	2.4
10-15 "	23.8	5.5	24.3	25.5	33.2	5.5	4.9	4.9	4.3	4.2	3.5
15-20 "	21.6	9.4	30.5	23.8	25.0	5.8	5.5	5.4	4.9	4.7	3.9
20-25 "	14.7	7.4	18.8	16.0	22.6	6.0	5.4	5.5	5.1	5.0	4.3
25-30 "	14.6	7.0	14.1	16.1	20.3	5.9	5.4	5.4	5.1	5.1	4.3
30-35 "	14.6	6.2	12.5	12.6	14.3	4.7	4.5	4.5	4.3	4.3	3.8
35 miles and over	11.9	3.8	9.4	13.5	26.6	6.2	5.7	5.8	5.4	5.4	4.6

has been noted previously. It is also to be observed that maximum rates have been held, for the most part, within 20 miles of central cities. This inner portion of satellite area has contained in all census years at least 70 per cent of all incorporated places in Standard Metropolitan Areas, but less than 50 per cent in Extended Metropolitan Areas.

Figs. 8 and 9 describe growth rates for different sizes of places, by distance zone, for selected decades. Large increases of growth rates in unincorporated areas are apparent in all but the farthest distance zone. On the other hand, no clear trend of change in incorporated places of less than 1,000 population is observable. The gradient pattern of growth in this size class is clearly marked. With each increase in size above 1,000 population the tendency for growth rates to decline in later years becomes increasingly pronounced. In the largest size classes, 25,000 and over, while rates have been reduced, it also seems that high growth rates have shifted to more distant mile zones. In fact, in all sizes of incorporated places gradients have tended to flatten; that is, growth rates in outlying zones have approximated those in inner zones.

The data shown in Figs. 10 and 11, however, indicate that increases in growth rates, relative to central city rates, have occurred in all satellite places up to 5,000 population and in places of 10,000-25,000 population. In some of the largest satellites increases in relative rates have taken place in outlying distance zones. The largest changes occurred in the smallest places, and within 15 miles of central cities in most size classes of incorporated places. But the spread of metropolitan influence on the growth of satellite places is clearly revealed.

The effects of differential rates of change on the satellite composition of each distance zone are shown in Figs. 12 and 13. The proportion of the population in unincorporated area declined in every distance zone from 1900 through 1930. After that it increased, returning to its 1900 level only in the 0-5 mile zone. No doubt the post-1930 trends of increase in the unincorporated area beyond the 0-5 mile zone will continue in the decades after 1950. Incorporated places of less than 2,500 population in Standard Metropolitan areas contained a progressively smaller proportion of the population of each zone, the amount of the decline varying with distance from the central city. Satellite places of this size in Extended Metropolitan Areas, however, held a fairly constant share of the population of each zone. The proportion of the population contained in satellite places of the 2,500-10,000 class remained rather stable in the 0-5 mile zone but increased in all other zones. The largest changes have occurred in the proportion within satellites of 25,000 or more population particularly in outlying zones.

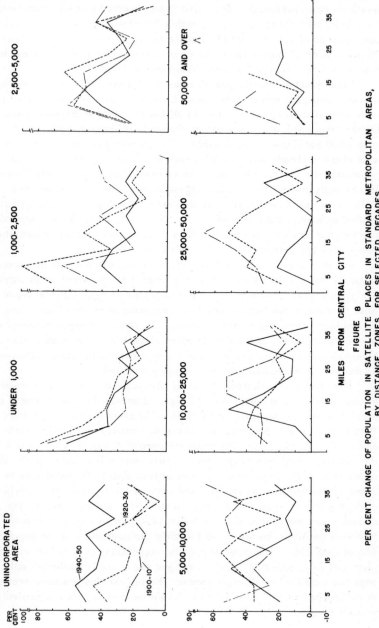

FIGURE 8

PER CENT CHANGE OF POPULATION IN SATELLITE PLACES IN STANDARD METROPOLITAN AREAS,
BY DISTANCE ZONES, FOR SELECTED DECADES

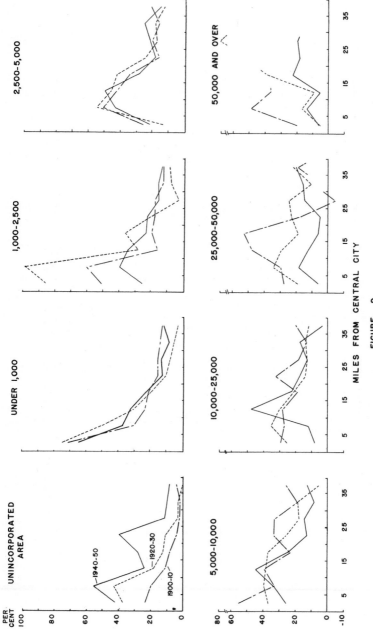

FIGURE 9

PER CENT CHANGE OF POPULATION IN SATELLITE PLACES IN EXTENDED METROPOLITAN AREAS,
BY DISTANCE ZONES, FOR SELECTED DECADES

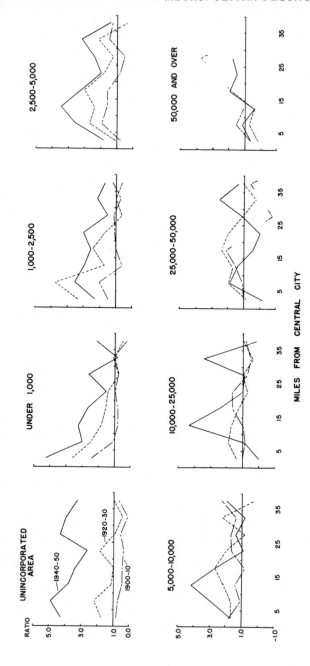

FIGURE 10

RATIO OF RATE OF CHANGE IN SATELLITE PLACES TO RATE OF CHANGE IN CENTRAL CITIES IN STANDARD METROPOLITAN AREAS, BY DISTANCE ZONES, FOR SELECTED DECADES

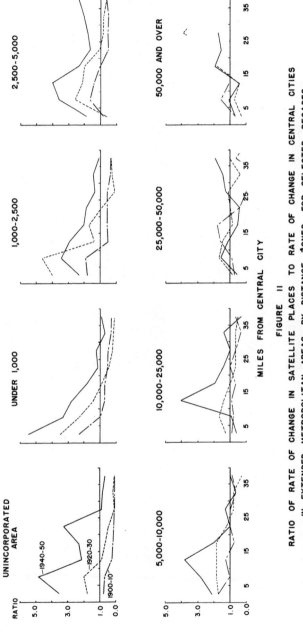

FIGURE II

RATIO OF RATE OF CHANGE IN SATELLITE PLACES TO RATE OF CHANGE IN CENTRAL CITIES
IN EXTENDED METROPOLITAN AREAS, BY DISTANCE ZONES, FOR SELECTED DECADES

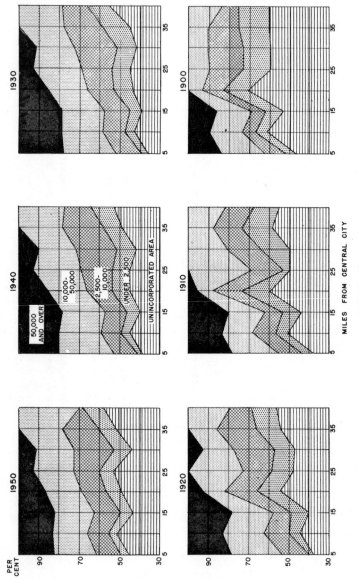

FIGURE 12

PER CENT DISTRIBUTION OF POPULATION IN DISTANCE ZONES OF STANDARD METROPOLITAN AREAS,
BY SIZE AND TYPE OF SATELLITE PLACE, 1900-1950

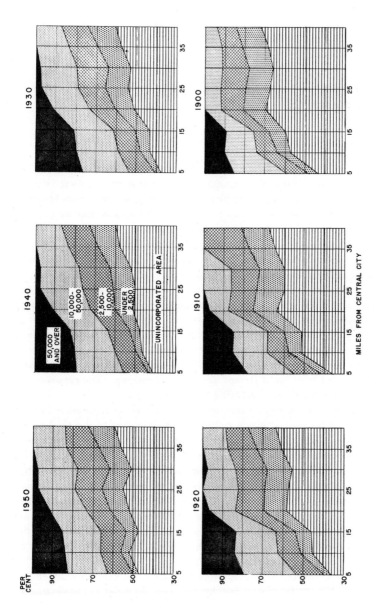

FIGURE 13

PER CENT DISTRIBUTION OF POPULATION IN DISTANCE ZONES OF EXTENDED METROPOLITAN AREAS, BY SIZE AND TYPE OF SATELLITE PLACE, 1900-1950

CHAPTER III

SIZE OF CENTRAL CITY AND POPULATION
REDISTRIBUTION

It was pointed out in the preceding chapter that rapid growth is associated with a concentration tendency. A small area, for example, is
perhaps a newly emergent metropolitan area and therefore may be in a
rapid growth phase. On the other hand, a large area, having attained a
greater maturity, may be near the completion of its growth cycle. Maturity
may mean, among other things, the development of a high population density in the inner zones, an effect of which may be to encourage an acceleration of growth in the outlying parts of the area. Maturity may also
mean, however, a more fully developed transportation system and a more
ramified network of intra-area relationships. Thus there is the further
probability that the larger the area the greater is its scope of influence
as reflected in a centrifugal movement of population. Thus a direct relationship between population redistribution and size of metropolitan area
may be inferred from two different sets of assumptions. The present
chapter is concerned with exploring this hypothesis.

The population size of a metropolitan area may be represented either
by the size of its central city population or by the size of the total population of the area. But while the ratio of the one measure of size to the
other varies considerably in comparisons of individual areas, a classification based on one measure of size produces a distribution which differs
in only a few respects from that obtained by the use of the other. Hence
either measure may be used without appreciably altering the results. Because many of the characteristics of metropolitan areas later to be analyzed are also characteristics of central cities it seems advisable, in the
interest of consistency, to employ size of central city as the basis for a
size classification of metropolitan areas.

Table 9 shows the size classification of central cities employed and
the number of areas in each class, by decades. In order to obtain true
measures of change for each decade metropolitan areas are reclassified

for each inter-censal interval on the basis of size of central city at the beginning of the respective decade. The "under 100,000" class merits special comment. This includes all metropolitan areas with central cities of less than 100,000, even though many such cities in census years prior to 1940 were too small to have qualified as central cities of metropolitan areas, i.e., less than 50,000 population. Since this report is concerned with the growth history of all places classified as metropolitan in 1950, these areas are included.

TABLE 9. NUMBER OF METROPOLITAN AREAS IN STUDY, BY SIZE OF CENTRAL CITY, AND BY DECADE, 1900 - 1950

Size of central city	1940-1950	1930-1940	1920-1930	1910-1920	1900-1910
Total	143	157	155	153	148
1,000,000 and over	5	5	4	3	3
500,000 - 1,000,000	10	10	8	6	3
250,000 - 500,000	11	15	7	8	11
100,000 - 250,000	41	41	37	24	15
Under 100,000	76	86	99	112	116

Central Cities and Satellite Areas

In Table 10 it is evident that there is no clear relationship between size of central city and rate of population change in metropolitan areas. High rates prevailed in the largest, the middle-sized, and the smallest areas, while the two intervening size classes grew at comparatively low rates. The 250,000-500,000 class alternates with the 1,000,000 and over class as the most rapidly growing class of metropolitan areas.

A more consistent variation with size appears in the rates of change of parts of areas. The rates of population change in central cities tend to vary inversely with size, though the 1,000,000 and over and the 250,000-500,000 classes, particularly the former, are exceptions to this generalization. Conversely, growth rates in satellite areas vary directly with size of central city. The principal exception in this instance is the 250,000-500,000 class. Especially noteworthy are the high rates of growth in both central cities and satellite areas of that class in the 1930-40 decade. But much of the exceptional character of the middle-sized class seems to disappear when the boundaries of Extended rather

Table 10. Per Cent Change of Population, by Size of Central City, Distance Zone, Type of Metropolitan Area, and Decade, 1900-1950

Size of central city and distance zone	Standard Metropolitan Areas					Extended Metropolitan Areas				
	1940-1950	1930-1940	1920-1930	1910-1920	1900-1910	1940-1950	1930-1940	1920-1930	1910-1920	1900-1910
1,000,000 and over	18.0	7.8	30.0	22.0	33.5	18.3	8.1	29.9	21.6	33.3
Central cities	9.4	5.6	24.0	19.3	32.2	9.4	5.6	24.0	19.3	32.2
Satellite area	33.0	11.8	43.8	28.5	36.7	33.2	12.5	42.6	26.9	35.8
0-5 miles	3.2	-1.0	11.4	21.4	39.0	3.2	-1.0	11.4	21.4	39.0
5-10 miles	28.6	10.8	55.5	37.2	46.6	28.6	10.8	55.5	37.2	46.6
10-15 miles	34.8	9.9	36.6	29.1	39.8	34.8	9.9	36.6	29.1	39.8
15-20 miles	40.7	17.8	68.9	38.8	48.0	40.7	17.8	68.9	38.8	48.0
20-25 miles	41.2	17.1	67.3	29.0	38.7	41.4	17.1	67.3	29.0	38.7
25-30 miles	32.8	13.0	41.4	29.2	36.3	35.4	13.1	40.8	27.8	34.2
30-35 miles	43.8	13.9	26.9	26.0	18.3	44.5	14.1	27.8	24.0	19.4
35 miles and over	26.9	10.6	26.6	8.2	15.5	27.9	10.8	23.9	5.9	17.8
500,000 - 1,000,000	20.9	4.9	20.3	20.3	20.5	20.0	4.9	19.1	18.7	18.9
Central cities	8.9	1.0	11.4	19.8	16.5	8.9	1.0	11.4	19.8	16.5
Satellite area	36.2	10.1	32.9	21.0	26.5	32.0	9.4	28.5	17.5	22.1
0-5 miles	10.4	2.2	19.4	24.2	29.0	10.4	2.2	19.4	24.2	29.0
5-10 miles	41.6	11.8	51.0	22.5	37.8	41.7	11.7	50.9	22.4	37.5
10-15 miles	51.7	14.6	35.2	15.2	19.7	51.6	14.8	34.6	14.8	18.8
15-20 miles	35.8	11.2	30.2	27.8	16.9	33.9	11.4	27.8	22.9	15.1
20-25 miles	31.5	10.8	11.7	20.9	4.3	28.1	10.7	9.4	15.0	-4.2
25-30 miles	20.4	6.6	17.6	19.9	-3.5	16.7	5.7	11.1	10.8	-27.1
30-35 miles	31.8	2.3	4.1	3.8	21.9	14.0	2.8	5.3	8.4	5.0
35 miles and over	33.2	6.4	11.7	5.1	8.2	5.1	3.9	5.1	4.8	-0.3
250,000 - 500,000	23.4	13.2	23.3	34.9	31.8	20.0	11.2	19.5	31.0	28.1
Central cities	17.7	9.3	16.8	34.2	29.0	17.7	9.3	16.7	34.2	29.0
Satellite area	34.3	22.7	50.8	36.8	37.9	22.2	13.5	24.8	25.2	27.0
0-5 miles	21.7	11.1	47.2	73.2	39.5	22.0	11.1	47.2	73.2	39.5
5-10 miles	48.0	29.2	72.2	36.7	60.0	49.9	29.1	72.0	36.6	59.5
10-15 miles	24.1	26.4	39.2	39.4	26.1	23.5	22.1	32.5	34.1	23.5
15-20 miles	42.8	14.2	11.7	26.9	34.3	27.3	8.9	12.3	19.8	24.6
20-25 miles	31.1	35.1	12.6	35.1	30.6	12.8	9.0	2.8	20.8	18.2
25-30 miles	9.5	14.7	-1.0	0.4	27.1	8.2	6.1	1.8	1.1	17.0
30-35 miles	----	12.2	-4.4	5.8	16.7	7.7	5.0	-0.3	-3.7	11.6
35 miles and over	----	----	----	5.5	3.5	3.0	3.2	0.3	0.1	23.5
100,000 - 250,000	19.9	5.9	21.5	20.0	22.5	16.9	5.2	15.7	13.5	14.2
Central cities	12.7	2.7	20.6	22.4	24.1	12.7	2.7	20.6	22.4	24.1
Satellite area	30.8	11.1	23.2	15.4	19.1	19.8	7.0	11.9	7.2	7.7
0-5 miles	39.4	14.4	31.9	27.6	27.0	39.4	14.4	32.2	27.8	26.9
5-10 miles	38.8	15.2	30.1	17.1	22.2	37.9	14.6	29.1	17.0	20.5
10-15 miles	23.7	5.8	10.4	11.2	13.9	23.3	6.6	9.2	8.3	9.7
15-20 miles	15.9	11.9	19.2	3.5	2.1	16.9	7.1	11.3	2.4	4.9
20-25 miles	9.5	3.7	22.7	-5.1	-3.8	11.2	-6.4	4.4	3.4	3.0
25-30 miles	7.8	-0.5	1.0	-4.4	-2.9	7.9	6.3	2.6	0.1	-0.8
30-35 miles	9.2	2.9	1.4	-2.5	-12.0	6.7	3.6	5.2	5.4	3.6
35 miles and over	-7.3	-0.4	-2.9	-1.9	-9.3	-1.3	0.2	-1.5	-1.7	-1.7
Under 100,000	20.7	10.8	24.2	28.0	28.7	14.6	8.6	15.2	17.0	16.6
Central cities	18.1	8.2	29.2	38.5	42.0	18.1	8.2	29.2	38.5	42.0
Satellite area	23.3	13.8	18.6	17.2	17.2	13.2	8.8	9.6	9.4	9.3
0-5 miles	29.9	19.2	29.9	28.3	22.7	30.6	19.2	30.2	28.4	22.6
5-10 miles	29.1	17.3	23.9	16.7	14.1	27.3	15.8	21.9	15.5	13.7
10-15 miles	19.5	11.4	15.3	15.0	18.2	16.8	9.3	11.7	11.9	13.3
15-20 miles	13.6	6.2	7.4	12.4	11.5	9.3	6.1	6.9	7.3	8.0
20-25 miles	10.6	8.7	18.2	10.7	13.3	8.2	7.4	7.0	4.5	7.4
25-30 miles	-0.3	6.3	9.6	14.6	12.5	6.1	6.8	4.4	6.8	6.7
30-35 miles	-4.6	9.2	-5.2	-1.6	-0.2	4.6	5.2	5.1	5.5	4.4
35 miles and over	57.1	11.0	0.1	14.7	80.1	5.7	3.6	1.8	6.0	6.9

than Standard Metropolitan Areas are used. It is possible that the definition of the Standard Metropolitan Area is more selective of rapidly growing
places in the 250,000-500,000 class than in the other four size classes.

When the 50-year trends of growth rates in metropolitan areas are
analyzed, it is apparent that there are certain differentials in the general
tendency to decline that was noted in the preceding chapter. Growth rates
in areas with central cities of 1,000,000 population or more declined by almost half from 1900 to 1950, though the trend was irregular. No appreciable difference exists between Standard and Extended Metropolitan Areas
in this respect. But in the former, areas with central cities of 500,000-
1,000,000 population maintained a relatively constant growth rate, if the
1930-40 decade may be treated as an unrepresentative period, on the other
hand, in the Extended Metropolitan Areas of the same size class, a trend
toward increasing rates of growth is observable. In the third size class,
250,000-500,000 population, growth rates in both types of metropolitan
areas increased in the second decade of the 50-year period after which
they dropped by about 33 per cent. No trend of change is evident after
1920. The pattern of changes in growth rates in the 100,000-250,000 size
class of Standard Metropolitan Areas is very similar to that in the largest
size class. The trend for this same size class of Extended Metropolitan
Areas, however, was in the direction of increasing rates of growth. And
in the smallest size class growth rates declined through the period, though
by a greater extent in Standard than in Extended Metropolitan Areas.

All sizes of central cities experienced declining rates of growth. The
greatest amounts of reduction occurred in the largest and in the smallest
central cities. The least reduction of growth rate over the 50-year period
occurred in central cities of 250,000-500,000 population. It was also in
this size class that the retardation of growth of the 1930-40 decade was
least.

Growth rate trends in satellite areas display no consistent pattern. In
metropolitan areas with central cities of 1,000,000 population and over, and
in those of 250,000-500,000 the tendency was toward reduction, though the
peak rates of growth took place in 1920-30. All other size classes show
rising growth rates in satellite areas, with somewhat larger increases in
those of the Extended Metropolitan Areas.

The rates of change in each distance zone, shown in Table 10, reveal
several kinds of variation with size of central city. In the largest size
classes rates of increase have declined steadily in the innermost zones.
The zone of decline extends out to 10 miles from centers in the 1,000,000
and over areas, but to only 5 miles in areas with central cities of 250,000
to 1,000,000 population. Areas with central cities below 250,000 population, however, had trends of increase in rates of change within the 0-5 mile

and adjacent zones. A second characteristic is that the larger the size of central city the more extensive is the area over which growth rates were equal to or in excess of the average growth of satellite areas. For the largest size class that included all area within 30 miles, in 1900-10, and most of the satellite territory beyond 10 miles of central cities after 1930. In the 500,000-1,000,000 metropolitan areas the average growth was exceeded within a lengthening radius, beginning at 10 miles, in 1900-10, and embracing more distant zones in succeeding decades. A similar change took place in the 250,000-500,000 with the difference that at no time did the zone of greater than average growth reach beyond 30 miles of the central city. In the next smaller size class that radius changed from 10 miles at the beginning of the period to 20 miles at the end, while in metropolitan areas of the under 100,000 class the radius moved from 5 miles or less to 15 miles.

The small, and frequently negative, rates of change in the more remote distance zones, especially in the smaller areas, suggest that in the formative stages of metropolitan development central cities and inner zones grew at the expense in part at least, of their outlying zones. Apparently only in areas with central cities greater than 500,000, and there only since 1930, has growth occurred without loss to distance zones near metropolitan peripheries.

That the differences in growth rates in different size classes of metropolitan areas may be due partly to variations in densities of population is indicated by Table 11. The variation of density with size, both in central cities and in each distance zone, is close, much closer in fact than in the relationship between rate of change and size. The linear correlation coefficient for density (1940) and rate of change (1940-50) in Standard Metropolitan Areas is -.358, and in Extended Metropolitan Areas -.240. Although these values reveal the type of relationships expected, they are not high. Variations in density do not account for more than 13 per cent of the variations in rate of change. Most of the variation, therefore, is a function of other factors.

A comparison of rates of change in parts of metropolitan areas with rates of change in the total population of the nation casts further light on size variations. According to Table 12 there is no clear relationship between the ratios and sizes of areas, though there is some evidence of a direct association in the satellite areas. Growth seems to have favored first one size class of metropolitan areas and then another in different decades. Thus the highest relative rates of change in 1,000,000 and over areas occurred in 1920-30; the 500,000-1,000,000 areas attained their peak growth, relative to that of the nation, in 1940-50, as did also the 100,000-250,000 class of areas; while the remaining two classes of areas had their

TABLE 11. POPULATION PER SQUARE MILE IN METROPOLITAN AREAS, BY SIZE OF CENTRAL CITY, AND DISTANCE ZONE, 1940

Type of metropolitan area	Total	Central cities	Distance from central city									All satellite areas
			0-5	5-10	10-15	15-20	20-25	25-30	30-35	35 and over	
Standard Metropolitan Areas												
1,000,000 and over	1,359	13,846	11,143	3,915	1,977	841	458	289	186	100	530
500,000 - 1,000,000	732	11,397	4,552	1,133	365	259	778	107	97	46	342
250,000 - 500,000	619	6,198	1,736	369	142	65	59	29	—	4	205
100,000 - 250,000	249	5,422	555	184	179	55	34	29	25	17	103
Under 100,000	134	4,882	341	105	58	43	27	47	14	18	65
Extended Metropolitan Areas												
1,000,000 and over	1,172	13,846	11,143	3,915	1,977	841	458	297	194	94	463
500,000 - 1,000,000	460	11,397	4,552	1,087	319	207	129	95	80	61	229
250,000 - 500,000	195	6,198	1,454	346	115	64	64	57	64	49	94
100,000 - 250,000	123	5,422	555	175	108	69	59	49	59	30	73
Under 100,000	64	4,882	290	89	48	42	34	39	34	28	44

TABLE 12. RATIO OF RATE OF POPULATION CHANGE IN METROPOLITAN AREAS TO RATE OF CHANGE OF TOTAL UNITED STATES POPULATION, BY TYPE OF PLACE, SIZE OF CENTRAL CITY, TYPE OF METROPOLITAN AREA, AND DECADE, 1900-1950

Type of place and size of central city	Standard Metropolitan Areas					Extended Metropolitan Areas				
	1940-50	1930-40	1920-30	1910-20	1900-10	1940-50	1930-50	1920-30	1910-20	1900-10
Total area										
1,000,000 and over	1.24	1.08	1.86	1.48	1.60	1.26	1.13	1.86	1.45	1.59
500,000 - 1,000,000	1.44	.68	1.26	1.36	.98	1.38	.68	1.19	1.26	.90
250,000 - 500,000	1.61	1.83	1.45	2.32	1.51	1.38	1.56	1.21	2.08	1.34
100,000 - 250,000	1.37	.82	1.34	1.34	1.07	1.17	.72	.98	.91	.68
Under 100,000	1.43	1.50	1.50	1.88	1.37	1.01	1.19	.94	1.14	.79
Central cities										
1,000,000 and over	.65	.78	1.49	1.30	1.53	.65	.78	1.49	1.30	1.53
500,000 - 1,000,000	.61	.14	.71	1.33	.79	.61	.14	.71	1.33	.79
250,000 - 500,000	1.22	1.29	1.04	2.30	1.38	1.22	1.29	1.04	2.30	1.38
100,000 - 250,000	.88	.38	1.28	1.50	1.15	.88	.38	1.28	1.50	1.15
Under 100,000	1.25	1.14	1.81	2.58	2.00	1.25	1.14	1.81	2.58	2.00
Satellite areas										
1,000,000 and over	2.28	1.64	2.72	1.91	1.75	2.29	1.74	2.65	1.81	1.70
500,000 - 1,000,000	2.50	1.40	2.04	1.41	1.26	2.21	1.31	1.77	1.17	1.05
250,000 - 500,000	2.37	3.15	3.16	2.47	1.80	1.53	1.88	1.54	1.69	1.29
100,000 - 250,000	2.12	1.54	1.44	1.03	.91	1.37	.97	.74	.48	.37
Under 100,000	1.61	1.92	1.16	1.15	.82	.91	1.22	.60	.63	.44

highest ratios in the 1910-20 decade. All sizes of central cities had
reached their highest relative growth rates by 1920, their ratios declining
rapidly after that date. The ratios for satellite areas increased over the
period, and for most of the areas the highest ratios occurred in the last
10-year interval. Both the largest and the middle-sized areas, however,
maintained high ratios for satellite areas throughout the period. It is of
interest to note that not until after 1930 did growth rates in the satellite
areas of the two smallest classes of Extended Metropolitan Areas rise a
above the national average.

Differentials in the centrifugal movement of population are described
in detail in Figs. 14 and 15. The metropolitan areas with central cities of
1,000,000 or more population have maintained higher than average growth
rates over most of their satellite areas throughout the 50-year period. Low
ratios are found in the extreme distance zones in the first two decades,
and ratios in the innermost zones dropped below unity after 1920. The
progressive spread of higher than average growth rates over satellite areas
is more clearly apparent in the 500,000 to 1,000,000 size class. In the
next smaller size class that trend of change is observable only at the
centers and the extremities of metropolitan areas: central city ratios declined while ratios in the zones beyond 25 miles showed some tendency to
increase. The patterns of centrifugal change are similar in the two smallest size classes, though the area over which higher than average rates
prevailed is greater by 5 miles in the larger of the two classes of areas.
In general, the larger the size of central city the more extensive has been
the area over which growth rates exceeded the decennial rate of the total
population of the nation.

The ratio of satellite growth rates to central city rates provides, however, a better measure of centrifugal movement of population. Measured on
this basis the rate of deconcentration appears to vary rather closely with
size of central city in all decades but 1930-40, as may be seen in Table
13. Correspondingly, deconcentration has tended to accelerate in successive decades, with the 1930-40 decade off-setting the trend. There is also
a noticeable tendency for the rates of deconcentration to have increased by
larger amounts, over the five decades, in small than in large metropolitan
areas. This is most apparent in Extended Metropolitan Areas.

Figs. 16 and 17, in which the ratios of distance zone rates to central
city rates are presented, reveal that in metropolitan areas with central cities
of over 1,000,000 the gradient aspect of deconcentration, such as is apparent
in all other classes of areas, is lacking. Although the ratios have increased
in successive decades, there are but slight variations among distance zones.
The exceptional growth of satellite relative to central city population in the

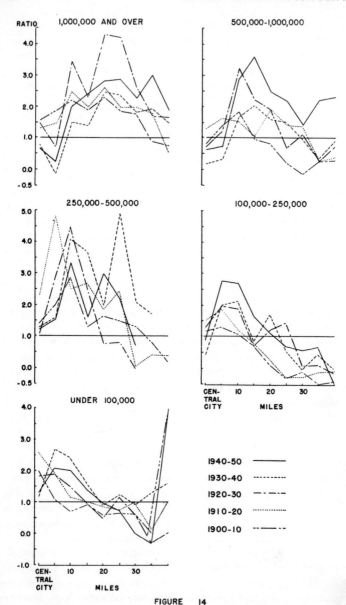

FIGURE 14

RATIO OF RATE OF POPULATION CHANGE IN STANDARD METROPOLITAN AREAS
TO RATE OF CHANGE OF TOTAL UNITED STATES POPULATION, BY SIZE OF
CENTRAL CITY AND BY DISTANCE ZONE, 1900-1950

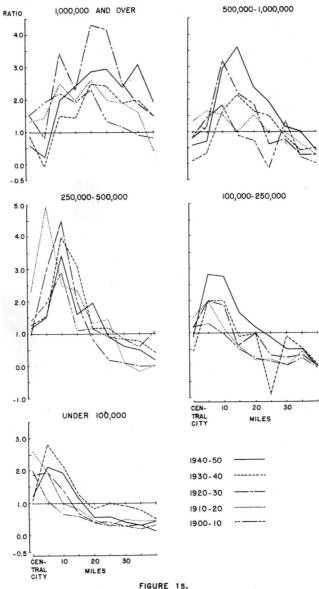

FIGURE 15.

RATIO OF RATE OF POPULATION CHANGE IN EXTENDED METROPOLITAN AREAS
TO RATE OF CHANGE OF TOTAL UNITED STATES POPULATION, BY SIZE OF
CENTRAL CITY AND BY DISTANCE ZONE, 1900-1950

500,000-1,000,000 and the 100,000-250,000 areas during the 1930-40 decade results from a defect of the ratio rather than from unusually high satellite growth rates. As the central city growth rate approaches zero the ratios assume increasingly larger values. It was shown in Table 10 that the 1930-40 rate for central cities of 500,000-1,000,000 was only 1.0 per cent, and the rate for central cities of 100,000-250,000 was 2.7 per cent. Actually the 1930-40 satellite growth rates in these two classes of metropolitan areas were slightly below those for other size classes. Thus a high ratio may be due to a failure of central city growth as well as to a relatively high rate of satellite growth.

TABLE 13. RATIO OF RATE OF CHANGE IN SATELLITE AREAS TO RATE OF CHANGE IN CENTRAL CITIES, BY TYPE OF METROPOLITAN AREA, SIZE OF CENTRAL CITY, AND DECADE, 1900-1950

Metropolitan area and size of central city	1940-50	1930-40	1920-30	1910-20	1900-10
Standard Metropolitan Areas	2.68	2.47	1.45	.86	.83
1,000,000 and over	3.51	2.11	1.83	1.48	1.14
500,000 - 1,000,000	4.07	10.10	2.89	1.06	1.61
250,000 - 500,000	1.94	2.44	3.02	1.08	1.31
100,000 - 250,000	2.43	4.11	1.13	.69	.79
Under 100,000	1.29	1.68	.64	.45	.41
Extended Metropolitan Areas	1.97	1.90	.88	.51	.47
1,000,000 and over	3.53	2.23	1.78	1.39	1.11
500,000 - 1,000,000	3.60	9.40	2.50	.88	1.34
250,000 - 500,000	1.25	1.45	1.49	.74	.93
100,000 - 250,000	1.56	2.59	.58	.32	.32
Under 100,000	.73	1.07	.33	.24	.22

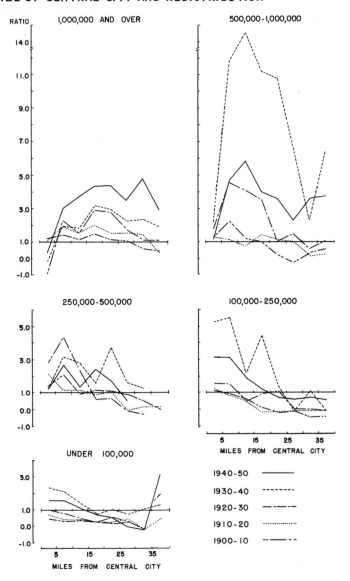

FIGURE 16
RATIO OF RATE OF POPULATION CHANGE IN SATELLITE AREA OF STANDARD
METROPOLITAN AREAS TO RATE OF CHANGE IN CENTRAL CITY, BY SIZE
OF CENTRAL CITY AND BY DISTANCE ZONE, 1900-1950

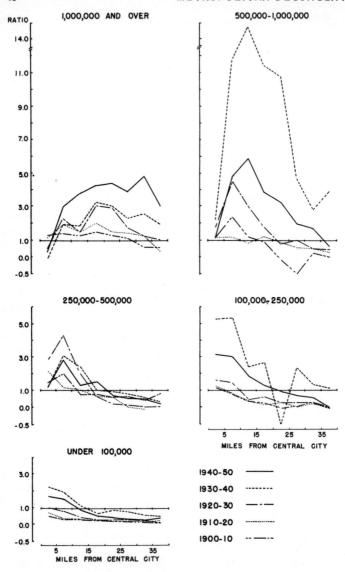

FIGURE 17.
RATIO OF RATE OF POPULATION CHAN   IN SATELLITE AREA OF EXTENDED
METROPOLITAN AREAS TO RATE OF CHANGE IN CENTRAL CITY, BY SIZE
OF CENTRAL CITY AND BY DISTANCE ZONE, 1900-1950

The proportion of all population increase that accrued to central cities shows, in Table 14, a rough correspondence with city size. And the amount of decline in this respect, from 1900 through 1950, shows some tendency to vary inversely with size of area. Central cities of 250,000-500,000 were unusually successful in maintaining a large proportion of all increase in their areas. The proportions of growth attracted to satellite areas conform to a converse pattern.

Although satellite areas received increasingly large shares of all growth, most of the increase was contained within a closely circumscribed space, as Table 15 clearly shows. The 10-15 mile distance zone, in the largest class of metropolitan areas, has consistently absorbed the largest proportion of all satellite growth. In the four other size classes the 5-10 mile zone has continued to attract the largest share of growth occurring outside central cities. But while there has been concentration of population increase within a given zone, there also have been rapid increases in the proportions received by more distant zones. Size of central city appears to have been an important factor in the radius over which population increments have been scattered.

Differences in rates of change have not been large enough to significantly alter the distribution of population within metropolitan areas. The cumulative percentage distributions, shown in Table 16, demonstrate that in few instances has the distance required to contain any given proportion of the total population shifted by more than five miles. This applies not only to each decade, but to the entire 50-year period as well. In several cases the shifts have been toward reduction rather than increase of the distance.

It will be observed that in Extended Metropolitan Areas, concentration varies directly with size of area. This, of course, is largely a result of the direct variation of the proportion of population in central cities with size of central city. Such an association appears only as a tendency in Standard Metropolitan Areas.

Coefficients of redistribution, shown graphically in Fig. 18, indicates that the highest incidence of redistribution occurred in the 250,000-500,000 class. Referring to Table 16 it will be seen that movement in that size class of areas was toward concentration. Relatively constant rates of redistribution obtained in the two smallest size classes, and the data in Table 16 show very slight shifts toward a scattering or deconcentration of population. The rather erratic patterns of redistribution shown for the remaining two classes of metropolitan areas are due largely to sharp declines in the proportions of population within 10 miles of central cities.

TABLE 14. PER CENT DISTRIBUTION OF POPULATION INCREASE BY TYPE OF PLACE, AND BY SIZE OF CENTRAL CITY, TYPE OF METROPOLITAN AREA, AND DECADE, 1900-1950

Size of central city and type of place	Standard Metropolitan Areas					Extended Metropolitan Areas				
	1940-50	1930-40	1920-30	1910-20	1900-10	1940-50	1930-40	1920-30	1910-20	1900-10
1,000,000 and over	100.0	100.0	100.0	100.0	100.0	100.0	100.0	100.0	100.0	100.0
Central cities	33.3	46.8	55.6	61.7	68.4	32.2	45.7	54.9	61.6	67.4
Satellite areas	66.7	53.2	44.4	38.3	31.6	67.8	54.3	45.1	38.4	32.6
500,000 - 1,000,000	100.0	100.0	100.0	100.0	100.0	100.0	100.0	100.0	100.0	100.0
Central cities	23.8	11.9	33.1	57.3	47.9	22.9	11.0	32.9	56.6	49.9
Satellite areas	76.2	88.1	66.9	42.7	52.1	77.1	89.0	67.1	43.4	50.1
250,000 - 500,000	100.0	100.0	100.0	100.0	100.0	100.0	100.0	100.0	100.0	100.0
Central cities	50.2	50.3	58.0	70.5	62.0	44.0	44.8	56.3	70.9	59.6
Satellite areas	49.8	49.7	42.0	29.5	38.0	56.0	55.2	43.7	29.1	40.4
100,000 - 250,000	100.0	100.0	100.0	100.0	100.0	100.0	100.0	100.0	100.0	100.0
Central cities	38.4	28.1	61.9	74.1	72.4	30.9	22.1	57.2	69.0	67.4
Satellite areas	61.6	71.9	38.1	25.9	27.6	69.1	77.9	42.8	31.0	32.6
Under 100,000	100.0	100.0	100.0	100.0	100.0	100.0	100.0	100.0	100.0	100.0
Central cities	45.0	40.4	63.8	69.7	67.8	36.5	28.6	54.7	59.4	56.6
Satellite areas	55.0	59.6	36.2	30.3	32.2	63.5	71.4	45.3	40.6	43.4

Table 15. Percentage Distribution of Population Increase in Standard Metropolitan Areas, by Distance Zone, by Size of Central City, Type of Metropolitan Area, and Decade, 1900-1950

Size of central city and distance zone	Standard Metropolitan Areas					Extended Metropolitan Areas				
	1940-1950	1930-1940	1920-1930	1910-1920	1900-1910	1940-1950	1930-1940	1920-1930	1910-1920	1900-1910
1,000,000 and over	100.0	100.0	100.0	100.0	100.0	100.0	100.0	100.0	100.0	100.0
Central cities	33.3	46.8	55.6	61.7	68.4	32.2	45.7	54.9	61.6	67.4
0-5 miles	0.4	-0.3	1.1	2.4	2.7	0.4	-0.3	1.0	2.3	2.6
5-10 miles	12.3	10.2	9.9	8.3	6.2	11.9	10.0	9.7	8.2	6.1
10-15 miles	18.1	11.9	10.7	11.6	9.9	12.5	11.6	10.6	11.6	9.8
15-20 miles	14.2	13.1	9.0	6.2	4.6	13.7	12.7	8.7	6.2	4.5
20-25 miles	7.1	8.0	6.9	3.8	3.2	8.9	7.9	6.8	3.8	3.2
25-30 miles	4.5	4.0	2.9	2.8	2.2	5.2	4.3	3.2	2.9	2.3
30-35 miles	4.3	3.0	1.5	2.0	1.0	4.6	3.2	1.7	2.1	1.2
35 miles and over	3.8	3.3	2.4	1.2	1.8	5.6	4.9	3.2	1.3	2.9
500,000 - 1,000,000	100.0	100.0	100.0	100.0	100.0	100.0	100.0	100.0	100.0	100.0
Central cities	23.8	11.9	33.1	57.3	47.9	22.9	11.0	32.9	56.6	49.9
0-5 miles	3.0	2.9	6.7	10.5	17.9	2.9	2.7	6.6	10.3	18.6
5-10 miles	36.6	41.1	36.2	13.9	22.9	35.5	38.3	36.0	13.8	23.8
10-15 miles	18.3	20.6	11.1	5.2	6.9	18.3	20.0	11.1	5.2	7.1
15-20 miles	8.9	12.0	7.9	6.5	3.5	9.4	12.8	7.8	6.2	3.7
20-25 miles	4.9	7.1	2.1	3.5	0.4	5.6	7.9	2.0	3.1	-0.6
25-30 miles	2.3	3.1	2.2	2.6	-0.1	3.2	3.8	2.0	2.3	-2.8
30-35 miles	1.2	0.4	0.2	0.3	0.4	1.4	1.1	0.6	1.3	0.3
35 miles and over	1.0	0.9	0.5	0.2	0.2	0.8	2.4	1.0	1.2	-----
250,000 - 500,000	100.0	100.0	100.0	100.0	100.0	100.0	100.0	100.0	100.0	100.0
Central cities	50.2	50.3	58.0	70.5	62.0	44.0	44.8	56.3	70.9	59.6
0-5 miles	8.3	6.5	10.6	7.5	4.2	7.6	5.9	10.3	7.5	4.0
5-10 miles	26.3	26.2	24.5	12.0	17.8	24.2	23.8	23.7	12.1	17.1
10-15 miles	8.2	12.3	5.8	4.3	4.5	8.3	11.5	6.4	4.3	4.3
15-20 miles	5.5	2.2	0.8	2.7	4.6	7.5	3.6	2.3	2.8	4.4
20-25 miles	1.4	2.2	0.3	2.8	3.6	3.4	3.7	0.5	2.6	3.2
25-30 miles	0.1	0.3	0.0	0.0	2.5	2.4	3.0	0.5	0.1	3.3
30-35 miles	-----	0.0	0.0	0.1	0.7	1.9	2.2	-0.1	-0.3	1.6
35 miles and over	-----	0.0	-----	0.1	0.1	0.7	1.5	0.1	-----	2.5
100,000 - 250,000	100.0	100.0	100.0	100.0	100.0	100.0	100.0	100.0	100.0	100.0
Central cities	38.4	28.1	61.9	74.1	72.4	30.9	22.1	57.2	69.0	67.4
0-5 miles	18.0	20.5	11.9	8.9	9.8	14.5	16.2	11.3	8.5	9.2
5-10 miles	29.8	33.1	17.3	12.0	12.7	24.9	27.0	16.7	12.1	12.4
10-15 miles	10.4	8.7	4.6	4.8	5.2	12.6	11.2	5.2	4.9	5.7
15-20 miles	2.8	8.8	3.0	0.5	0.2	7.7	10.8	5.0	1.3	2.7
20-25 miles	0.6	0.9	1.3	-0.2	-0.1	4.6	4.2	1.9	2.0	1.9
25-30 miles	0.3	-0.1	0.0	-0.1	0.0	2.9	3.7	1.0	0.1	-0.4
30-35 miles	0.1	0.1	0.0	0.0	-0.1	2.4	4.6	2.3	2.9	1.9
35 miles and over	-0.4	-0.1	0.0	0.0	-0.1	-0.5	0.2	-0.6	-0.8	-0.8
Under 100,000	100.0	100.0	100.0	100.0	100.0	100.0	100.0	100.0	100.0	100.0
Central cities	45.0	40.4	63.8	69.7	67.8	36.5	28.6	54.7	59.4	56.6
0-5 miles	18.3	19.9	11.8	9.7	7.6	15.4	14.3	10.3	8.4	6.3
5-10 miles	18.3	20.3	12.3	8.1	8.0	16.2	15.3	11.2	7.3	7.3
10-15 miles	9.8	10.6	6.6	6.2	8.1	10.3	9.5	6.9	6.7	7.8
15-20 miles	3.4	3.1	2.0	3.1	3.1	6.2	7.0	4.8	4.7	5.4
20-25 miles	2.2	3.3	2.9	1.3	1.6	5.9	9.2	5.0	2.8	5.1
25-30 miles	0.0	1.0	0.7	1.0	0.9	4.4	8.2	3.2	4.5	4.8
30-35 miles	-0.1	0.4	-0.1	-----	-----	2.5	4.9	2.9	3.0	2.7
35 miles and over	3.1	1.0	-----	0.9	2.9	2.6	3.0	1.0	3.2	4.0

Table 16. Cumulative Percentage Distribution of Population in Standard Metropolitan Areas, by Distance Zone, Size of Central City, Type of Metropolitan Area, and Decade, 1900-1950.

Size of central city and distance zone	Standard Metropolitan Areas						Extended Metropolitan Areas					
	1950	1940	1930	1920	1910	1900	1950	1940	1930	1920	1910	1900
1,000,000 and over												
Central city	59.0	63.7	65.0	69.5	70.4	71.1	58.0	62.7	64.0	68.3	69.1	69.6
0-5 miles	61.0	65.9	67.4	72.3	72.8	73.4	59.9	64.9	66.4	71.1	71.5	71.9
5-10 miles	69.4	73.6	74.8	77.6	77.7	77.8	68.2	72.5	73.7	76.3	76.3	76.3
10-15 miles	80.1	82.9	84.1	86.4	86.5	86.2	78.7	81.7	82.8	84.9	84.9	84.5
15-20 miles	87.6	89.2	89.8	90.3	90.0	89.4	86.0	87.8	88.4	88.8	88.3	87.6
20-25 miles	92.4	93.2	93.4	93.4	92.9	92.2	90.7	91.7	92.0	91.8	91.1	90.3
25-30 miles	95.2	95.7	95.8	95.5	95.0	94.3	93.8	94.4	94.6	94.1	93.4	92.6
30-35 miles	97.3	97.5	97.5	97.2	96.7	96.2	96.1	97.3	96.4	95.9	95.3	94.7
35 miles and over	100.0	100.0	100.0	100.0	100.0	100.0	100.0	100.0	100.0	100.0	100.0	100.0
500,000 - 1,000,000												
Central city	50.4	56.0	57.3	58.8	58.4	59.7	47.0	51.8	53.6	55.0	53.5	57.2
0-5 miles	55.9	62.0	63.8	65.8	67.1	72.4	5.2	57.3	59.7	61.5	61.5	69.3
5-10 miles	77.4	80.4	81.0	80.2	79.6	84.8	72.2	74.3	75.8	75.0	73.1	81.3
10-15 miles	86.7	87.8	87.9	86.6	86.5	91.9	81.1	81.4	82.5	81.1	79.7	88.5
15-20 miles	92.6	93.0	93.1	91.9	91.3	96.2	87.3	87.0	88.0	86.5	84.8	93.1
20-25 miles	96.1	96.2	96.3	95.6	94.8	98.3	91.6	91.0	91.6	90.5	88.7	95.8
25-30 miles	98.4	98.5	98.5	98.1	97.4	99.1	95.3	94.8	94.9	94.0	92.7	97.8
30-35 miles	99.3	99.3	99.3	99.2	98.8	99.5	97.3	96.9	96.9	96.3	95.5	98.9
35 miles and over	100.0	100.0	100.0	100.0	100.0	100.0	100.0	100.0	100.0	100.0	100.0	100.0
250,000 - 500,000												
Central city	63.1	66.1	71.2	80.8	72.0	68.1	48.6	49.5	54.1	65.6	64.2	57.9
0-5 miles	71.9	75.0	78.9	86.0	75.5	71.4	55.6	56.4	60.1	69.9	67.4	60.7
5-10 miles	87.2	87.8	90.7	93.9	86.9	80.8	67.9	66.3	69.3	76.3	77.6	68.8
10-15 miles	95.2	95.7	96.8	97.4	90.7	86.3	75.2	73.4	75.2	80.2	81.5	74.0
15-20 miles	98.6	98.7	98.9	98.9	94.2	90.6	81.0	78.8	79.8	83.8	85.8	79.1
20-25 miles	99.8	99.8	99.7	99.5	97.0	94.3	86.0	84.1	84.4	87.3	89.7	84.0
25-30 miles	100.0	100.0	100.0	100.0	98.5	97.3	91.2	89.9	89.8	92.6	93.3	89.4
30-35 miles	-----	-----	-----	-----	99.6	98.7	95.6	94.9	94.8	96.1	96.0	93.3
35 miles and over	-----	-----	-----	-----	100.0	100.0	100.0	100.0	100.0	100.0	100.0	100.0
100,000 - 250,000												
Central cities	56.2	60.2	61.8	64.6	66.2	67.6	39.6	41.0	42.5	43.7	41.6	39.8
0-5 miles	67.2	69.3	70.2	72.6	72.7	75.7	47.0	47.2	48.3	49.2	45.7	44.7
5-10 miles	84.9	84.6	83.2	85.0	86.8	88.6	60.1	58.3	57.9	58.2	55.3	53.2
10-15 miles	93.8	93.3	92.0	94.4	95.4	97.0	69.7	67.4	66.6	67.1	63.3	61.6
15-20 miles	96.2	96.8	96.4	97.8	98.5	99.1	77.4	75.1	74.5	74.0	70.5	69.5
20-25 miles	97.3	98.0	97.8	99.0	99.3	99.5	83.9	82.0	81.2	80.8	78.7	78.4
25-30 miles	98.0	98.8	98.8	99.7	99.8	99.7	89.6	88.2	87.6	87.2	86.1	86.0
30-35 miles	98.2	99.0	99.0	99.9	99.9	99.9	95.2	94.3	94.1	94.0	93.3	93.5
35 miles and over	100.0	100.0	100.0	100.0	100.0	100.0	100.0	100.0	100.0	100.0	100.0	100.0
Under 100,000												
Central cities	50.1	51.2	53.3	52.9	50.8	46.4	30.4	29.5	30.0	28.4	26.3	22.3
0-5 miles	63.7	63.8	64.5	62.4	60.4	56.0	38.8	36.9	36.4	33.6	31.3	26.9
5-10 miles	77.6	76.8	77.2	74.9	73.9	72.2	48.4	45.6	44.7	41.3	39.5	35.7
10-15 miles	87.9	87.2	87.3	85.4	85.6	85.0	57.5	54.5	53.5	50.2	48.8	45.5
15-20 miles	92.8	92.4	92.8	92.0	92.5	92.7	66.7	64.1	63.4	60.8	59.7	56.7
20-25 miles	96.8	96.7	96.9	95.8	95.8	96.2	76.6	74.6	74.1	71.7	70.4	68.1
25-30 miles	98.2	98.4	98.6	97.6	97.7	98.3	86.4	85.2	84.6	82.7	81.5	80.0
30-35 miles	98.6	98.9	99.0	98.1	98.3	99.0	93.8	93.3	92.7	91.4	90.9	90.2
35 miles and over	100.0	100.0	100.0	100.0	100.0	100.0	100.0	100.0	100.0	100.0	100.0	100.0

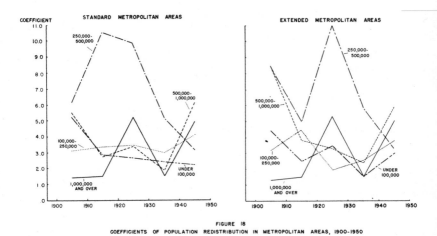

FIGURE 18
COEFFICIENTS OF POPULATION REDISTRIBUTION IN METROPOLITAN AREAS, 1900-1950

The comparisons of Standard and Extended Metropolitan Areas have shown, by virtually all measures, a more pronounced gradient aspect in the latter than in the former. And this is indicative of the inclusion within Standard Metropolitan Areas of most of the rapidly growing territories surrounding central cities. Even so, the difference between comparable zones have been small in most cases. It seems unnecessary, therefore, to carry the Extended Metropolitan Area concept beyond the present point.

Size and Type of Satellite Place

It is of interest to know whether the trends of change in metropolitan areas that were observed when all satellite population was considered apply to population in each size and type of satellite place. That they do not apply uniformly is apparent in Table 17. For example, while there has been a general tendency for rates of change in all sizes and types of places to vary with the size of central city, that association has been most definite among small incorporated places and unincorporated areas. Perhaps such places are more dependent on and therefore more responsive to central city influence than are large satellite places. Unfortunately the data at hand do not permit direct observation of that relationship.

TABLE 17. PER CENT CHANGE OF POPULATION IN STANDARD
METROPOLITAN AREAS, BY SIZE AND TYPE OF SATELLITE
PLACE, BY SIZE OF CENTRAL CITY AND DECADE
1900 - 1950

Size of central city and size and type of satellite place	1940-50	1930-40	1920-30	1910-20	1900-10
1,000,000 and over					
50,000 and over	9.6	1.3	11.1	17.1	31.4
25,000 - 50,000	12.7	5.1	40.2	28.4	53.3
10,000 - 25,000	23.9	12.2	50.2	55.0	36.3
5,000 - 10,000	37.1	14.8	61.5	33.1	52.0
2,500 - 5,000	45.6	12.8	66.7	30.1	46.8
1,000 - 2,500	44.6	18.4	110.5	47.1	46.4
Under 1,000	58.2	26.0	84.3	38.9	52.1
Unincorporated area	70.5	27.5	60.2	23.9	29.7
500,000 - 1,000,000					
50,000 and over	13.0	2.5	20,8	11.7	22.2
25,000 - 50,000	16.2	0.0	30.2	8.9	26.0
10,000 - 25,000	24.1	7.1	24.4	30.3	33.6
5,000 - 10,000	39.0	9.4	37.9	31.3	22.9
2,500 - 5,000	40.3	15.0	74.1	42.5	88.1
1,000 - 2,500	48.2	16.2	55.1	42.4	68.1
Under 1,000	36.1	17.9	30.8	32.3	28.1
Unincorporated area	57.6	18.1	33.6	17.1	20.8
250,000 - 500,000					
50,000 and over	5.9	-3.2	14.2	34.4	124.3
25,000 - 50,000	7.6	-0.3	1.5	34.5	19.7
10,000 - 25,000	27.8	15.1	57.1	46.7	50.9
5,000 - 10,000	31.7	11.6	62.3	40.7	51.4
2,500 - 5,000	54.3	15.9	62.4	154.1	61.3
1,000 - 2,500	63.9	26.5	48.7	54.8	50.7
Under 1,000	42.3	20.4	63.5	28.0	36.4
Unincorporated area	39.8	32.3	55.6	16.0	25.7
100,000 - 250,000					
50,000 and over	17.1	-6.3	4.3	11.8	–
25,000 - 50,000	11.4	1.5	23.1	24.8	33.1
10,000 - 25,000	3.7	-1.6	14.8	12.3	28.7
5,000 - 10,000	4.2	2.1	20.6	7.5	32.0
2,500 - 5,000	17.9	1.0	17.8	3.2	40.2
1,000 - 2,500	14.9	10.0	26.6	20.5	26.6
Under 1,000	17.4	8.2	33.9	15.5	32.3
Unincorporated area	46.6	19.6	27.8	17.0	14.2
Under 100,000					
50,000 and over	–	–	–	–	–
25,000 - 50,000	5.5	4.1	9.4	25.6	47.0
10,000 - 25,000	11.6	5.7	24.0	22.2	20.9
5,000 - 10,000	11.2	-3.8	15.0	21.9	30.5
2,500 - 5,000	26.6	9.6	6.7	23.0	27.5
1,000 - 2,500	11.3	9.1	20.6	14.2	25.1
Under 1,000	22.4	7.1	16.6	14.5	22.5
Unincorporated area	27.9	18.1	20.0	15.9	13.4

In all metropolitan area size classes, satellite incorporated places of 25,000 or more population have experienced declining rates of growth continuously since 1900. That trend reaches into satellite places of 10,000-25,000 population in metropolitan areas with central cities of less than 250,000 population. In all other sizes of incorporated places the trend has been irregular. Growth rates reached their highest point in the 1920-30 decade in most instances and then subsided. Only in unincorporated areas have growth rates shown any tendency toward continuous increase. For the most part, 1940-50 and 1930-40 growth rates varied inversely with size of incorporated place and were highest in unincorporated area. But in earlier decades that pattern of variation obtained only among incorporated places of 2,500 population and over, and only in metropolitan areas with central cities of 250,000 or more population.

The rates of change of all incorporated population, by distance zones, as shown in Table 18, reveal few instances of uninterrupted increase. Irregularity of rate from decade to decade has been the prevalent characteristic. The most notable instances of consistent change are found in the 0-5 and 5-10 mile zones where the trend has been downward. In these zones are located most of the large satellites, i.e., 25,000 population and over, which have been growing at progressively lower rates. Sharp declines are also observable in the outermost zones of the smaller metropolitan areas in which small incorporated places predominate. The zones between 10 and 20 miles from central cities, where the concentration of satellite incorporated places is pronounced (Table 19), have generally maintained the highest rates.

No clear association of rates of change of incorporated population with size of central city is observable for any distance zone in Table 18. The highest rates occurred in the 250,000-500,000 class, while in the two adjacent size classes rates are relatively low. It is apparent, however, that the larger the central city the more distant from it are the zones of highest rates of change.

The relation of growth rates in satellite places to size of central city is made clearer when they are expressed as ratios to central city growth rates, as in Fig. 19. It is immediately apparent that the smaller the size of central city the lower has been the relative growth rates of all sizes and types of satellite places. This is true of each of the three decades shown. Only in a few instances, and those mainly in 1900-10, do any of the curves for the 1,000,000 and over class of areas drop below unity. A striking exception to the general pattern in that size class is presented by the satellites of 50,000 or more population the ratios of which are below unity in the inner zones and above unity in outer zones. In the 500,000-1,000,000

TABLE 18. PER CENT CHANGE OF SATELLITE INCORPORATED POPULATION IN STANDARD METROPOLITAN AREAS, BY SIZE OF CENTRAL CITY, DISTANCE ZONES, AND DECADE, 1900-1950

Size of central city and distance zones	1940-50	1930-40	1920-30	1910-20	1900-10
1,000,000 and over	20.4	7.2	39.1	30.0	39.9
0 - 5 miles	-15.5	-1.8	15.6	20.5	32.4
5 - 10 "	17.5	8.1	47.2	34.2	38.1
10 - 15 "	24.3	5.8	30.1	29.0	40.4
15 - 20 "	31.1	12.5	65.1	39.6	64.7
20 - 25 "	22.4	9.8	59.3	28.5	44.2
25 - 30 "	22.6	7.7	39.3	42.8	40.7
30 - 35 "	32.3	5.8	31.3	28.6	31.5
35 miles and over	18.3	3.7	24.5	10.4	23.5
500,000 - 1,000,000	23.1	5.9	32.6	23.7	29.4
0 - 5 miles	9.3	1.4	18.2	22.1	29.1
5 - 10 "	25.0	6.8	44.8	26.0	36.7
10 - 15 "	48.9	9.0	33.2	15.7	27.9
15 - 20 "	19.3	8.9	49.3	49.5	24.9
20 - 25 "	14.3	7.2	11.5	24.1	16.9
25 - 30 "	11.4	1.2	15.8	19.2	-2.6
30 - 35 "	9.5	1.4	17.9	3.6	37.8
35 miles and over	52.3	9.6	16.3	2.5	43.1
250,000 - 500,000	25.4	8.6	45.7	51.6	53.3
0 - 5 miles	15.0	5.7	39.7	78.8	38.7
5 - 10 "	41.7	12.2	67.3	43.0	81.9
10 - 15 "	20.5	6.5	23.7	50.7	30.9
15 - 20 "	70.1	8.8	17.9	44.2	37.4
20 - 25 "	-51.0	22.4	5.7	64.9	52.0
25 - 30 "	30.8	7.6	3.1	5.7	39.8
30 - 35 "	—	—	-13.9	23.8	38.4
35 miles and over	—	—	—	16.1	0.0
100,000 - 250,000	10.6	1.3	17.0	13.2	31.6
0 - 5 miles	16.4	6.0	18.1	16.1	47.1
5 - 10 "	7.3	0.2	20.2	12.7	30.0
10 - 15 "	10.3	-0.8	13.5	18.1	22.7
15 - 20 "	17.5	2.4	25.2	-2.2	2.5
20 - 25 "	4.6	0.8	12.1	-5.1	-2.9
25 - 30 "	10.6	-1.4	7.0	2.2	14.2
30 - 35 "	12.5	4.4	1.9	-0.7	-7.0
35 miles and over	-5.7	-2.7	-9.7	12.8	8.2
Under 100,000	14.2	5.4	16.1	19.8	27.2
0 - 5 miles	19.8	5.0	21.7	18.5	25.2
5 - 10 "	11.7	1.3	14.5	18.9	22.9
10 - 15 "	19.0	7.7	24.9	28.2	36.0
15 - 20 "	16.3	7.7	7.9	17.1	13.6
20 - 25 "	-4.2	7.9	12.1	14.6	35.8
25 - 30 "	0.6	3.3	10.1	10.1	17.7
30 - 35 "	4.5	-11.4	4.1	2.5	8.8
35 miles and over	8.3	19.9	-4.9	19.0	72.1

class there are also few cases in which the curves fall below unity. The gradients, however, are steeper than are those of the 1,000,000 and over class, i.e., ratios change more rapidly with distance. The 250,000-500,000 class, which has had the most rapid growth of satellite population of any size class (See Tables 10 and 18), nevertheless had ratios below those of the two larger classes of metropolitan areas. In the two smallest size classes of metropolitan areas, high relative rates of growth in satellite places have been held within 20 miles of central cities for the most part, though only in two or three cases have the ratios exceeded 2.0.

Increases of ratios, from 1900-10 to 1940-50, have been general over all size classes of metropolitan areas and in most sizes and types of satellite places. The increases are particularly striking in areas with central cities of 1,000,000 or more population, especially in unincorporated areas. On the other hand, increases have been moderate in small metropolitan areas. The largest satellite places have been least affected by the tendency toward increase of relative growth rates. In the three smallest metropolitan areas the trend has actually worked in the opposite direction. It is also noteworthy that the largest increases of ratios have occurred within 15 miles of central cities. And at greater distances, particularly in small metropolitan areas, 1940-50 ratios frequently drop below those of earlier decades.

The changing patterns of population distribution in each distance zone are shown in Fig. 20. The proportion of the population occupying unincorporated area, as well as that in incorporated places of less than 10,000 population, decreases with increases in the size of central cities. These differences tend to diminish as distance from the central city is lengthened. The proportion represented by the population in incorporated places of 10,000 or more population varies directly with size of city.

In large metropolitan areas, those with central cities of 500,000 or more population, the proportion of the population in unincorporated area in each distance zone declined from 1900 to 1950. The proportions in incorporated places of less than 2,500 population increased to 1910 and then declined through the next four decades. Increases in places of 2,500 or more population were sustained throughout the period.

Unincorporated areas in the 250,000-500,000 class gained increased proportions more or less steadily. In fact, it appears that the proportions in unincorporated areas were enlarged at the expense of all sizes of incorporated satellite places. The principal change of unincorporated area population in metropolitan areas with central cities of 100,000-250,000 population involved increase within inner zones and decline in outer zones. This was accompanied by a decline in the proportion in places

TABLE 19. AVERAGE NUMBER OF SATELLITE INCORPORATED
PLACES IN STANDARD METROPOLITAN AREAS, BY SIZE OF
CENTRAL CITY, DISTANCE ZONE, AND CENSUS YEAR, 1900-1950

Size of central city and distance zone	1950	1940	1930	1920	1910	1900
1,000,000 and over	149.4	144.8	174.5	197.6	141.3	107.0
0 - 10 miles	21.6	22.2	27.2	30.3	21.3	17.0
10 - 20 "	59.0	56.8	67.6	72.0	51.0	36.0
20 - 30 "	36.4	35.6	42.5	48.3	36.0	27.3
30 miles and over	32.4	30.2	37.2	47.0	33.0	26.7
500,000 - 1,000,000	45.8	44.9	59.6	65.0	92.7	20.3
0 - 10 miles	18.7	15.4	19.5	20.5	29.0	7.7
10 - 20 "	14.2	14.5	19.1	19.8	25.7	5.0
20 - 30 "	9.8	11.5	15.0	17.0	28.0	4.3
30 miles and over	3.1	3.5	6.0	7.7	10.0	3.3
250,000 - 500,000	15.3	11.4	29.7	14.2	16.1	23.6
0 - 10 miles	7.3	6.7	16.5	7.3	5.8	6.5
10 - 20 "	6.6	4.0	11.1	4.8	4.9	6.7
20 - 30 "	1.2	.7	2.1	2.0	3.1	7.1
30 miles and over	.2	—	—	.1	2.3	3.3
100,000 - 250,000	9.7	11.3	12.2	14.1	13.5	6.7
0 - 10 miles	3.4	3.8	4.0	5.2	5.3	3.0
10 - 20 "	4.3	5.1	5.5	6.9	6.5	3.0
20 - 30 "	1.3	1.5	1.8	1.8	1.5	.5
30 miles and over	.7	.9	.9	.2	.2	.2
Under 100,000	9.4	7.3	6.4	7.1	7.7	6.7
0 - 10 miles	3.6	2.8	2.4	2.5	2.7	2.4
10 - 20 "	4.1	3.2	2.8	3.2	3.4	3.0
20 - 30 "	1.2	.9	.8	.9	1.0	.9
30 miles and over	.5	.4	.4	.5	.6	.4

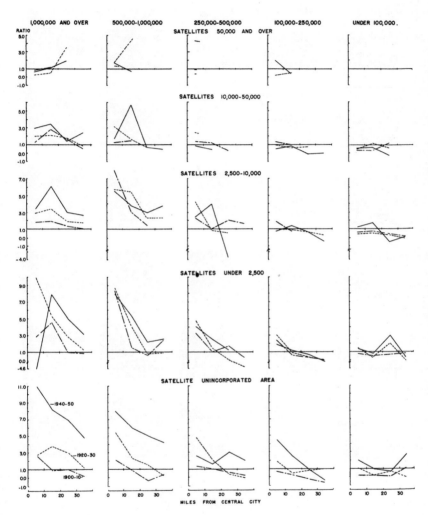

FIGURE 19

RATIO OF RATE OF CHANGE IN SATELLITE PLACES TO RATE OF CHANGE IN CENTRAL CITIES OF
STANDARD METROPOLITAN AREAS, BY SIZE OF CENTRAL CITY AND BY DISTANCE ZONE, FOR
SELECTED DECADES

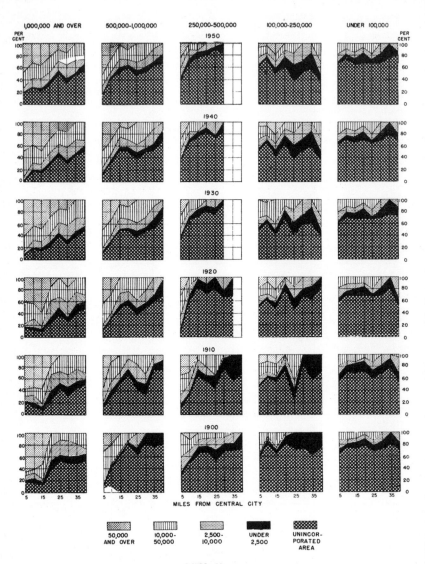

FIGURE 20

PER CENT DISTRIBUTION OF POPULATION IN DISTANCE ZONES OF STANDARD METROPOLITAN AREAS,
BY SIZE AND TYPE OF SATELLITE PLACE AND BY SIZE OF CENTRAL CITY, 1900-1950

of less than 2,500 population and a rapid increase of the proportions in
places over 2,500 population, especially in zones beyond 20 miles from
central cities.

The distribution of satellite population shows the least change in
the smallest class of metropolitan areas. It is evident, however, that
unincorporated areas declined to 1920 and then regained their 1900 proportions by 1950. These shifts concerned the zones within 10 miles and
beyond 35 miles of central cities. There was also some increase in proportions contained by satellites of 10,000 population and over.

CHAPTER IV

AVERAGE ANNUAL GROWTH OF CENTRAL CITY AND POPULATION REDISTRIBUTION

The suggestion was made in the preceding chapter that rate of growth of central city may influence population redistribution. Evidence of this relationship was observed in the ratios of satellite growth to central city growth for successive decades: satellite area growth rates varied inversely with central city growth rates. But whether this association was the result of changing historical circumstances or an effect of central city growth rates remains to be determined. There is also the possibility that the irregularities in the relationship of population redistribution with size of central city observed in Chapter III may be a function of differences in growth rates. If so those irregularities should disappear when the factor of central city growth rate is controlled. The present chapter will attempt to answer both of these questions.

For the purposes of the following analysis, central city growth rate is defined as the 50-year average annual rate of increase. Central cities were ranked on this basis, and the rank array was divided into three approximately equal parts to provide high, medium, and low classes of central city growth rates. The ranges for each class are:

High	6.14 and over
Medium	2.28 - 6.13
Low	2.27 and under

Table 20 indicates the number of metropolitan areas in each central city growth rate class.[1]

Central Cities and Satellite Areas

That the rate of inter-censal growth of the total metropolitan population is associated with the long-run growth experience of central cities is clearly indicated in Table 21. Areas whose central cities have had the lowest average annual increase have grown more slowly in every decade than have metropolitan areas with more rapidly growing central cities. This direct relationship is not, as might reasonably have been expected, entirely a function of central city rates of increase. Growth rates in satellite areas, after 1910, also varied directly with central city growth trends. The tendency toward an inverse relationship in 1900-10 is a departure from the pattern established during succeeding decades.

TABLE 20. NUMBER OF STANDARD METROPOLITAN AREAS BY AVERAGE ANNUAL RATE OF CENTRAL CITY CHANGE, SIZE OF CENTRAL CITY, AND DECADE, 1900 - 1950

Average annual rate of change and size of central city	1940-50	1930-40	1920-30	1910-20	1900-10
Total	143	157	155	153	148
High	43	51	50	48	44
1,000,000 and over	2	2	1	-	-
500,000 - 1,000,000	-	-	-	-	-
250,000 - 500,000	2	4	-	1	1
100,000 - 250,000	11	10	7	1	-
Under 100,000	28	35	42	46	43
Medium	51	54	54	54	54
1,000,000 and over	1	1	1	1	1
500,000 - 1,000,000	6	5	3	2	-
250,000 - 500,000	5	6	4	4	6
100,000 - 250,000	14	15	14	10	5
Under 100,000	25	27	32	37	42
Low	49	52	51	51	50
1,000,000 and over	2	2	2	2	2
500,000 - 1,000,000	4	5	5	4	3
250,000 - 500,000	4	5	3	3	4
100,000 - 250,000	16	16	16	13	10
Under 100,000	23	24	25	29	31

TABLE 21. PER CENT CHANGE OF POPULATION IN STANDARD
METROPOLITAN AREAS, BY TYPE OF PLACE, AVERAGE
ANNUAL RATE OF CENTRAL CITY CHANGE, AND DECADE,
1900-1950

Type of place and average annual rate of change	1940-50	1930-40	1920-30	1910-20	1900-10
Actual					
Total					
High	37.1	16.7	46.6	55.2	42.0
Medium	18.9	8.2	25.7	24.3	34.7
Low	12.0	3.9	17.8	18.1	22.9
Central cities					
High	27.9	11.5	53.4	73.8	72.9
Medium	9.9	6.2	21.6	24.8	37.6
Low	5.6	0.8	11.7	17.5	20.9
Satellite areas					
High	50.5	25.5	35.2	32.1	17.0
Medium	35.4	11.9	34.3	23.1	29.3
Low	19.8	8.0	27.3	19.0	25.9
Adjusted[a]					
Total					
High	30.1	13.3	39.4	33.8	17.9
Medium	19.8	8.5	26.3	26.3	30.3
Low	12.7	3.9	18.4	18.6	23.3
Central cities					
High	22.2	9.0	39.4	33.8	30.0
Medium	10.1	6.2	21.6	26.2	34.1
Low	5.7	0.8	12.0	17.6	22.4
Satellite areas					
High	41.6	20.5	39.7	22.9	7.8
Medium	37.4	13.0	36.2	26.3	23.2
Low	21.2	8.6	28.5	20.1	24.7

[a]Adjusted for size of central city. Size distribution of all areas used
as the standard.

An examination of the adjusted rates in Table 21 reveals that the association observed in the unadjusted rates is independent of variations in the size of central city population. The adjustment of rates in each growth class to a standard distribution of central city sizes introduces a number of minor changes, however. For example, the amount of difference in rates is reduced in almost every type of place and decade series. The most striking change of this kind occurs in the central city rates for the first three decades of the period. Evidently the very large proportion of metropolitan areas with small central cities that fell into the high growth class (see Table 20) exaggerated the unadjusted rates for that class. The direct relationship of population change with average annual growth rate of central city observable in the unadjusted rates for all metropolitan areas in 1900-10 disappears when rates are adjusted. That seems to be due to the widened spread of rates for satellite areas. In view of the failure of the adjustment of rates to have added any important correction of the observed relationship, no further adjustment of the data seems necessary.

Growth rates of total populations have declined more or less steadily through the 50-year period regardless of the trends that prevailed in central cities. It is to be noted, furthermore, that the unevenness of decline, which has been attributed to the unique historical events of the 1910-20 and the 1930-40 decades, has not been eliminated by controlling the rate of central city growth. In satellite areas the trend of decline is evident only in the low class and the trend there is irregular.

The direct relationship between average annual rate of central city growth and the growth of population in satellite areas is shown in Fig. 21 and appears to hold in most distance zones after 1910. The relationship is reversed in the 1900-10 decade. Areas with slowly growing central cities started the 50-year period with comparatively high rates in all zones and ended the half century with relatively low rates of increase. Growth rates moved in an opposite direction in the satellite zones of areas with rapidly growing central cities, not, however, without some unevenness. In the medium class the trend has corresponded fairly closely with that of the high areas.

It is only in the 1900-1910 decade that Fig. 21 lends even partial support to the hypothesis that central cities grow at the expense of satellite areas; the record of the following decades appears to contradict the hypothesis. Yet, although the expected effect of central city growth on satellite growth is not perceptible in comparisons of absolute rates, it may emerge when those rates are reduced to relative values.

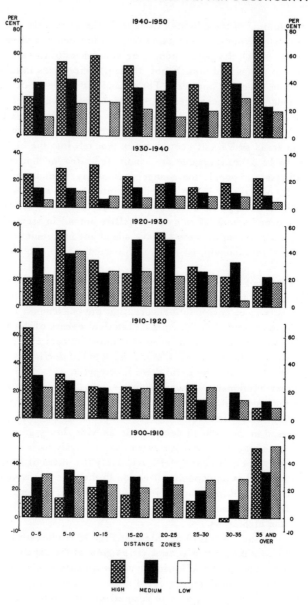

FIGURE 21

PER CENT CHANGE OF POPULATION IN DISTANCE ZONES OF STANDARD
METROPOLITAN AREAS, BY AVERAGE ANNUAL RATE OF CHANGE OF CEN-
TRAL CITY POPULATION AND BY DECADE, 1900-1950

The ratios of satellite rates to central city rates of change reveal a clear inverse relationship between the relative growth of satellite population and the average annual increase of central city population. Table 22 reveals exceptions only in the last two decades of the period under study. In other words, deconcentration has proceeded most rapidly where the central city has grown most slowly. It seems quite probable, therefore, that satellite growth is an inverse function of central city growth; as one increases the other tends to decrease or to grow at a reduced rate. The figures support the assumption that metropolitan growth is a unitary phenomenon rather than an arithmetic summation of two or more growth tendencies.

The ratios for distance zones, described in Fig. 22, conform to the pattern observed in Table 22, despite many overlappings of the curves. Not until after 1930 do the ratios for areas with the most rapidly growing central cities rise above unity in any zone. On the other hand, in the areas with the slowest growing central cities ratios fall below unity only in zones beyond 30 miles from metropolitan centers in the early decades. A conspicuous feature of Fig. 22 is the lack of clear cut gradients in the distributions of ratios. Even the comparatively flat gradients observed in Fig. 6 appear to have been vitiated by the subdivision of all Standard Metropolitan Areas into classes based on average annual rate of central city change.

A comparison of the distributions of the amounts of population increase in each decennial period reveals a marked centrifugal tendency in all classes of areas. As may be observed in Table 23, 78 per cent of all increase in high areas accrued to central cities in 1900-10, while in medium areas the proportion was 71 per cent and in low areas it was 56 per cent.

TABLE 22. RATIO OF RATE OF POPULATION CHANGE IN SATEL-
LITE AREAS TO RATE OF CHANGE IN CENTRAL CITIES OF
STANDARD METROPOLITAN AREAS, BY AVERAGE ANNUAL
RATE OF CENTRAL CITY CHANGE AND BY DECADE,
1900 - 1950

Average annual rate of central city change	1940-50	1930-40	1920-30	1910-20	1900-10
All areas	2.7	2.5	1.4	0.9	0.8
High	1.8	2.2	0.7	0.4	0.2
Medium	3.6	1.9	1.6	0.9	0.8
Low	3.5	10.0	2.3	1.1	1.2

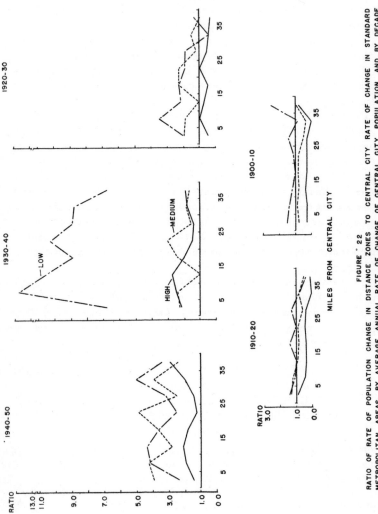

FIGURE 22

RATIO OF RATE OF POPULATION CHANGE IN DISTANCE ZONES TO CENTRAL CITY RATE OF CHANGE IN STANDARD METROPOLITAN AREAS, BY AVERAGE ANNUAL RATE OF CHANGE OF CENTRAL CITY POPULATION AND BY DECADE, 1900-1950

In 1940-50 these proportions had declined to 44, 34, and 26, respectively.
But in 1940-50 a radius of more than 10 miles was required to contain the
proportion of the increment claimed by central cities of both high and
medium areas in 1900-10. In low areas a radius of less than 10 miles contained in 1940-50 the proportion of the increase that went to central cities
in the first decade. Thus while the core parts of metropolitan areas with
slowly growing central cities received relatively small shares of the gains,
the dispersion of the increases to population at least within a 15-mile ra
radius proceeded more rapidly in areas with rapidly growing central cities.
Actually, however, dispersion over the total metropolitan area moved at a
faster pace in low than in either medium or high areas. In spite of the
centrifugal tendencies of growth, the fact remains that the more rapid the
rate of central city growth the smaller is the proportion of all growth attracted to satellite areas. Needless to say, this adds further confirmation
to the inferences that central city growth detracts from satellite area
growth.

Despite the uninterrupted dispersion of population increase there has
been a concentration of population through part of the 50-year period at
least in each class of metropolitan areas. In the high areas, Table 24
shows, concentration continued to 1930, after which deconcentration set
in. Concentration in the medium areas gave way to deconcentration after
1920. And in the low areas concentration within a radius of 15 miles
ended in 1910, but in the more distant zones the centripetal trend persisted
to 1920. The rates of redistribution are more clearly visible in Fig. 23.
It will be observed that each of the three classes of areas began the study
period with declining rates of redistribution. In each case the decline
ended in the decade in which concentration yielded to deconcentration.
Thereafter the rate of redistribution increased as deconcentration progressed. Steeper rises for low and medium than for high areas are
apparent.

Size and Type of Satellite Places

In general, all sizes and types of satellite places have grown at rates
which vary directly with the average annual rate of central city growth. As
Table 25 shows, that association is repeated in the data for every decade.
Frequently, however, rates of change are higher in the medium than in the
high class of metropolitan areas, especially in the 20-30 mile zones.

A more or less consistent pattern of change in the rates of change is
observable in each of the three classes of metropolitan areas. Unincorporated area rates increased over the 50 years and the rates of change in

TABLE 23. CUMULATIVE PERCENTAGE DISTRIBUTION OF
POPULATION INCREASE IN STANDARD METROPOLITAN
AREAS, BY AVERAGE ANNUAL RATE OF CENTRAL CITY
CHANGE, DISTANCE FROM CENTRAL CITY, AND
DECADE, 1900 - 1950

Average annual rate of central city change and distance from central city	1940-50	1930-40	1920-30	1910-20	1900-10
High					
Central cities	44.5	43.3	71.5	74.0	77.7
0 - 5 miles	50.3	51.2	74.8	82.2	80.8
5 - 10 "	68.7	69.4	84.9	88.8	85.6
10 - 15 "	84.1	85.4	91.7	93.9	92.9
15 - 20 "	92.5	93.9	94.9	97.4	96.5
20 - 25 "	95.7	97.2	98.8	99.1	97.7
25 - 30 "	97.0	98.3	99.5	99.8	98.3
30 - 35 "	98.1	99.0	99.7	99.8	98.3
35 miles and over	100.0	100.0	100.0	100.0	100.0
Medium					
Central cities	33.7	49.7	56.9	68.7	70.7
0 - 5 miles	41.2	55.7	61.9	72.7	73.6
5 - 10 "	66.1	74.5	76.6	83.6	83.7
10 - 15 "	78.2	81.4	84.9	92.0	91.5
15 - 20 "	86.8	89.2	91.7	95.2	94.8
20 - 25 "	93.9	95.0	96.0	97.4	96.9
25 - 30 "	96.1	96.8	97.6	98.3	98.0
30 - 35 "	98.2	98.2	98.8	99.1	98.4
35 miles and over	100.0	100.0	100.0	100.0	100.0
Low					
Central cities	25.8	12.1	39.9	58.7	56.1
0 - 5 miles	35.8	24.5	50.9	69.1	66.8
5 - 10 "	61.1	58.9	75.1	80.3	80.1
10 - 15 "	78.4	75.6	85.4	87.4	87.9
15 - 20 "	87.3	84.7	92.1	93.0	92.2
20 - 25 "	91.3	91.5	95.7	96.0	95.3
25 - 30 "	94.9	95.9	98.3	98.5	97.7
30 - 35 "	97.3	97.8	98.6	99.3	98.6
35 miles and over	100.0	100.0	100.0	100.0	100.0

TABLE 24. CUMULATIVE PERCENTAGE DISTRIBUTION OF
POPULATION IN STANDARD METROPOLITAN AREAS, BY
AVERAGE ANNUAL RATE OF CENTRAL CITY CHANGE,
DISTANCE ZONE, AND CENSUS YEAR, 1900 - 1950

Average annual rate of central city change, and distance zone	1950	1940	1930	1920	1910	1900
High						
Central cities	55.3	59.3	62.9	62.3	55.3	44.8
0 - 5 miles	61.0	65.0	68.3	69.7	62.1	53.7
5 - 10 "	75.2	77.7	79.0	78.3	73.3	67.9
10 - 15 "	86.5	87.5	87.7	87.7	85.4	82.7
15 - 20 "	93.3	93.6	94.0	94.0	93.7	92.3
20 - 25 "	96.8	97.2	97.3	97.4	96.6	96.0
25 - 30 "	98.0	98.4	98.6	98.6	98.1	97.9
30 - 35 "	98.8	99.1	99.2	99.0	98.6	98.6
35 miles and over	100.0	100.0	100.0	100.0	100.0	100.0
Medium						
Central cities	59.6	64.5	65.5	67.7	67.2	65.3
0 - 5 miles	63.9	68.2	69.1	70.9	70.4	69.0
5 - 10 "	77.4	79.6	80.0	80.8	80.3	79.1
10 - 15 "	86.7	88.4	89.1	90.1	89.6	89.1
15 - 20 "	92.0	93.0	93.4	93.7	93.3	92.9
20 - 25 "	95.5	95.8	96.0	96.0	95.6	95.3
25 - 30 "	97.3	97.5	97.6	97.6	97.3	97.2
30 - 35 "	98.5	98.5	98.6	98.5	98.3	98.3
35 miles and over	100.0	100.0	100.0	100.0	100.0	100.0
Low						
Central cities	52.0	55.1	57.7	60.8	60.8	61.3
0 - 5 miles	61.4	64.4	66.6	69.3	69.2	69.3
5 - 10 "	75.8	77.5	79.2	79.9	80.0	79.7
10 - 15 "	85.3	86.1	87.0	87.3	87.3	87.0
15 - 20 "	91.0	91.4	92.0	92.0	91.9	91.7
20 - 25 "	94.5	94.8	95.2	95.1	95.0	94.8
25 - 30 "	97.0	97.2	97.4	97.2	97.1	96.8
30 - 35 "	98.2	98.2	98.4	98.3	98.2	98.0
35 miles and over	100.0	100.0	100.0	100.0	100.0	100.0

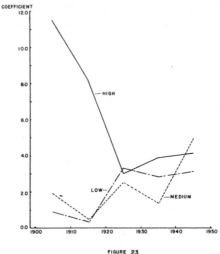

FIGURE 23
COEFFICIENTS OF POPULATION REDISTRIBUTION IN STANDARD
METROPOLITAN AREAS, BY AVERAGE ANNUAL RATE OF CHANGE
OF CENTRAL CITY POPULATION, 1900-1950

in incorporated places decreased. The largest declines occurred in the
biggest satellite incorporated places. In areas with slow growing central
cities incorporated places of 10,000 or more population lost population
with increasing frequency in the later decades. Changes in the rates of
change appear to have been most extreme where the average rate of central city growth has been highest. That appears with greatest clarity at
the extremes of the satellite size range, that is, in the rates of unincorporated area and of the largest incorporated places.

But, as previously observed, when rates of change are expressed as
ratios to central city rates the direct relationship with average annual rate
of central city growth becomes an inverse relationship (Table 26). A
notable exception, though not an entirely consistent one, is supplied by
the incorporated places of 10,000 or more population. Ratios for such
places tend to increase with the rate of central city growth.

In metropolitan areas with low rates of central city growth the highest
ratios moved from incorporated places of less than 10,000 population to
unincorporated area. This shift seems to have been completed in 1930-40.
A similar change occurred in areas with central cities that had medium
growth rates, but it was not until 1940-50 that unincorporated area emerged
as, in relative terms, the most rapidly growing type of satellite place.
Likewise, in areas with central cities that had the highest average annual
rates of change such a change was in the making, though it had not been
consumated by 1940-50.

Table 25. Per Cent Change of Satellite Population in Standard Metropolitan Areas, by Size and Type of Satellite Place, Distance Zone, Average Annual Rate of Central City Change, and Decade, 1900-1950

Size and type of place and distance zone	High					Medium					Low				
	1940-1950	1930-1940	1920-1930	1910-1920	1900-1910	1940-1950	1930-1940	1920-1930	1910-1920	1900-1910	1940-1950	1930-1940	1920-1930	1910-1920	1900-1910
50,000 and over															
0-10 miles	21.5[a]	10.1[a]	---	---	---	13.2	-1.3	13.9	21.2[a]	46.7[a]	5.2	-0.3	7.3	11.9	23.5
10-20 miles	46.0[a]	15.7[a]	---	---	---	4.2	0.2	13.7	19.0	35.5	4.7	-1.6	5.5[a]	21.6[a]	---
20-30 miles	10.6[a]	2.6[a]	---	---	---	---	---	---	---	---	18.2[a]	10.3[a]	81.3[a]	---	---
30 miles and over	---	---	---	---	---	---	---	---	---	---	---	---	---	---	---
10,000 - 50,000															
0-10 miles	35.7	17.1	41.2	63.9[a]	90.5[a]	14.4	26.2	44.7	24.1	41.3[a]	0.5	-10.7	25.1	22.7	23.0
10-20 miles	50.4[a]	17.8	41.1[a]	36.1[a]	10.8[a]	19.7	7.9	44.9	307.2	206.3[a]	31.6	3.4	24.2	-16.5	37.3
20-30 miles	42.0[a]	5.5[a]	89.4[a]	---	---	13.8	12.0	21.7	35.2[a]	26.2[a]	-0.5	-0.3	21.6	38.5	46.4[a]
30 miles and over	42.6[a]	5.3[a]	---	---	---	30.4	0.2	2.0[a]	27.6[a]	27.2[a]	12.5	1.9	25.8	15.2	18.3[a]
2,500 - 10,000															
0-10 miles	84.8	13.6	65.9	167.7	29.8	43.2	18.1	54.6	47.2	62.3	7.2	3.0	29.2	20.7	39.8
10-20 miles	90.4	29.0	54.7	41.5	35.1[a]	42.6	14.2	57.2	29.5	-49.1	21.3	6.4	45.4	32.0	42.5
20-30 miles	6.9	7.8	40.3[a]	---	48.8[a]	30.3	7.3	24.1	15.6	2.2	12.1	6.0	37.5	18.2	42.1
30 miles and over	61.0	76.3[a]	-2.8[a]	-28.6[a]	---	18.5	4.4	34.7	23.0	47.4	17.3	3.6	15.0	10.9	39.0
Under 2,500															
0-10 miles	49.8	26.4	170.7	22.1	38.2	52.9	25.7	104.6	44.1	64.0	23.1	13.6	41.2	34.7	51.6
10-20 miles	38.7	20.2	25.7	34.1	20.8	36.7	16.5	54.8	26.0	33.2	27.1	7.6	35.5	27.4	21.1
20-30 miles	24.3	15.8	12.6	19.3	16.8	37.3	12.3	30.2	28.9	28.5	18.3	10.2	25.0	21.0	38.2
30 miles and over	24.5	17.5	17.7	-15.1	5.4	19.5	6.9	14.1	27.2	35.5	20.6	5.3	16.0	5.5	21.6
Unincorporated area															
0-10 miles	54.6	38.3	23.9	30.2	9.3	73.4	16.7	42.8	26.4	18.3	38.4	25.6	50.1	20.5	30.5
10-20 miles	53.4	31.7	24.8	20.1	17.8	70.1	18.4	25.3	-15.1	31.8	22.9	12.3	19.9	34.8	10.1
20-30 miles	43.2	21.6	44.5	32.1	10.5	58.4	20.7	28.6	8.3	38.7	25.8	13.4	19.6	8.9	12.9
30 miles and over	87.6	24.4	17.6	18.1	41.4	34.7	17.7	31.0	7.4	17.0	30.5	10.4	0.7	7.5	10.4

[a] Based on less than five incorporated places.

Table 26. Ratio of Rate of Change of Satellite Population to Central City Rate of Change in Standard Metropolitan Areas, by Size and Type of Satellite Place, Distance Zone, Average Annual Rate of Central City Change, and Decade, 1900-1950

Size and type of satellite place and distance zone	High					Medium					Low				
	1940-1950	1930-1940	1920-1930	1910-1920	1900-1910	1940-1950	1930-1940	1920-1930	1910-1920	1900-1910	1940-1950	1930-1940	1920-1930	1910-1920	1900-1910
50,000 and over															
0-10 miles	0.8	0.9	---	---	---	1.3	-0.2	0.6	0.9	1.2	0.9	-0.4	0.6	0.7	1.1
10-20 miles	1.7	1.4	---	---	---	0.4	0.0	0.6	0.8	0.9	0.8	-2.0	0.5	1.2	---
20-30 miles	0.4	0.2	---	---	---	---	---	---	---	---	3.2	12.9	6.9	---	---
30 miles and over	---	---	---	---	---	---	---	---	---	---	---	---	---	---	---
10,000 - 50,000															
0-10 miles	1.3	1.5	0.8	0.9	1.2	1.5	4.2	2.1	1.0	1.1	0.1	-13.4	2.1	1.3	1.1
10-20 miles	1.8	1.5	0.8	0.5	0.1	2.0	1.3	2.1	12.4	5.5	5.6	4.2	2.1	-0.9	1.8
20-30 miles	1.5	0.5	1.7	---	---	1.4	1.9	1.0	1.4	0.7	-0.1	-0.4	1.8	2.2	2.2
30 miles and over	1.5	0.5	---	---	---	3.1	0.0	0.1	1.1	0.7	2.2	2.4	2.2	0.9	0.9
2,500 - 10,000															
0-10 miles	3.0	1.2	1.2	2.3	0.4	4.4	2.9	2.5	1.9	1.7	1.3	3.8	2.5	1.2	1.9
10-20 miles	3.2	2.5	1.0	0.6	0.5	4.3	2.3	3.1	1.2	-1.3	3.8	8.0	3.9	1.8	2.0
20-30 miles	0.2	0.7	0.8	---	0.7	3.1	1.2	1.1	0.6	0.1	2.2	7.5	3.2	1.0	2.0
30 miles and over	2.2	6.6	-0.1	0.4	---	1.9	0.7	1.6	0.9	1.3	3.1	4.5	1.3	0.6	1.9
Under 2,500															
0-10 miles	1.8	2.3	3.2	0.3	0.5	5.3	4.1	4.8	1.8	1.7	4.1	17.0	3.5	2.0	2.5
10-20 miles	1.4	1.8	0.5	0.5	0.3	3.7	2.7	2.4	1.0	0.9	4.8	9.5	3.0	1.6	1.0
20-30 miles	0.9	1.4	0.2	0.3	0.2	3.8	2.0	1.4	1.2	0.8	3.3	12.8	2.1	1.2	1.8
30 miles and over	0.9	1.5	0.3	-0.2	0.1	2.0	1.0	0.7	1.1	0.9	3.7	6.6	1.4	0.3	1.0
Unincorporated area															
0-10 miles	2.0	3.3	0.4	0.4	0.1	7.4	2.7	2.0	1.1	0.5	6.9	32.0	4.3	1.2	1.5
10-20 miles	1.9	2.8	0.5	0.3	0.2	7.1	3.0	1.2	-0.6	0.8	4.1	15.4	1.7	2.0	0.5
20-30 miles	1.5	1.9	0.8	0.4	0.1	5.9	3.3	2.7	0.3	1.0	4.6	16.8	0.5	0.5	0.6
30 miles and over	3.1	2.1	0.3	0.2	0.6	3.5	2.9	1.4	0.3	0.5	5.4	13.0	0.1	0.4	0.5

It is apparent, therefore, that deconcentration has progressed most rapidly in areas with slow growing central cities and that it has been directed mainly toward the small incorporated places and unincorporated area. The trends in areas with higher rates of central city growth, however, indicate an accelerating deconcentration and with similar results.

In view of the differentials in rates of deconcentration that have been described, the percentage distributions by size and type of satellite place within each distance zone, as shown in Table 27, contain a number of points of interest. For example, the concentration of population in large incorporated places, i.e., 10,000 or more population, has been highest where the average annual rate of central city change has been lowest. On the other hand, the proportion of population in unincorporated area has varied directly with the rate of central city change. In this connection it should be noted that in all classes of metropolitan areas the proportions in unincorporated areas declined from 1900 to 1930 and then increased through the following census years. These facts, together with the growing tendency for unincorporated area to increase more rapidly than other types of satellite places, make it seem doubtful that the proportion of all population in unincorporated areas will ever drop to as low a figure in the high class of metropolitan areas as it has been in the class of areas with low rates of central city change. This depends somewhat on the observed tendency of large satellite places to continue the relatively high growth rates in metropolitan areas with high average annual rates of central city change.

Table 22. Per Cent Distribution of Satellite Population in Standard Metropolitan Areas, by Size and Type of Satellite Place, Census Year, Average Annual Rate of Central City Change, and Distance Zone, 1900-1950

Census year and size and type of satellite place	High				Medium				Low			
	Miles from central city				_Miles from central city_				_Miles from central city_			
	0-10 miles	10-20 miles	20-30 miles	30 miles and over	0-10 miles	10-20 miles	20-30 miles	30 miles and over	0-10 miles	10-20 miles	20-30 miles	30 miles and over
1950												
Total	100.0	100.0	100.0	100.0	100.0	100.0	100.0	100.0	100.0	100.0	100.0	100.0
50,000 and over	10.4	10.9	---	---	21.3	27.9	22.9	---	16.8	8.2	13.6	---
10,000 - 50,000	18.6	15.0	9.5	13.9	17.6	23.4	16.9	15.3	19.6	17.3	20.9	28.5
2,500 - 10,000	10.0	13.3	8.3	9.7	10.9	12.4	7.6	20.9	11.2	12.7	17.8	12.4
Under 2,500	2.9	4.8	8.5	10.4	4.1	6.5	7.6	7.3	3.5	7.9	9.3	10.9
Unincorporated area	58.1	56.0	68.9	66.0	46.1	29.8	52.6	56.5	48.9	53.9	38.4	48.2
1940												
Total	100.0	100.0	100.0	100.0	100.0	100.0	100.0	100.0	100.0	100.0	100.0	100.0
50,000 and over	12.7	11.4	---	---	26.5	34.6	28.1	---	19.0	9.6	13.0	---
10,000 - 50,000	20.4	15.5	11.6	16.5	21.7	25.3	18.1	15.2	23.2	16.1	24.3	31.0
2,500 - 10,000	8.1	10.8	7.8	10.2	10.7	11.3	7.6	22.8	12.4	12.8	18.3	13.0
Under 2,500	2.8	5.4	10.7	14.0	3.7	6.2	7.6	7.9	3.4	7.7	9.1	11.0
Unincorporated area	56.0	56.9	64.7	59.3	37.4	22.6	46.2	54.1	42.0	53.8	35.3	45.0
1930												
Total	100.0	100.0	100.0	100.0	100.0	100.0	100.0	100.0	100.0	100.0	100.0	100.0
50,000 and over	16.2	8.3	---	---	28.5	36.6	26.2	---	20.5	10.1	12.1	---
10,000 - 50,000	18.7	14.5	12.5	18.8	21.5	21.4	21.3	16.7	23.8	21.9	24.4	31.4
2,500 - 10,000	9.7	11.1	8.2	1.8	10.4	6.6	8.3	23.4	12.4	13.4	17.5	12.9
Under 2,500	3.8	6.5	10.6	22.1	3.2	6.6	8.3	8.6	3.6	8.0	9.5	11.9
Unincorporated area	51.6	59.6	63.1	57.3	36.4	25.0	44.2	51.3	39.7	46.6	36.5	43.8
1920												
Total	100.0	100.0	100.0	100.0	100.0	100.0	100.0	100.0	100.0	100.0	100.0	100.0
50,000 and over	17.2	17.5	---	---	30.0	36.1	23.8	---	16.5	5.7	4.9	---
10,000 - 50,000	9.8	6.7	12.1	---	17.0	14.1	23.3	16.1	27.3	20.7	26.5	26.1
2,500 - 10,000	5.3	10.4	4.6	3.5	10.1	9.8	9.9	20.7	14.6	14.8	16.4	12.7
Under 2,500	---	---	7.7	23.4	4.9	8.2	9.9	10.3	4.7	9.3	11.5	12.4
Unincorporated area	67.7	65.4	75.6	73.1	38.0	31.8	43.0	52.9	36.9	49.5	40.7	48.8
1910												
Total	100.0	100.0	100.0	100.0	100.0	100.0	100.0	100.0	100.0	100.0	100.0	100.0
50,000 and over	---	---	---	---	26.3	33.2	23.8	---	4.7	3.4	4.9	---
10,000 - 50,000	4.7	3.0	12.1	---	15.1	5.5	18.6	11.7	17.1	23.4	26.5	24.9
2,500 - 10,000	10.2	5.2	4.6	27.5	9.9	8.8	13.0	20.0	23.7	28.3	16.4	17.8
Under 2,500	6.3	10.8	7.7	5.7	5.6	8.9	13.0	11.7	13.8	13.7	11.5	14.3
Unincorporated area	78.8	81.2	75.6	66.8	43.1	43.6	44.6	56.6	40.7	31.2	40.7	43.0
1900												
Total	100.0	100.0	100.0	100.0	100.0	100.0	100.0	100.0	100.0	100.0	100.0	100.0
50,000 and over	---	---	---	---	20.7	24.9	17.1	---	---	---	---	---
10,000 - 50,000	2.8	1.8	---	---	13.8	0.9	27.1	9.3	13.3	29.3	9.1	24.9
2,500 - 10,000	5.9	5.1	6.6	---	6.4	8.0	10.9	14.2	25.6	13.7	23.4	10.4
Under 2,500	5.5	8.2	10.3	21.9	5.6	8.6	---	14.7	10.7	11.3	14.3	12.9
Unincorporated area	85.8	84.9	83.1	78.1	53.5	57.6	44.9	61.8	44.7	43.3	44.5	51.8

CHAPTER V

DISTANCE BETWEEN CENTRAL CITIES AND POPULATION REDISTRIBUTION

It is possible that some of the variation in patterns of population re-distribution within metropolitan areas may be affected by the distances between areas. Where areas are located in close proximity to one another the advantages of accessibility to two or more centers rather than to one only may be manifested in a more pronounced tendency to deconcentration than occurs where areas are widely spaced. The presence of two or more metropolitan areas within short distances of one another suggests, too, that the extent of metropolitan development in that locality may have advanced further than where areas are located far apart. If so, the tendency of population to settle in satellite zones is apt to be stronger.

Proximity is measured by air-line distances between central cities.[1] The range of distances is subdivided into three classes and all metropolitan areas are sorted accordingly. The three classes are: (1) centers within 50 miles; (2) centers more than 50 miles but less than 100 miles apart; and (3) centers 100 or more miles apart. Table 28 reports the num-of areas in each class. It would have been desirable also to control the size of central city from which distance is measured. Unfortunately, the number of metropolitan areas is too small to permit so extensive a subdivision of the data.

Central Cities and Satellite Areas

Except for the years between 1910 and 1930 the highest growth rates occurred in the most remotely located Standard Metropolitan areas, i.e., those 100 or more miles from other metropolitan areas measured from their centers. And, as may be observed in Table 29, the lowest actual rates of change were had in areas situated within 50 miles of other metropolitan areas. A trend of decline is evident in the data for areas within 100 miles of other areas, but the most distantly located areas show no clear trend

TABLE 28. NUMBER OF STANDARD METROPOLITAN AREAS,
BY DISTANCE BETWEEN CENTRAL CITIES, SIZE OF
CENTRAL CITY, AND DECADE, 1900 - 1950

Distance between and size of central city	1940-50	1930-40	1920-30	1910-20	1900-10
Total	143	157	155	153	148
Centers within 50 miles	74	75	75	75	75
1,000,000 and over	1	1	1	1	1
500,000 - 1,000,000	8	7	5	4	2
250,000 - 500,000	4	7	4	5	7
100,000 - 250,000	25	22	24	12	9
Under 100,000	36	38	41	53	56
Centers more than 50 but less than 100 miles	52	59	58	58	56
1,000,000 and over	4	4	3	2	2
500,000 - 1,000,000	1	2	2	1	1
250,000 - 500,000	6	7	3	3	3
100,000 - 250,000	13	15	10	9	5
Under 100,000	28	31	40	43	45
Centers 100 miles or more	17	23	22	20	17
250,000 and over[a]	2	2	1	1	1
100,000 - 250,000	3	4	3	3	1
Under 100,000	12	17	18	16	15

[a]Includes one metropolitan area with a central city of 500,000 - 1,000,000
population.

toward declining rates. Moreover, the last named class was least affected
by the retarding influences on growth incident to the 1930-1940 decade.
The growth rates of central cities in the three proximity classes maintained the same relative positions observed in the data for total populations. In this respect, however, the tendency of rates of increase to
decline operated in all classes, though the decline was least in the areas
farthest removed from other areas.

The adjustment of rates leaves the described relationship of growth
with distance between central cities undisturbed in the first three decades
of the fifty-year period. But contrary to the findings based on unadjusted

rates, the same pattern extends into the 1930-1940 decade. In the 1940-1950 decade growth rates tended to vary inversely with distance between centers. Thus the expectation of higher growth rates where the distances between metropolitan centers are least finds greater support in the adjusted than in the unadjusted rates. Even so, however, the relationship is not as definite as was anticipated.

Growth in satellite areas presents several interesting departures from the patterns in total and in central city populations. While the size of the growth rate has been directly related to the distance separating areas in three of the five decades, that relationship was sustained by rather diverse trends. For example, in areas with centers within 50 miles of other centers the growth rates of satellite populations were comparatively stable, at least the amount of increase was very slight. In areas with central cities 50 to 100 miles from other metropolitan centers satellite population reached its highest rate of growth in 1920-30 after which the rate subsided. Finally, in the most isolated areas satellite growth rates declined to 1930 and then accelerated rapidly in the last two decades.

Fig. 24 indicates that the effect of distance between metropolitan centers on rates of change in satellite areas has not penetrated far from centers. In 1930-40 and 1940-50 the direct relationship is apparent in the 0-5 mile and the 5-10 mile zones; in 1910-20 and 1920-30 the association seems to have been confined mainly to the 0-5 mile zone; and the 1900-10 decade rates tend to be inversely related to proximity between centers. No clear relationship is evident in most zones beyond 10 miles from centers, except in the 35 mile and over zone where the direct relationship appears in the first two and the last decades. If, however, attention is directed only to the within 50 miles and the 50 to 100 mile classes, growth rates are found to be directly related to proximity in virtually all satellite zones after 1910. It seems quite possible, therefore, that the diffusion of metropolitan influence as reflected in high rates of growth is of recent origin in the most isolated metropolitan areas and consequently has not reached far into hinterlands. The passing of another decade or two may produce a consistent relationship in all satellite zones.

There were negligible differences in the relative growth rates of satellite areas in 1900-10 and 1910-20. Differentiation set in, the unstandardized ratios in Table 30 show, in the 1920-30 decade and persisted to 1950. Beginning in 1920, ratios have varied inversely with distance between central cities. That relationship was somewhat indefinite, however, in the most recent inter-censal period. Thus it

TABLE 29. PER CENT CHANGE OF POPULATION IN STANDARD
METROPOLITAN AREAS, BY TYPE OF PLACE, DISTANCE
BETWEEN CENTRAL CITIES, AND DECADE, 1900-1950

Type of place and distance between central cities	1940-50	1930-40	1920-30	1910-20	1900-10
Actual					
Total					
Central cities within 50 miles	18.7	6.4	20.2	23.4	26.9
" " 50 to 100 "	19.6	8.6	29.1	25.9	31.3
" " 100 or more "	29.0	14.8	27.3	22.3	35.7
Central cities					
Central cities within 50 miles	10.6	2.9	15.2	25.3	27.6
" " 50 to 100 "	11.4	6.0	25.4	26.7	34.2
" " 100 or more "	23.0	11.6	32.2	23.4	40.4
Satellite Areas					
Central cities within 50 miles	28.5	10.9	27.3	20.8	26.0
" " 50 to 100 "	34.1	13.5	37.3	24.3	25.7
" " 100 or more "	41.1	21.6	18.0	20.1	28.0
Adjusted[a]					
Total					
Central cities within 50 miles	22.1	4.5	19.3	22.5	25.4
" " 50 to 100 "	19.2	8.3	26.5	26.1	29.2
" " 100 or more "	11.2	5.8	12.9	12.1	23.0
Central cities					
Central cities within 50 miles	18.0	2.0	13.3	23.5	26.2
" " 50 to 100 "	11.2	5.3	23.2	28.5	33.5
" " 100 or more "	8.7	4.5	15.6	12.1	21.4
Satellite areas					
Central cities within 50 miles	27.1	10.1	28.0	21.2	24.4
" " 50 to 100 "	33.3	14.0	33.7	21.1	20.8
" " 100 or more "	16.4	8.7	8.0	12.1	25.7

[a]Adjusted for size of central city. Size distribution of all areas used
as the standard.

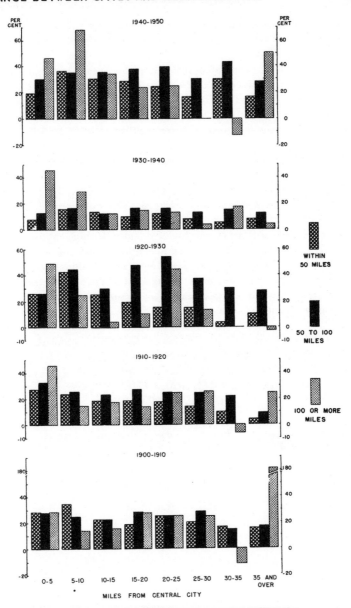

FIGURE 24
PER CENT CHANGE OF POPULATION IN DISTANCE ZONES OF STANDARD METROPOLITAN
AREAS, BY DISTANCE BETWEEN CENTRAL CITIES, AND BY DECADES, 1900-1950

appears that, at least during the last 30 years, satellite areas tended to have the highest relative growth rates where the distance between central cities are least.

The absence of consistent differences between relative growth rates during the first two decades of the 50-year period applies to all distance zones, as may be noted in Fig. 25. Barring occasional deviations, zonal rates of those decades were less than the rates of their respective central cities in all proximity classes. After 1920 the relative growth of satellite population in metropolitan areas 100 or more miles from other areas lagged behind comparable rates in less isolated areas, and the lag grew larger with distance away from central cities. Nevertheless, between 1920 and 1950 the satellite area over which rates exceeded central city rates in that proximity class was greatly enlarged. The variations of ratios with distance in metropolitan areas located within 100 miles or less of one another are particularly noteworthy. Evidently the high ratios in satellite territories of areas 50 miles or less from other areas, observed in Table 30, were due mainly to high relative growth rates within 15 miles of central cities. At greater distances during most of the period after 1920 ratios were highest in metropolitan areas located 50 to 100 miles from the nearest competing areas.

TABLE 30. RATIO OF RATES OF CHANGE IN SATELLITE AREAS TO RATES OF CHANGE IN CENTRAL CITIES OF STANDARD METROPOLITAN AREAS, BY DISTANCE BETWEEN CENTRAL CITIES AND BY DECADE, 1900 - 1950

Distance between central cities	1940-50	1930-40	1920-30	1910-20	1900-10
All areas	2.7	2.5	1.4	0.9	0.8
Within 50 miles	2.7	3.8	1.8	0.8	0.9
50 to 100 "	3.0	2.2	1.5	0.9	0.8
100 or more miles	1.8	1.9	0.6	0.8	0.7

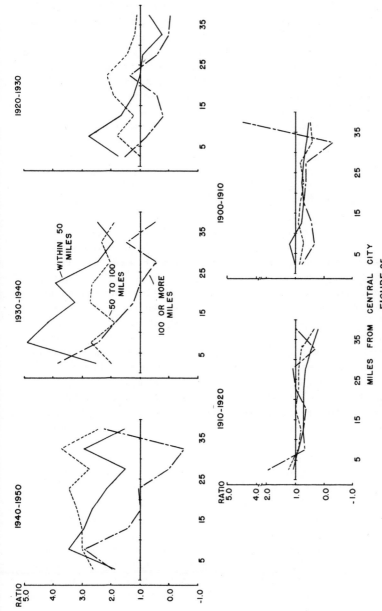

FIGURE 25
RATIO OF RATE OF POPULATION CHANGE IN DISTANCE ZONES TO CENTRAL CITY RATE OF CHANGE IN
STANDARD METROPOLITAN AREAS, BY DISTANCE BETWEEN CENTRAL CITIES, AND BY DECADES, 1900-1950

Additional light is shed on the relationship between population redistribution and the distance separating metropolitan centers by an analysis
of the distribution of decennial increments as presented in Table 31. Conspicuous in the data is the fact that, since 1920, the closer are central
cities to one another the smaller was the proportion of all increase gained
by central cities and, conversely, the larger was the proportion absorbed
by satellite areas. This was, at best, but a tendency prior to 1920. The
dispersion of population growth, however, has been widest and has proceeded with fewest interruptions in areas with central cities 50 to 100
miles from other central cities. In that class a radius of almost 15 miles
was required in 1950 to embrace the proportion of increase received by
central cities alone in 1900. But in the other proximity classes the 1900
proportion of increase received by central cities had, by 1950, dispersed
over an area with a radius of less than 10 miles.

Smaller changes have occurred in the distributions of the total populations. Table 32 indicates, however, that in each proximity class a
slightly different pattern of change has been followed. In areas located
within 50 miles of other areas concentration was the prevailing trend
down to 1930 after which deconcentration set in. In areas 50 to 100
miles from other areas the concentration phase ended in 1920. But in
the most distant areas deconcentration characterized redistribution from
1900 to 1920, following which was a decade of concentration, with a return to deconcentration characterizing the last decade. The most important shifts in all proximity classes were from central cities to satellite zones within 10 miles of central cities. For example, in areas nearest to other areas the proportion in central cities declined by 6 percentage points, or about 12 per cent; but this loss was almost entirely
absorbed by the 0-5 and 5-10 mile zones. A similar shift took place
in the most remotely located areas. Metropolitan areas 50 to 100 miles
from other areas are distinguished by the fact that central city losses
were spread over a larger part of the satellite area, to a distance of
approximately 20 miles.

The coefficients of redistribution, shown in Fig. 26, display considerable irregularity in metropolitan areas whose central cities are 50
to 100 miles and 100 or more miles from other central cities. In both
cases redistribution slowed appreciably between 1910 and 1920 and
again between 1930 and 1940, both of which were decades of reduced
metropolitan growth. Of the two classes only that comprising areas with
central cities 50 to 100 miles from other metropolitan centers shows any
tendency toward an increasing rate of redistribution over the entire 50-
year period. Increase is even more pronounced, however, in areas having

TABLE 31. CUMULATIVE PERCENTAGE DISTRIBUTION OF
POPULATION CHANGE IN STANDARD METROPOLITAN
AREAS, BY DISTANCE BETWEEN CENTRAL CITIES,
DISTANCE FROM CENTRAL CITY, AND DECADE,
1900 - 1950

Distance between central cities, and satellite distance zone	1940-50	1930-40	1920-30	1910-20	1900-10
Within 50 miles					
Central cities	30.7	25.4	44.4	62.2	58.2
0 - 5 miles	40.0	35.8	55.4	72.4	67.3
5 - 10 "	71.2	68.5	81.5	85.6	83.5
10 - 15 "	86.6	85.4	91.9	92.6	91.1
15 - 20 "	93.2	91.7	96.0	96.1	94.5
20 - 25 "	96.6	96.6	98.2	98.2	97.2
25 - 30 "	98.1	98.5	99.5	99.4	98.8
30 - 35 "	99.3	99.2	99.6	99.8	99.4
35 miles and over	100.0	100.0	100.0	100.0	100.0
50 - 100 miles					
Central cities	37.3	45.9	59.6	69.9	72.1
0 - 5 miles	43.0	51.3	63.1	74.6	75.6
5 - 10 "	59.0	67.6	74.6	82.2	82.1
10 - 15 "	74.1	77.8	82.8	89.6	90.4
15 - 20 "	85.3	88.3	90.3	94.3	94.4
20 - 25 "	91.7	93.6	95.2	96.8	96.6
25 - 30 "	94.8	96.1	97.2	98.4	98.2
30 - 35 "	97.4	97.9	98.3	99.3	98.8
35 miles and over	100.0	100.0	100.0	100.0	100.0
100 or more miles					
Central cities	52.8	53.3	77.1	68.9	70.7
0 - 5 miles	62.2	67.4	84.0	75.7	74.1
5 - 10 "	81.3	81.5	90.2	80.8	77.5
10 - 15 "	87.7	90.5	91.1	87.2	81.4
15 - 20 "	90.6	94.3	92.9	90.7	85.9
20 - 25 "	94.7	98.2	99.8	93.4	87.6
25 - 30 "	94.7	98.7	100.6	95.5	89.0
30 - 35 "	94.5	99.1	100.6	95.4	88.8
35 miles and over	100.0	100.0	100.0	100.0	100.0

TABLE 32. CUMULATIVE PERCENTAGE DISTRIBUTION OF
POPULATION IN STANDARD METROPOLITAN AREAS,
BY DISTANCE BETWEEN CENTRAL CITIES, DISTANCE
ZONE, AND CENSUS YEAR, 1900 - 1950

Distance between central cities, and distance zone	1950	1940	1930	1920	1910	1900
Within 50 miles						
Central cities	50.7	54.4	56.5	58.9	57.5	56.7
0 - 5 miles	59.9	63.6	65.6	67.6	66.2	65.4
5 - 10 "	78.4	79.7	80.6	80.5	79.4	78.2
10 - 15 "	88.8	89.2	89.6	89.2	88.4	87.8
15 - 20 "	93.6	93.7	93.9	93.6	93.0	92.7
20 - 25 "	96.6	96.6	96.7	96.5	96.0	95.8
25 - 30 "	98.4	98.4	98.4	98.3	98.0	97.9
30 - 35 "	99.2	99.2	99.2	99.2	99.0	98.9
35 miles and over	100.0	100.0	100.0	100.0	100.0	100.0
50 to 100 miles						
Central cities	59.6	64.0	65.5	68.4	67.9	66.1
0 - 5 miles	63.6	67.7	69.3	72.4	71.6	70.2
5 - 10 "	74.0	77.1	78.4	80.1	79.6	78.7
10 - 15 "	83.8	85.8	86.8	88.3	88.0	87.2
15 - 20 "	90.6	91.7	92.4	92.8	92.5	91.7
20 - 25 "	94.4	94.9	95.4	95.4	95.1	94.5
25 - 30 "	96.6	96.9	97.2	97.1	96.8	96.3
30 - 35 "	98.0	98.1	98.3	98.1	97.9	97.5
35 miles and over	100.0	100.0	100.0	100.0	100.0	100.0
100 or more miles						
Central cities	63.6	66.7	68.0	65.4	65.5	62.6
0 - 5 miles	70.3	72.7	72.7	69.3	68.9	66.9
5 - 10 "	81.0	81.0	80.1	76.6	76.8	76.7
10 - 15 "	86.9	86.7	86.4	84.5	85.2	86.6
11 - 20 "	90.3	90.3	90.3	89.3	91.2	92.6
20 - 25 "	95.1	95.3	95.0	93.7	93.6	95.1
25 - 30 "	96.0	96.4	96.5	95.4	95.4	97.2
30 - 35 "	96.3	96.8	96.9	95.9	95.8	97.8
35 miles and over	100.0	100.0	100.0	100.0	100.0	100.0

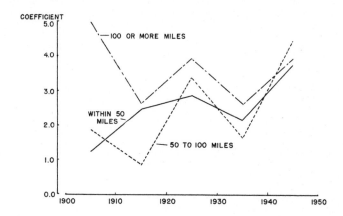

FIGURE 26
COEFFICIENTS OF POPULATION REDISTRIBUTION IN STANDARD
METROPOLITAN AREAS, BY DISTANCE BETWEEN CENTRAL CITIES,
1900-1950

central cities within 50 miles of their own centers. The increase is reversed in only one decade, 1930-40, and the decline is comparatively small. Although the rates of redistribution in the most distantly located metropolitan areas exhibit no trend of increase, they have been the highest rates down to the last decade.

Size and Type of Satellite Place

Growth rates of satellite places of different sizes and types, described in Table 33, have changed over the five decade period showing a relationship to the distances between central cities. Although rates for satellite places of 10,000 or more population have declined, the numbers of places represented by the rates are so small that no reliable conclusion regarding the effect of distance can be drawn. Rates for satellite incorporated places of 2,500 to 10,000 population have declined rapidly in metropolitan areas whose centers are within 50 miles of other centers, and relatively slowly in areas whose centers are 50 to 100 miles from other centers. But in the most isolated metropolitan areas the rates of population growth in satellites of 2,500-10,000 population, within 20 miles of central cities, have increased strikingly. Beyond 20 miles, however, declining trends have prevailed.

Table 33. Per Cent Change of Satellite Population in Standard Metropolitan Areas,
by Size and Type of Satellite Place, Distance Zone, Distance Between Central Cities, and Decades, 1900-1950

Size and type of place and distance zone	Within 50 miles					50 to 100 miles					100 or more miles				
	1940-1950	1930-1940	1920-1930	1910-1920	1900-1910	1940-1950	1930-1940	1920-1930	1910-1920	1900-1910	1940-1950	1930-1940	1920-1930	1910-1920	1900-1910
50,000 and over															
0-10 miles	19.0	1.6	16.7	21.7	41.4[a]	-0.3	0.7	3.4	10.0	27.1[a]	---	---	---	---	---
10-20 miles	2.5[a]	0.7[a]	2.0[a]	---	---	10.3	1.2	13.2	19.2	35.5[a]	---	---	---	---	---
20-30 miles	10.6[a]	2.6[a]	---	---	---	21.8[a]	10.3[a]	81.3[a]	---	---	---	---	---	---	---
30 miles and over	---	---	---	---	---	---	---	---	---	---	---	---	---	---	---
10,000 - 50,000															
0-10 miles	14.9	0.2	27.8	18.3	29.2	5.2	11.3	37.2	29.6	27.2	40.0[a]	3.9[a]	64.3[a]	27.0[a]	---
10-20 miles	23.0	4.2	20.5	26.2	22.2	34.3	10.7	50.7	47.8	63.7	---	---	---	---	---
20-30 miles	4.1[a]	3.6	11.0	18.1	28.8	13.2	6.9	41.9	55.2	42.0	---	---	---	---	---
30 miles and over	6.0[a]	1.6[a]	1.0[a]	23.7[a]	13.9[a]	25.3	1.5	23.8	17.2	21.4	0.4[a]	3.7[a]	---	---	---
2,500 - 10,000															
0-10 miles	22.2	6.2	29.5	51.4	46.9	40.1	13.2	60.6	69.7	39.5	87.3	22.4	35.6	-73.5[a]	10.9[a]
10-20 miles	25.1	6.3	40.6	29.1	34.2	57.7	18.6	73.5	36.6	59.4	60.3	26.5	0.1	11.4[a]	-24.4[a]
20-30 miles	6.8	6.2	19.6	19.8	33.6	29.8	7.7	44.4	13.4	48.5	4.0[a]	-5.8[a]	-41.5[a]	---	---
30 miles and over	23.3	4.6	15.0	5.4	47.3	25.2	5.7	41.1	18.4	28.6	-6.7	2.3	-4.7	25.0	123.5[a]
Under 2,500															
0-10 miles	37.7	18.3	64.2	33.1	44.1	33.8	20.9	130.5	42.6	72.5	77.4	30.5	42.6	37.0	65.2
10-20 miles	18.5	8.7	20.7	21.1	21.5	49.4	18.1	64.6	37.7	31.0	54.5	19.0	37.1	37.0	65.2
20-30 miles	16.0	8.3	9.5	23.4	41.6	39.1	15.6	43.2	20.1	23.1	-5.6	4.7	4.0	55.7	35.5
30 miles and over	14.6	1.8	10.9	2.3	16.4	52.9	21.5	47.8	13.5	16.9	1.9	5.5	-9.1	32.9	92.0
Unincorporated area															
0-10 miles	42.4	22.5	43.9	21.5	26.4	73.6	28.0	42.3	20.3	16.5	55.2	44.9	26.0	107.7	13.7
10-20 miles	36.3	16.3	20.0	12.6	17.4	54.8	25.3	33.4	12.8	9.5	22.0	17.5	3.6	15.3	20.7
20-30 miles	37.2	16.2	16.5	10.9	11.8	52.9	21.5	47.8	13.5	16.9	22.0	11.6	37.8	19.8	23.6
30 miles and over	28.0	8.4	4.0	5.7	10.8	41.2	20.9	27.3	8.9	7.3	102.4	8.7	-2.1	16.9	159.9

[a] Based on less than five incorporated places.

In the next smaller size class of satellite places, those with less than 2,500 population, rates have also declined within areas the centers of which are not more than 50 miles from other centers. But in areas comprising the 50 to 100 mile class, rates for the small incorporated places declined only in the 0-10 mile zone. Elsewhere their rates increased quite rapidly. And in the most remote metropolitan areas the smallest incorporated satellites within 20 miles of central cities grew with increasing rates. In distance zones beyond 20 miles from central cities their rates of change fell off sharply between 1900 and 1950.

Unincorporated area population grew at progressively higher rates in the within 50 mile and the 50-100 mile classes, the greatest changes occurring in the latter group of metropolitan areas. In the areas that are 100 or more miles distant from other areas increasing rates occurred in the 0-10 mile zone, while in the outlying zones the trends were erratic.

In summary, areas within 50 miles of other areas experienced increasing rates of change in unincorporated population, and those were rather moderate. Areas 50 to 100 miles of other areas had, by comparison, rapid increases of growth rates in incorporated places of less than 2,500 population and in unincorporated area. The largest increases of rates of change in the satellite population of areas 100 or more miles removed from other areas occurred in incorporated places of less than 10,000 population located within 20 miles of central cities. In this class of areas, in other words, there appears to have been a marked centripetal movement of satellite population directed mainly to incorporated places.

The ratios of satellite rates of change to central city rates, presented in Table 34, indicate that change has accelerated from 1900 to 1950 in all satellite places with less than 10,000 population. In the two least isolated groups of metropolitan areas the amount of change in ratios increased with distance from central city. It is also to be noted that the highest relative rates of growth passed from incorporated places to unincorporated areas. Metropolitan areas 100 or more miles removed from other areas are unique in two respects. There has been no tendency for relative growth rates to accelerate more rapidly in outer than in inner distance zones: in fact, the contrary is true. Nor have ratios for unincorporated areas exceeded those for incorporated places.

Metropolitan areas 100 or more miles distant from other centers have had, in all decades, larger proportions of their populations in unincorporated areas than have any other class of areas, as indicated in Table 35. The 30 mile and over zone, however, is an exception to that rule. It is not unlikely that in such areas that zone has not been subject to the influence of central cities. Population concentration has declined in

Table 34. Ratio of Rate of Change of Satellite Population to Central City Rate of Change in Standard Metropolitan Areas, by Size and Type of Satellite Place, Distance Zone, Distance Between Central Cities, and Decades, 1900-1950

Size and type of place and distance zone	Within 50 miles					50 to 100 miles					100 or more miles				
	1940-1950	1930-1940	1920-1930	1910-1920	1900-1910	1940-1950	1930-1940	1920-1930	1910-1920	1900-1910	1940-1950	1930-1940	1920-1930	1910-1920	1900-1910
50,000 and over															
0-10 miles	10.6	2.9	15.2	25.3	27.6	11.4	6.0	25.4	26.7	34.2	23.0	11.6	32.2	23.4	40.4
10-20 miles	1.8	0.6	1.1	0.9	1.5	0.0	-0.1	0.1	0.4	0.8	---	---	---	---	---
20-30 miles	0.2	0.2	0.1	---	---	0.9	0.2	0.5	0.7	1.0	---	---	---	---	---
30 miles and over	1.0	0.9	---	---	---	1.9	1.7	3.2	---	---	---	---	---	---	---
10,000 - 50,000															
0-10 miles	1.4	0.1	1.8	0.7	1.1	0.5	1.8	1.5	1.5	0.8	1.7	0.3	2.0	1.2	---
10-20 miles	2.2	1.4	1.3	1.0	0.8	3.0	1.8	2.0	1.8	1.9	---	---	---	---	---
20-30 miles	0.4	1.2	0.7	0.7	1.0	1.2	1.1	1.6	2.1	1.2	---	---	---	---	---
30 miles and over	0.6	0.6	0.1	0.9	0.5	2.2	0.2	0.9	0.6	0.6	0.0	0.3	---	---	---
2,500 - 10,000															
0-10 miles	2.1	2.1	1.9	2.0	1.7	3.5	2.2	2.4	2.6	1.2	3.8	1.9	1.1	-3.1	0.3
10-20 miles	2.4	2.2	2.7	1.2	1.2	5.1	3.1	2.9	1.4	1.7	2.6	2.3	0.0	0.5	-0.6
20-30 miles	0.6	2.1	1.3	0.8	1.2	2.6	1.3	1.7	0.5	1.4	0.2	-0.5	1.3	1.1	---
30 miles and over	2.2	1.6	1.0	0.2	1.7	2.2	0.9	1.6	0.7	0.8	-0.3	0.2	-0.1	1.1	3.1
Under 2,500															
0-10 miles	3.6	6.3	4.2	1.3	1.6	3.0	3.5	5.1	1.6	2.1	3.4	2.6	1.3	1.6	1.6
10-20 miles	1.7	3.0	1.4	0.8	0.8	4.3	3.0	2.5	1.4	0.9	2.4	1.6	1.2	0.8	0.7
20-30 miles	1.5	2.9	0.6	0.9	1.5	3.4	2.6	1.7	0.8	0.7	-0.2	0.4	0.1	2.4	0.9
30 miles and over	1.4	0.6	0.7	0.1	0.6	2.5	2.1	0.9	0.5	0.7	0.1	0.5	-0.3	1.4	2.3
Unincorporated area															
0-10 miles	4.0	7.8	2.9	2.8	1.0	6.5	4.7	1.7	0.8	0.5	2.4	3.9	0.8	4.6	0.3
10-20 miles	3.4	5.6	1.3	0.5	0.6	4.8	4.2	1.3	0.5	0.3	1.0	1.5	0.1	0.7	0.5
20-30 miles	3.5	5.6	1.1	0.4	0.4	4.6	3.6	1.9	0.5	0.5	1.0	1.0	1.2	0.8	0.6
30 miles and over	2.6	2.9	0.3	0.2	0.4	3.6	3.5	1.1	0.3	0.2	4.5	0.7	-0.1	0.7	4.0

Table 35. Per Cent Distribution of Satellite Population in Standard Metropolitan Areas, by Census Year, Size and Type of Satellite Place, Distance Between Central Cities, and Distance Zone, 1900-1950

Census year and size and type of place	Within 50 miles — Miles from central city				50 to 100 miles — Miles from central city				100 or more miles — Miles from central city			
	0-10 miles	10-20 miles	20-30 miles	30 miles and over	0-10 miles	10-20 miles	20-30 miles	30 miles and over	0-10 miles	10-20 miles	20-30 miles	30 miles and over
1950	100.0	100.0	100.0	100.0	100.0	100.0	100.0	100.0	100.0	100.0	100.0	100.0
50,000 and over	17.6	2.4	4.7	--	18.6	29.0	9.9	--	--	--	--	--
10,000 - 50,000	17.1	21.1	23.2	9.4	22.0	18.7	18.8	25.6	12.5	--	--	16.4
2,500 - 10,000	12.0	11.5	16.8	14.6	8.4	13.7	16.2	16.1	15.4	12.8	3.7	14.9
Under 2,500	4.1	7.5	8.4	12.1	2.6	5.6	7.5	8.3	4.3	11.2	5.4	8.0
Unincorporated area	49.2	57.5	46.9	63.9	48.4	33.0	47.6	50.0	67.8	76.0	90.9	60.7
1940	100.0	100.0	100.0	100.0	100.0	100.0	100.0	100.0	100.0	100.0	100.0	100.0
50,000 and over	19.2	3.0	5.1	--	24.8	35.6	11.0	--	--	--	--	--
10,000 - 50,000	19.3	22.2	26.6	10.9	27.7	18.8	22.5	27.1	14.2	10.3	4.2	23.4
2,500 - 10,000	12.7	11.9	18.8	14.6	7.9	11.7	16.9	17.1	13.0	9.3	6.8	22.7
Under 2,500	3.9	8.2	8.7	13.0	2.6	5.1	7.3	8.6	3.8	--	--	11.2
Unincorporated area	44.9	54.7	40.6	61.5	37.0	28.8	42.3	47.2	69.0	80.4	89.0	42.7
1930	100.0	100.0	100.0	100.0	100.0	100.0	100.0	100.0	100.0	100.0	100.0	100.0
50,000 and over	20.8	3.3	5.4	--	27.0	35.5	10.9	--	--	--	--	--
10,000 - 50,000	20.7	23.7	26.2	11.4	25.1	18.9	22.1	29.3	15.9	9.7	4.4	23.4
2,500 - 10,000	12.5	11.9	19.5	14.0	9.2	11.7	18.0	16.1	14.2	7.9	7.1	23.0
Under 2,500	4.1	8.7	9.3	14.3	2.7	5.8	7.8	10.6	3.9	--	--	10.8
Unincorporated area	41.9	52.4	39.6	60.3	36.0	28.1	41.2	44.0	66.0	82.4	88.5	42.8
1920	100.0	100.0	100.0	100.0	100.0	100.0	100.0	100.0	100.0	100.0	100.0	100.0
50,000 and over	17.2	2.0	--	--	24.1[b]	34.6	5.7	--	--	--	--	--
10,000 - 50,000	23.3	20.6	25.3	16.1	22.5	16.3	26.0	26.1	10.0	6.9	2.9	25.0
2,500 - 10,000	13.0	12.6	18.8	13.3	11.8	10.8	12.9	14.8	9.4	7.6	10.9	8.7
Under 2,500	5.2	10.3	9.5	14.7	3.9	8.0	11.4	11.6	8.5	--	--	--
Unincorporated area	41.3	54.5	46.4	55.9	37.7	30.3	39.0	47.5	72.1	85.5	86.2	66.3
1910	100.0	100.0	100.0	100.0	100.0	100.0	100.0	100.0	100.0	100.0	100.0	100.0
50,000 and over	15.9	--	--	--	25.0	32.5	24.6	--	--	--	--	--
10,000 - 50,000	21.3	17.3	20.4	10.5	14.9	14.3	15.3	25.1	9.9	--	--	32.8
2,500 - 10,000	11.1	12.4	18.7	9.5	11.0	9.2	14.5	13.6	39.6	2.7	15.1	11.0
Under 2,500	6.0	11.7	13.0	14.9	5.1	9.3	--	13.0	6.1	5.9	--	--
Unincorporated area	45.7	58.6	47.9	65.1	44.0	34.7	45.6	48.3	44.4	91.4	84.9	56.2
1900	100.0	100.0	100.0	100.0	100.0	100.0	100.0	100.0	100.0	100.0	100.0	100.0
50,000 and over	12.2	--	--	--	19.0	22.7	11.8	--	--	--	--	--
10,000 - 50,000	21.2	13.3	11.3	4.6	17.0	15.4	16.9	21.2	2.1	4.7	--	23.9
2,500 - 10,000	9.9	10.4	18.4	9.5	7.3	7.8	--	13.5	7.1	3.5	7.7	18.5
Under 2,500	5.9	11.0	14.7	13.7	5.0	8.6	13.0	13.0	--	--	--	--
Unincorporated	50.8	65.3	55.6	72.2	51.7	45.5	58.3	53.0	90.8	91.8	92.3	57.6

unincorporated areas, while the proportion of population in incorporated places of 2,500 or more people have increased more or less steadily. Thus it appears that the distribution of satellite population among the various sizes and types of places in the most isolated areas has been undergoing a radical change since 1900.

The smallest proportions of unincorporated population existed in metropolitan areas located 50 to 100 miles from other areas. Unincorporated area in the 0-10 mile zone had the smallest share of the zone's total population, partly because of the relatively large concentration in places of 50,000 or more population. Places of 10,000-50,000 size gained at the expense of all other types of satellite places from 1900 to 1940 in the 0-10 mile zone and from 1900 to 1920 in the two outermost zones. In later years the resurgence of unincorporated areas in those zones brought declines in the proportions in all incorporated places.

Likewise in metropolitan areas within 50 miles of other areas the proportions of unincorporated population in each distance zone declined from 1900 to about 1930, and then increased once more to the 1910 level. Incorporated places of less than 2,500 population sustained declining proportions throughout the 50 years, except in the 30 mile and over zone. Conversely, incorporated places of 2,500 or more population gained increased proportions until 1930 in inner zones and 1920 in the outer zones, after which their proportions were reduced through the remaining decades. These movements, as well as those in the more distant proximity classes, parallel the concentration and deconcentration phases of the distribution of total metropolitan area population. Concentration appears to deplete unincorporated areas in all distance zones. Deconcentration, on the other hand, seems to affect satellite incorporated places as well as central cities.

CHAPTER VI

SELECTED GEOGRAPHIC FEATURES AND POPULATION REDISTRIBUTION

The distribution of metropolitan population as well as changes in the distribution pattern doutblessly are affected by the presence or absence of of certain limiting factors in the geographic environment. For example, the location of a central city on a sea or lake coast confines its satellite area to, at most, three of its sides. Under such conditions the density of satellite population is probably greater and the growth rates in outlying distance zones are probably higher than where the central city is completely surrounded by habitable area. A river is also a barrier. But a river impedes rather than prevents the spread of metropolitan influence in all directions from a center. Hence it seems likely that distributional tendencies in areas with centers located on river banks may reflect the retarding influence of the river barrier. Still another type of central city location is that lacking any kind of water barrier. Presumably such a location would permit a more or less uniform spread of population about the central city. The greater abundance of satellite space or of easily accessible space may result in a lower density and perhaps a lower rate of change of satellite population.

Three types of locations relative to geographic features are recognized therefore. These are: (1) sea or lake coast; (2) river; and (3) other. The sea or lake coast locations present no serious problem of identification. International boundary lines, however, are treated as analogous to coastal lines. Accordingly Laredo and Detroit are included in the sea or lake coast location class. A river location is more difficult to define unequivocally. Any sized stream, even though it may be dry through part of each year, constitutes a barrier in some degree. But if no restrictions were put on the size of the river virtually all metropolitan areas would be included in the river location class. To avoid such inclusiveness and to distinguish only those areas in which a river represents a a major barrier, a river location is arbitrarily defined as a site on a navigable stream.[1] The third location class, i.e., all other, is accurately described by its designation. It does not comprise only areas with central cities situated on plains as may have been implied in the preceding paragraph. A few central cities are located at the bases of mountain ranges, such as Atlanta and Pueblo, which are no less effective as barriers than are navigable streams. But these are too few to treat separately, hence they are combined with all land-locked locations. The number of metropolitan areas having each type of central city location is shown in Table 36.

TABLE 36. NUMBER OF METROPOLITAN AREAS, BY TYPE OF LOCATION OF CENTRAL CITY, BY SIZE OF CENTRAL CITY, AND BY DECADE, 1900 - 1950

Type of location and size of central city	1940-50	1930-40	1920-30	1910-20	1900-10
Total	143	157	155	153	148
Sea or lake coast	34	37	36	35	35
1,000,000 and over	4	4	3	2	2
500,000 - 1,000,000	6	6	5	3	2
250,000 - 500,000	4	5	3	5	6
100,000 - 250,000	8	7	8	6	5
Under 100,000	12	15	17	19	20
River	36	40	40	40	40
500,000 and over[a]	5	5	4	4	2
250,000 - 500,000	3	4	3	3	5
100,000 - 250,000	13	14	13	8	5
Under 100,000	15	17	20	25	28
Other	73	80	79	78	73
250,000 - 500,000	4	6	1	–	–
100,000 - 250,000	20	20	16	10	5
Under 100,000	49	54	62	68	68

[a] Includes one area with a central city of 1,000,000 or more population (Philadelphia).

While this classification is adopted primarily to test the effects of geographic factors on population redistribution, it also bears a rough correspondence to a transport location classification. Central cities on sea or lake coasts are port cities with immediate access to deep water transport routes. Some port cities, however, such as Philadelphia and New Orleans, are located so far up a river's course that they are classified as having river locations. Most centers at river locations are oriented principally toward intra-continental exchanges. Both types of water locations, of course, are served also by rail and highway transportation. The class of all other locations, however, depend exclusively on railway and highway facilities with which to maintain inter-regional exchanges.[2] A time dimension is also represented in the classification. Many central cities at deep-water sites were among the first to attain large size. River cities flourished in the 19th century until the coming of the railroad. With the development of fast overland transportation made possible by the railroad and the highway river cities lost much of their former importance to a host of new cities that appeared at rail junctions as well as to coastal cities that gained quicker access to interior regions.[3] Thus central cities at other than water locations, are among the youngest of all metropolitan centers. Although most of the changes occasioned by major shifts in the means of inter-regional transportation occurred prior to 1900, many of the effects of those changes may have lingered on to account for some of the variations to be found in the following analysis. That is most probable of the other than water location class.

Central Cities and Satellite Areas

The lowest actual rates of change in metropolitan areas occurred, in all decades, in those areas having their central cities at river locations, as may be seen in Table 37. Rates for the other two classes were approximately the same. Central cities at river locations also grew slowly, while the highest rates of change were found in centers at other locations. Satellite area growth was most rapid in metropolitan areas at costal locations and slowest in areas at other locations from 1900 to 1930. After 1930 the relationship of satellite growth to type of location is uncertain.

Apparently most of the differences between location classes observed in the actual or unadjusted rates are due to differences in the size composition of the location classes. For when the growth rates are weighted by a standard size of area distribution, a clear and consistent relationship emerges. Total metropolitan area as well as both types of places within metropolitan areas are observed to have had the highest growth rates at costal locations and the lowest rates at other locations.

TABLE 37. PER CENT CHANGE OF POPULATION IN STANDARD
METROPOLITAN AREAS, BY TYPE OF LOCATION OF CENTRAL
CITY, TYPE OF PLACE, AND DECADE, 1900-1950

Type of place and type of location	1940-50	1930-40	1920-30	1910-20	1900-10
Actual					
Total					
Sea or lake coast	19.7	8.0	27.8	26.3	32.8
River	16.6	7.1	18.0	18.8	23.8
Other	23.7	9.2	27.6	29.2	30.5
Central cities					
Sea or lake coast	10.2	5.4	22.1	25.2	31.7
River	9.7	3.7	13.1	19.3	22.9
Other	18.8	6.2	31.4	38.9	49.2
Satellite areas					
Sea or lake coast	35.4	12.6	40.1	28.6	35.0
River	25.0	11.6	25.2	18.0	25.1
Other	31.2	14.3	21.8	16.9	13.2
Adjusted[a]					
Total					
Sea or lake coast	21.3	7.8	23.3	26.1	30.7
River	17.1	6.6	18.8	18.8	22.2
Other	9.7	4.0	13.1	11.2	11.2
Central cities					
Sea or lake coast	11.3	5.3	19.9	26.8	30.2
River	9.5	3.1	14.4	19.2	22.2
Other	7.1	2.6	12.9	13.7	16.3
Satellite areas					
Sea or lake coast	37.7	11.8	31.7	24.7	31.9
River	26.3	11.2	25.2	18.2	22.3
Other	13.6	6.4	13.5	7.9	6.4

[a]Adjusted for size of central city. Size distribution of all areas used
as the standard.

The declining rates of central cities at coastal and river locations were fairly well compensated by increasing rates in their respective satellite areas. This has not been true of metropolitan areas at other locations. Satellite area in that location class grew at increasing rates, but the increases were not sufficient to overcome the losses in central city rates, doubtlessly because of the relatively small satellite populations in such areas.

Differences in the patterns of growth within satellite areas, i.e., by distance zones, are much less simple. Until 1920, as may be noted in Fig. 27, satellite population in areas with central cities on coastal sites grew most rapidly in all distance zones; next in order of growth rate were areas with central cities on river sites: while the slowest growth rates obtained in the zones about central cities at other locations. In the next decade, 1920-30, that order of differences was reversed in the 0-5 mile zone, but it persisted in all other distance zones. The upsurge of growth of satellite population within 5 miles of central cities at other locations continued through the two following decades. Although growth rates of satellite population in areas with central cities at such locations showed a tendency to increase within a radius of 20 miles of centers, from 1920 to 1930, they lagged behind satellite rates in the two water location classes in all zones beyond 5 miles in 1920-30 and 1930-40, and, in all zones beyond 10 miles in 1940-50. Metropolitan areas with central cities on sea or lake coast retained through the last decades their high growth rates in the zones beyond 10 miles from their centers; in fact, rates in the outer zones increased while those of inner zones declined. In areas with central cities at river locations satellite growth rates increased in the 5-10 mile zone, rising above the rates of corresponding zones of other location classes, after 1930. Meanwhile, rates of change in outer zones declined.

Greater confidence may be placed in the descriptive accuracy of the foregoing observations regarding the shifts of growth patterns within satellite areas if they reappear when satellite rates are expressed as ratios of central city rates. First, however, it is well to note the differences in the relative growth rates of total satellite area. Table 38 shows that until 1930 there was no appreciable difference between the ratios in metropolitan areas with centers on river and coastal locations. But in 1930-40 the growth of population in satellite areas about centers at river locations surged well ahead of growth in satellite areas about centers at coastal locations. The latter attained their peak growth relative to central city growth in 1940-50, the ratio for the former having declined in that decade. Relative growth rates in satellite areas

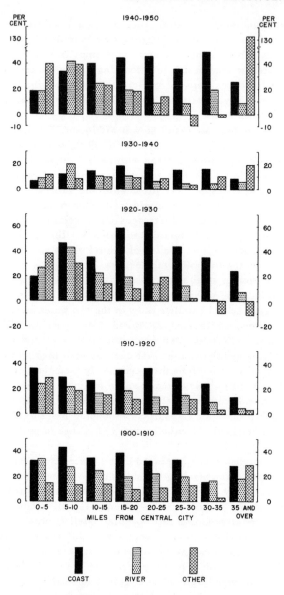

FIGURE 27
PER CENT CHANGE OF POPULATION IN DISTANCE ZONES
OF STANDARD METROPOLITAN AREAS, BY TYPE OF
LOCATION, AND BY DECADES, 1900-1950

TABLE 38. RATIO OF RATE OF CHANGE IN POPULATION IN
SATELLITE AREAS TO RATE OF CHANGE IN CENTRAL
CITIES IN STANDARD METROPOLITAN AREAS, BY TYPE
OF LOCATION, AND DECADE, 1900 - 1950

Type of Location	1940-50	1930-40	1920-30	1910-20	1900-10
Total	2.7	2.5	1.4	0.9	0.8
Sea or lake coast	3.5	2.3	1.8	1.1	1.1
River	2.6	3.1	1.9	0.9	1.1
Other	1.7	2.3	0.7	0.4	0.3

surrounding centers at other locations increased slowly until 1930, rose
abruptly to their maximum in 1930-40, and then subsided somewhat in the
1940-50 decade. Needless to say, ratios for total satellite area conceal
zonal differences.

Ratios by distance zones are shown in Fig. 28. It will be observed
that in 1900-10 and 1910-20 the three location classes stood in the same
positions relative to one another on the basis of ratios of zonal rates to
central city rates that they held on the basis of rates of change. During
those decades population deconcentration beyond the 15-mile radius took
place only in metropolitan areas with centers at coastal locations. Not
until the 1920-30 decade did satellite rates in areas at other than water
locations rise above central city rates, and that was limited to the 0-5
mile zone.

Three features of the trends through the last three decades of the 50-
year period are noteworthy. First is the rapid rise of ratios in the other
location class, particularly in the inner zones. Even so, the ratios for
this class surpassed those of metropolitan areas with centers at water
locations in just two zones: the 0-5 mile and the 35 mile and over zones.
The ratios for the latter were so extreme as to appear to have been chance
occurrences. Secondly, large increases occurred in the relative growth
rates of zones beyond 10 miles from centers at coastal locations. Population deconcentration advanced farthest and most rapidly in those areas.
Finally, the highest ratios of satellite growth in 5-10 mile zones was
found in areas at river locations. To what extent that is an effect of
river location cannot be inferred from the data presented thus far.

The distributions of the amounts of population change over metropolitan areas, by type of location, are shown in Table 39. In areas with

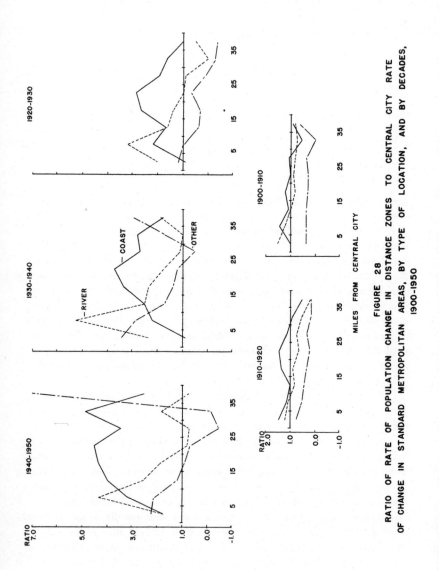

FIGURE 28

RATIO OF RATE OF POPULATION CHANGE IN DISTANCE ZONES TO CENTRAL CITY RATE
OF CHANGE IN STANDARD METROPOLITAN AREAS, BY TYPE OF LOCATION, AND BY DECADES,
1900-1950

TABLE 39. CUMULATIVE PERCENTAGE DISTRIBUTION OF POPULATION INCREASE IN STANDARD METROPOLITAN AREAS, BY TYPE OF LOCATION, DISTANCE ZONE, AND DECADE, 1900 - 1950

Type of location and distance zone	1940- 50	1930- 40	1920- 30	1910- 20	1900- 10
Sea or lake coast					
Central cities	32.1	43.2	53.9	65.7	66.6
0 - 5 miles	36.0	45.9	57.5	71.9	71.1
5 - 10 "	53.8	60.5	72.1	81.5	81.9
10 - 15 "	71.1	74.1	81.5	88.9	89.7
15 - 20 "	83.3	85.2	89.2	93.3	93.5
20 - 25 "	91.0	92.5	94.6	96.4	95.7
25 - 30 "	94.5	95.7	97.0	98.0	97.3
30 - 35 "	97.3	97.7	98.2	98.9	97.8
35 miles and over	100.0	100.0	100.0	100.0	100.0
River					
Central cities	32.0	29.7	43.1	60.1	55.8
0 - 5 miles	40.5	39.1	53.6	69.6	65.9
5 - 10 "	77.1	76.7	80.6	82.5	79.3
10 - 15 "	90.2	87.9	90.2	89.6	87.8
15 - 20 "	95.7	94.2	95.6	94.6	92.3
20 - 25 "	97.4	97.3	98.2	97.2	96.0
25 - 30 "	98.4	98.6	99.7	99.0	98.1
30 - 35 "	99.6	99.2	99.7	99.7	99.1
35 miles and over	100.0	100.0	100.0	100.0	100.0
Other					
Central cities	47.8	42.1	68.8	74.5	77.5
0 - 5 miles	62.8	60.6	78.9	81.8	82.0
5 - 10 "	83.9	81.6	90.8	89.7	88.6
10 - 15 "	93.3	92.6	96.5	96.5	95.3
15 - 20 "	96.2	96.9	98.5	98.9	97.7
20 - 25 "	97.8	98.8	100.2	99.4	98.7
25 - 30 "	97.9	99.1	100.3	100.0	99.4
30 - 35 "	97.9	99.4	100.2	100.0	99.5
35 miles and over	100.0	100.0	100.0	100.0	100.0

coastal locations there has been an uninterrupted dispersion of growth
through successive decades. Whereas almost 67 per cent of all increase
gathered in central cities in 1900-10, that proportion of the total increase
was spread over an area reaching to almost 15 miles of central cities in
1940-50. The dispersion of increase was more erratic in metropolitan
areas with river locations: dispersion was offset by centripetal tendencies
in 1910-20 and again in 1940-50. Of particular interest, however, is the
5-10 mile zone; its share of increase advanced from 13 per cent in 1900-10
to 37 per cent in 1930-40 and 1940-50. In neither of the other location
classes did the 5-10 mile zone attract more than 21 per cent of the total
increase. It is quite possible that the sharp rise of growth in the 5-10 mile
zone may have resulted from a recent overcoming of the river barrier through
the construction of additional bridges and the elimination of tolls. Dispersion of increase has been the trend also in metropolitan areas at other
than water locations, though that trend was reversed in the 1940-50 decade.
Central cities, however, have claimed larger shares of the increase than
has been true in either of the other location classes. It is largely for
this reason that the extent of dispersion has been least in that location
class.

Despite the dispersion of population increase that has taken place in
metropolitan areas at coastal locations, the central cities of such areas
have held larger proportions of the total area populations than have central cities at any other location. Nevertheless, a centrifugal drift has
operated throughout the five decades, as may be seen in Table 40.
Although most of the decline in the proportions within central cities
has been taken up by the 5-10 mile zone -- the proportion in the 0-5 mile
zone has remained unchanged, all zones beyond the 5-10 mile zone have
steadily increased their shares of the total population. In areas at river
locations the prevailing direction of population redistribution down to 1920
was toward concentration, after 1920 deconcentration set in and continued
to 1950. In the concentration phase losses were incurred in all zones beyond 5 miles from central cities. On the other hand, deconcentration was
largely a matter of shifting proportions from central cities to the 5-10 mile
zone. All zones beyond the 15 mile radius have had progressively smaller
proportions since 1900. Metropolitan areas situated at other than water
locations experienced population concentration from 1900 to 1930 and deconcentration in the remaining two decades. Again the principal shifts
involved central cities and 5-10 mile zones. The more distant zones had
declining proportions throughout the period under study.

The coefficients shown graphically in Fig. 29 describes the rates at
which redistribution occurred. Population in metropolitan areas at coastal

TABLE 40. CUMULATIVE PERCENTAGE DISTRIBUTION OF POPULATION IN STANDARD METROPOLITAN AREAS, BY TYPE OF LOCATION, DISTANCE ZONE, AND CENSUS YEAR, 1900 - 1950

Type of location and distance zone	1950	1940	1930	1920	1910	1900
Sea or lake coast						
Central cities	57.2	62.1	64.1	68.0	68.5	68.8
0 - 5 miles	61.5	66.5	68.6	72.9	73.0	73.5
5 - 10 "	73.6	77.5	79.1	81.7	81.8	81.6
10 - 15 "	83.5	85.9	87.1	89.2	89.2	89.0
15 - 20 "	90.2	91.5	92.1	92.9	92.7	92.4
20 - 25 "	94.2	94.8	95.0	95.3	95.0	94.7
25 - 30 "	96.4	96.8	96.9	96.9	96.5	96.3
30 - 35 "	97.8	97.9	98.0	97.8	97.5	97.4
35 miles and over	100.0	100.0	100.0	100.0	100.0	100.0
River						
Central cities	51.5	54.7	56.8	59.3	58.4	58.1
0 - 5 miles	59.9	63.1	64.8	66.7	65.8	65.1
5 - 10 "	77.8	77.8	78.6	78.2	77.3	76.8
10 - 15 "	87.4	86.8	87.0	86.4	85.7	85.2
15 - 20 "	92.6	92.0	92.1	91.6	91.0	90.8
20 - 25 "	95.9	95.6	95.7	95.3	94.9	94.7
25 - 30 "	98.0	97.9	98.0	97.7	97.4	97.3
30 - 35 "	99.1	99.0	99.1	99.0	98.8	98.8
35 miles and over	100.0	100.0	100.0	100.0	100.0	100.0
Other						
Central cities	57.9	60.3	62.4	60.4	56.0	48.1
0 - 5 miles	67.9	69.1	70.4	67.8	63.7	57.6
5 - 10 "	82.3	81.9	81.6	78.9	76.7	72.8
10 - 15 "	92.2	91.9	91.5	90.1	89.1	87.5
15 - 20 "	96.1	96.0	96.1	95.5	95.3	94.6
20 - 25 "	98.4	98.4	98.4	98.0	97.6	97.2
25 - 30 "	99.1	99.3	99.4	99.2	99.0	98.9
30 - 35 "	99.3	99.6	99.7	99.6	99.4	99.4
35 miles and over	100.0	100.0	100.0	100.0	100.0	100.0

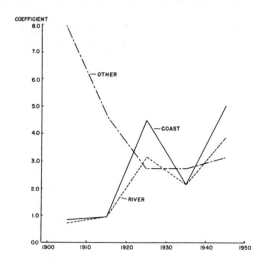

FIGURE 29
COEFFICIENTS OF POPULATION REDISTRIBUTION IN STANDARD
METROPOLITAN AREAS, BY TYPE OF LOCATION, 1900-1950

locations deconcentrated at an increasing rate. The 1920-30 and 1940-50 decades were periods of unusually rapid scatter, or, speaking more accurately, of high relative growth rates in outlying zones. This was noted in Fig. 28. Redistribution in metropolitan areas at river locations followed a similar pattern of variation, with the highest rates also in the 1920-30 and the 1940-50 decades. In this class of areas, however, 1920 marked the beginning of deconcentration. The most rapid redistribution occurred in metropolitan areas at other than water locations and during the period of population concentration. That period ended in 1930 and was followed by a comparatively slow deconcentration movement.

Satellite Area and River Locations

The effect of a river location on the changing distribution of population in metropolitan areas may be explored in another way, that is, by comparing growth tendencies in the parts of areas lying on the two sides of the rivers flowing through them. If the river is a barrier, higher growth rates should be found on the side on which the central city is situated than on the opposite side. Such a comparison obviously requires that the analysis be restricted to Standard Metropolitan areas which lie athwart rivers. The number satisfying that condition, shown in Table 41, is smaller than that of all areas with centers at river locations.

TABLE 41. NUMBER OF STANDARD METROPOLITAN AREAS AT RIVER LOCATIONS WITH PARTS ON OPPOSITE SIDES OF RIVERS, BY SIZE OF CENTRAL CITY, AND DECADE, 1900 - 1950

Size of Central city	1940-50	1930-40	1920-30	1910-20	1900-10
500,000 and over	5	5	4	4	2
250,000 - 500,000	2	3	3	3	5
100,000 - 250,000	11	12	11	7	3
Under 100,000	12	12	14	18	22

For the most part, since 1920, rates of change have been highest in the parts of metropolitan areas lying on the central city sides of rivers. That has been true of most distance zones as well as of total area, as shown in Table 42. The small differences between growth rates on the two sides of rivers in 1900-10 and 1910-20 may have been due to the early growth of twin cities immediately opposite metropolitan centers. If so, the influences of such rival centers did not last, for the barrier effect of rivers became prominent after 1920 despite the increases in the numbers and sizes of bridges and the eliminations of tolls. The irregularities in the data for zones beyond 25 miles of central cities are very likely a result of the small populations involved, particularly on the sides opposite central cities. For example, the 110.9 per cent growth of population in the 30-35 mile zone on the opposite river side, in the 1940-50 decade, was due almost entirely to the growth in one incorporated place in the Philadelphia metropolitan area. Excluding that one place, the average growth for the fragment of the zone was 2.5 per cent. Similar deviations occurred in other zones and decades where small populations existed.

In Table 43 it is apparent that satellite area on the central city sides of rivers commanded the largest share of the additions to population in all decades. The proportion increased steadily from 1900 to 1940, after which it declined slightly. In the 0-5 mile zone the largest proportion of increase frequently occurred on the sides opposite central cities. Still the proportion accruing to the central city side in that zone is noteworthy in view of the fact that a large part of the 0-5 mile zone is contained in central cities and is not therefore satellite area. The striking feature in Table 43, however, is the evidence of a gravitation of population increase to the 5-10 mile zone and especially to that part on the central city side. That trend

TABLE 42. PER CENT CHANGE OF SATELLITE POPULATION IN
STANDARD METROPOLITAN AREAS AT RIVER LOCATIONS, BY
DISTANCE ZONE, SIDE OF RIVER AND DECADE, 1900-1950

Distance zone and side of river	1940-50	1940-40	1920-30	1910-20	1900-10
All satellite area					
On central city side	40.1	11.3	27.8	18.6	23.5
On opposite side	22.1	5.5	13.2	17.5	24.4
0-5 mile zone					
On central city side	20.2	11.7	38.6	28.7	33.9
On opposite side	14.5	3.4	17.0	22.0	32.6
5-10 mile zone					
On central city side	87.6	19.3	40.4	20.6	26.0
On opposite side	37.2	13.8	22.6	19.8	23.1
10-15 mile zone					
On central city side	21.1	8.0	24.1	18.9	22.5
On opposite side	23.9	7.0	19.4	14.6	19.6
15-20 mile zone					
On central city side	16.9	8.3	16.4	18.7	12.1
On opposite side	7.6	7.8	9.1	12.8	20.7
20-25 mile zone					
On central city side	10.8	4.0	34.7	10.3	25.1
On opposite side	3.8	-12.7	8.3	17.9	24.4
25-30 mile zone					
On central city side	6.7	3.4	13.3	19.8	25.8
On opposite side	10.2	5.5	8.7	-4.7	13.7
30-35 mile zone					
On central city zone	8.9	4.3	3.6	8.1	21.0
On opposite side	110.9	-10.6	-12.9	22.5	-0.4
35 mile and over zone					
On central city side	8.8	6.8	4.6	4.5	12.5
On opposite side	20.7	-7.8	17.6	6.9	43.7

TABLE 43. PER CENT DISTRIBUTION OF POPULATION INCREASE
IN SATELLITE AREA OF STANDARD METROPOLITAN AREAS AT
RIVER LOCATIONS, BY DISTANCE ZONE, SIDE OF RIVER AND
DECADE, 1900-1950

Distance zone and side of river	1940-50	1930-40	1920-30	1910-20	1900-10
All satellite areas	100.0	100.0	100.0	100.0	100.0
On central city side	73.1	74.5	69.5	59.3	58.0
On opposite side	26.9	25.5	30.5	40.7	42.0
0-5 mile zone					
On central city side	4.4	9.1	10.4	10.0	9.4
On opposite side	4.9	4.5	9.2	14.3	14.3
5-10 mile zone					
On central city side	53.1	41.4	29.9	18.8	18.7
On opposite side	14.6	19.2	11.8	13.1	11.6
10-15 mile zone					
On central city side	8.9	11.9	13.9	13.6	12.2
On opposite side	4.2	4.6	5.2	5.0	5.2
15-20 mile zone					
On central city side	3.4	6.2	5.0	7.0	3.6
On opposite side	1.1	4.0	2.0	3.6	4.5
20-25 mile zone					
On central city side	1.5	2.0	6.7	3.0	5.5
On opposite side	0.4	-6.6	1.6	4.2	4.1
25-30 mile zone					
On central city side	0.8	1.7	2.8	5.1	4.9
On opposite side	0.4	0.7	0.5	-0.4	1.0
30-35 mile zone					
On central city side	0.6	1.1	0.4	1.3	2.6
On opposite side	1.0	-0.4	-0.3	0.6	0.0
35 mile and over zone					
On central city side	0.4	1.2	0.4	0.5	1.2
On opposite side	0.4	-0.6	0.5	0.3	1.2

reached its highest point in 1940-50 when 53 per cent of all satellite increase concentrated in the part of the 5-10 mile zone on the central city
side of rivers. Nevertheless, the effect of rivers on the distributions of
growth has extended 30 miles or more from central cities.

Size and Type of Satellite Place

It is not surprising in view of earlier findings to discover that the
growth rates of all sizes and types of satellite places located in metropolitan areas at coastal locations exceeded those of similar places in
other locations (Table 44). Moreover, high growth rates extended further
into outlying zones about centers at coastal locations than in other location classes. Growth rates in satellite places at both river and other
than water locations fell off abruptly beyond 20 miles from centers. But
metropolitan areas at all types of locations had in common the tendency
for rates of change to decline in incorporated places of 2,500 or more
population. Although there was some tendency in incorporated places of
less than 2,500 for the rates of change to increase, especially within 20
miles, the largest increases of growth rates occurred in unincorporated
area. The most rapid increase of this kind took place within areas at
other than water locations.

These comparisons stand out more sharply when rates of change are
expressed as ratios to central city rates, as in Table 45. The highest
relative rates of change occurred in areas at coastal locations and the
lowest developed at other than water locations. All types of satellite
places gained in the deconcentration of population within areas at coastal
locations; in fact, deconcentration accelerated over the years since 1900
in all types of places except those of 50,000 or more population. In the two
other location classes deconcentration affected all unincorporated areas
and incorporated places of less than 10,000 population which are within 20
miles of central cities. In the zones beyond 20 miles from centers the
effect of differential growth was to increase concentration at the centers
or within the 20 mile zones about centers.

Although unincorporated population in areas at coastal locations en-
joyed the highest growth rates, both absolute and relative, the proportion
unincorporated was of the total population in each zone never grew as
large as that in areas at river and other than water locations. The largest
proportions, Table 46 shows, consistently occurred in the satellite areas
of land-locked centers. This variation finds a parallel in incorporated
places of less than 2,500 population. Low proportions of population in
unincorporated areas and in small incorporated places are a function of
large proportions in large incorporated places, and, conversely, large

Table 44. Per Cent Change of Satellite Population in Standard Metropolitan Areas, by Size and Type of Satellite Place, Distance Zone, Type of Location, and Decade, 1900-1950

Size and type of satellite place and distance zone	Sea or lake coast					River					Other				
	1940-1950	1930-1940	1920-1930	1910-1920	1900-1910	1940-1950	1930-1940	1920-1930	1910-1920	1900-1910	1940-1950	1930-1940	1920-1930	1910-1920	1900-1910
50,000 and over															
0-10 miles	11.4	0.9	12.1	19.7	36.9	4.6	-1.7	6.0	6.5	25.5[a]	----	----	----	----	----
10-20 miles	10.6	1.8	13.7	19.0	35.5	3.6	-3.5	5.5	21.8[a]	----	----	----	----	----	----
20-30 miles	18.8	8.1	81.3	----	----	----	----	----	----	----	----	----	----	----	----
30 miles and over	----	----	----	----	----	----	----	----	----	----	----	----	----	----	----
10,000 - 50,000															
0-10 miles	13.5	7.7	40.1	34.6	35.0	7.2	3.2	14.9	11.9	22.5	13.2	-1.1	41.9	15.4	17.5[a]
10-20 miles	40.6	11.0	44.3	39.9	59.6	4.9	2.4	21.5	22.5	37.3	12.9	2.6	24.6	41.2	-54.7[a]
20-30 miles	14.3	6.9	32.2	46.3	38.4	9.8	2.3	15.6	17.4	41.7	-31.8	3.4	15.3	26.8	23.5[a]
30 miles and over	22.9	1.7	19.6	18.4	21.4	6.0	1.6	6.5	19.7	13.9	----	----	----	----	----
2,500 - 10,000															
0-10 miles	53.7	23.0	75.7	96.5	60.9	19.0	9.0	31.7	22.2	57.6	27.2	-3.1[a]	21.6	26.1	5.9[a]
10-20 miles	60.7	119.4	88.5	39.0	56.8	13.7	6.7	34.9	27.8	33.1	32.6	-58.1[a]	11.2	24.7	35.0[a]
20-30 miles	30.8	9.4	48.5	18.6	43.8	0.1	3.4	17.2	16.0	37.1	5.8[a]	2.5	10.0[a]	16.6[a]	30.3[a]
30 miles and over	24.3	4.5	33.6	22.2	41.2	9.6	4.0	7.9	85.6[a]	50.0[a]	4.8[a]	25.6[a]	-11.0[a]	-67.9[a]	23.7[a]
Under 2,500															
0-10 miles	75.7	37.4	214.1	76.1	77.0	36.5	18.2	62.1	39.0	57.2	26.9	14.3	41.4	17.2[a]	38.8[a]
10-20 miles	64.4	29.1	110.0	53.3	47.5	23.1	8.1	20.0	24.4	20.8	18.2	6.3	12.1	14.7	16.1[a]
20-30 miles	54.7	25.0	63.3	32.0	27.1	4.1	3.1	8.0	18.7	37.3[a]	14.1	4.5	1.5[a]	19.6[a]	34.4[a]
30 miles and over	29.5	12.4	25.6	18.6	31.2[a]	14.5	1.8	3.3	-4.6[a]	18.1[a]	-59.2[a]	2.9[a]	-2.5[a]	6.8[a]	11.8[a]
Unincorporated															
0-10 miles	59.2	20.8	42.9	21.9	37.5	54.1	28.0	52.9	29.5	23.7	46.7	27.2	32.7	21.6	12.2
10-20 miles	66.0	9.4	45.7	22.6	14.0	31.2	14.6	18.0	11.3	17.7	21.8	42.1	10.7	8.3	12.7
20-30 miles	73.2	33.3	73.4	26.0	26.8	10.1	7.7	10.2	9.2	11.3	26.5	7.9	16.5	1.3	2.7
30 miles and over	44.3	19.6	28.2	9.5	18.0	14.6	6.9	1.9	1.4	12.2	92.3	14.7	-12.8	36.6	16.4

[a] Based on less than 5 incorporated places.

Table 45. Ratio of Rate of Change of Satellite Population to Central City Rate of Change in Standard Metropolitan Areas, by Size and Type of Satellite Place, Distance Zone, Type of Location, and Decade, 1900-1950

Size and type of satellite place and distance zone	Sea or lake coast					River					Other				
	1940-1950	1930-1940	1920-1930	1910-1920	1900-1910	1940-1950	1930-1940	1920-1930	1910-1920	1900-1910	1940-1950	1930-1940	1920-1930	1910-1920	1900-1910
50,000 and over															
0-10 miles	1.1	0.2	0.6	0.8	1.2	0.5	-0.5	0.5	0.3	1.1	--	--	--	--	--
10-20 miles	1.0	0.3	0.6	0.8	1.1	0.4	-1.0	0.4	1.1	--	--	--	--	--	--
20-30 miles	1.8	1.5	3.7	--	--	--	--	--	--	--	--	--	--	--	--
30 miles and over	--	--	--	--	--	--	--	--	--	--	--	--	--	--	--
10,000 - 50,000															
0-10 miles	1.3	1.4	1.8	1.4	1.1	0.7	0.9	1.1	0.6	1.0	0.7	0.2	1.3	0.4	0.4
10-20 miles	4.0	2.0	2.0	1.6	1.9	0.5	0.6	1.6	1.2	1.6	0.7	0.4	0.8	1.1	-1.1
20-30 miles	1.4	1.3	1.5	1.8	1.2	1.0	0.6	1.2	0.9	1.8	-1.7	0.6	0.5	0.7	0.5
30 miles and over	2.2	0.3	0.9	0.7	0.7	0.6	0.4	0.5	1.0	0.6	--	--	--	--	--
2,500 - 10,000															
0-10 miles	5.3	4.3	3.4	3.8	1.9	2.0	2.4	2.4	1.2	2.5	1.4	-0.5	0.7	0.7	0.1
10-20 miles	6.0	22.1	4.0	1.6	1.8	1.4	1.8	2.7	1.4	1.4	1.7	-9.4	0.4	0.6	0.7
20-30 miles	3.0	1.7	2.2	0.7	1.4	0.0	0.9	1.3	0.8	1.6	0.3	-0.4	0.3	0.4	0.6
30 miles and over	2.4	0.8	1.5	0.9	1.3	1.0	1.1	0.6	4.4	2.2	0.3	4.1	-0.4	-1.8	0.5
Under 2,500															
0-10 miles	7.4	6.9	9.7	3.0	2.4	3.8	4.9	4.7	2.0	2.5	1.4	2.3	1.3	0.4	0.8
10-20 miles	6.3	5.4	5.0	2.1	1.5	2.4	2.2	1.5	1.3	0.9	1.0	1.0	4.0	0.4	0.3
20-30 miles	5.4	4.6	2.9	1.3	0.8	0.4	0.8	0.6	1.0	1.6	0.8	0.7	0.0	0.5	0.7
30 miles and over	2.9	2.3	1.2	0.7	1.0	1.5	0.5	0.2	-0.2	0.8	-3.2	0.5	0.0	0.2	0.2
Unincorporated															
0-10 miles	5.8	3.8	1.9	0.9	1.2	5.6	7.6	4.0	1.5	1.0	2.5	4.4	1.0	0.6	0.2
10-20 miles	6.5	1.7	2.1	0.9	0.4	3.2	4.0	1.4	0.6	0.8	1.2	6.8	0.3	0.2	0.3
20-30 miles	7.2	6.2	3.3	1.0	0.8	1.0	2.1	0.8	0.5	0.5	1.4	1.3	0.5	0.0	0.0
30 miles and over	4.3	3.6	1.3	0.4	0.6	1.5	1.9	0.2	0.1	0.5	4.9	2.4	-0.4	0.9	0.3

Table 46. Per Cent Distribution of Satellite Population in Standard Metropolitan Areas, by Census Year, Size and Type of Satellite Place, Type of Location, and Distance Zone, 1900–1950

Census year and size and type of satellite place	Sea or lake coast				River				Other			
	0-10 miles	10-20 miles	20-30 miles	30 miles and over	0-10 miles	10-20 miles	20-30 miles	30 miles and over	0-10 miles	10-20 miles	20-30 miles	30 miles and over
1950												
Total	100.0	100.0	100.0	100.0	100.0	100.0	100.0	100.0	100.0	100.0	100.0	100.0
50,000 and over	34.8	25.2	11.5	0.0	5.4	7.7	0.0	0.0	0.0	0.0	0.0	0.0
10,000 - 50,000	23.6	22.3	21.1	24.4	19.7	13.1	18.7	13.1	8.3	16.2	10.4	0.0
2,500 - 10,000	7.4	13.8	16.0	17.4	15.3	11.9	16.1	12.0	11.4	10.2	12.9	6.2
Under 2,500	1.5	4.0	6.6	8.5	4.9	8.3	11.1	14.9	5.5	13.1	10.1	1.9
Unincorporated area	32.7	34.7	45.4	49.7	54.7	59.0	54.1	60.0	74.8	60.5	66.6	91.9
1940												
Total	100.0	100.0	100.0	100.0	100.0	100.0	100.0	100.0	100.0	100.0	100.0	100.0
50,000 and over	40.0	32.3	13.7	0.0	6.8	9.0	0.0	0.0	0.0	0.0	0.0	0.0
10,000 - 50,000	26.5	22.5	26.2	26.5	24.3	15.3	18.4	13.9	10.3	17.3	17.1	0.0
2,500 - 10,000	6.1	12.2	17.4	18.7	17.0	12.8	17.3	12.4	12.5	9.3	13.7	10.1
Under 2,500	1.1	3.4	7.5	8.8	4.8	8.2	11.4	14.7	6.0	13.4	10.0	8.0
Unincorporated area	26.3	29.6	37.2	46.0	47.1	54.7	52.9	59.0	71.2	60.0	59.2	81.9
1930												
Total	100.0	100.0	100.0	100.0	100.0	100.0	100.0	100.0	100.0	100.0	100.0	100.0
50,000 and over	43.1	34.7	14.8	0.0	9.2	9.3	0.0	0.0	0.0	0.0	0.0	0.0
10,000 - 50,000	25.4	23.1	26.4	28.8	24.8	17.4	20.8	13.7	11.7	16.8	9.2	0.0
2,500 - 10,000	5.9	6.5	19.2	9.9	17.1	14.3	16.4	10.9	5.9	13.4	10.0	8.9
Under 2,500	1.1	3.9	6.0	9.9	5.2	8.2	11.5	17.6	13.5	20.8	14.4	9.2
Unincorporated area	24.5	31.8	33.6	43.0	43.7	50.8	51.3	57.8	68.9	49.0	66.4	81.9
1920												
Total	100.0	100.0	100.0	100.0	100.0	100.0	100.0	100.0	100.0	100.0	100.0	100.0
50,000 and over	35.3	34.8	5.8	0.0	11.7	7.8	0.0	0.0	0.0	0.0	0.0	0.0
10,000 - 50,000	29.8	20.7	34.4	26.6	22.2	15.9	17.9	9.8	10.0	13.8	9.0	0.0
2,500 - 10,000	7.1	11.6	19.1	17.2	18.7	14.2	16.9	12.9	12.8	7.9	13.4	8.4
Under 2,500	1.9	5.4	8.1	10.9	7.0	8.8	12.7	14.8	6.9	15.2	11.4	15.4
Unincorporated area	25.9	27.5	32.6	45.3	40.4	53.3	52.5	62.5	70.3	63.1	66.2	76.2
1910												
Total	100.0	100.0	100.0	100.0	100.0	100.0	100.0	100.0	100.0	100.0	100.0	100.0
50,000 and over	34.6	33.6	0.0	0.0	13.1	4.5	0.0	0.0	0.0	0.0	0.0	0.0
10,000 - 50,000	25.1	19.3	34.5	23.8	20.9	11.8	13.2	8.8	5.1	12.2	9.2	0.0
2,500 - 10,000	7.7	10.6	16.6	16.2	16.7	12.8	18.2	5.6	12.7	7.0	10.4	28.7
Under 2,500	2.1	6.7	12.0	12.7	7.6	10.1	14.5	14.7	8.8	15.6	16.1	14.9
Unincorporated area	30.5	29.8	36.9	47.3	41.7	60.8	54.1	70.9	73.4	65.2	64.3	56.4
1900												
Total	100.0	100.0	100.0	100.0	100.0	100.0	100.0	100.0	100.0	100.0	100.0	100.0
50,000 and over	30.9	26.5	0.0	0.0	7.7	0.0	0.0	0.0	0.0	0.0	0.0	0.0
10,000 - 50,000	26.3	20.9	16.6	20.4	23.0	13.8	3.9	5.3	3.5	3.6	4.3	0.0
2,500 - 10,000	6.0	8.5	22.0	13.7	11.4	9.3	17.3	9.9	8.7	9.0	17.0	4.9
Under 2,500	2.6	6.3	10.7	13.8	7.4	9.5	15.8	13.5	7.3	13.8	14.5	14.8
Unincorporated area	34.2	37.8	50.7	52.1	50.5	67.4	63.0	71.3	80.5	73.6	64.2	80.3

proportions in the smallest or least densely settled places are made possible by a lack of development, if not an absence, of large incorporated
satellites. Thus areas at coastal locations have had a comparatively full
complement of satellite places, while areas at other than water locations
have stood at the other extreme in this respect. The proportions of zonal
populations contained within satellites of over 10,000 population have declined since 1930, however, particularly in the inner zones.

Transportation Access to Central City

An implicit assumption in much of the preceding discussion is that
some of the variation in the territorial extent and the rate of population redistribution among differenc classes of metropolitan areas is due to differences in the development of transportation access from satellite zones to
central cities. This factor has been referred to as an element in the concept of metropolitan maturity, which in turn has been associated with the
"age" of metropolitan areas. It seems appropriate at this point to bring
the matter out of the realm of speculation and into that of observation.

To test the influence of intramural transportation access a thirty-three
per cent sample of minor civil divisions was drawn from thirteen metropolitan areas with central cities of 250,000 or more population in 1940. [4]
These were sorted into four types of transportation classes; namely, highway and railway, highway only, railway only, and neither highway nor railway. A highway location was identified as a location on a hard-surfaced
national or state highway leading directly to the central city. This is ex-
clusive of locations on lateral roads and township and county roads. Where
the minor civil division was not an incorporated place the unit was classed
as having a highway location when the route passed through or near its
geometric center. A rail location was defined also as a location on a
direct rail route to the central city. A township was identified as having
such a location when an incorporated place near its geometric center was
located on a direct rail route to the center. Needless to say, this classification by type of transportation access, based as it is on 1940 maps, is
not entirely satisfactory. No allowance is made for the length of time a
given type of access has been in existence. Nor is there any control over
the frequency and quality of railway service. The difficulties involved in
standardizing such variables are probably too obvious to require mention.
While it may be possible to find ways of discounting the deficiencies, it
seems better to turn directly to the data to see what they indicate.

It is evident in Table 47 that from 1900 to 1930 the most rapidly
growing satellite places were those served by both highways and railways.

TABLE 47. PER CENT CHANGE OF POPULATION IN A SAMPLE
OF SATELLITE PLACES IN STANDARD METROPOLITAN AREAS
WITH CENTRAL CITIES OF 250,000 OR MORE POPULATION, BY
TYPE OF TRANSPORTATION ACCESS, DISTANCE ZONE, AND
DECADE, 1900 - 1950

Type of transportation access and distance zone	1940-50	1930-40	1920-30	1910-20	1900-10
Highway and railway					
5 - 10 miles	37.9	17.4	57.2	22.3	38.9
10 - 15 "	59.6	17.8	62.1	27.5	16.5
15 - 20 "	23.4	14.7	39.3	28.2	24.3
20 - 25 "	50.4	7.3	36.4	35.3	13.2
25 - 30 "	24.8	12.2	37.1	44.8	46.5
30 - 35 "	24.5	7.3	5.1	18.9	29.8
35 miles and over	45.3	6.4	13.1	14.4	6.7
Highway only					
5 - 10 miles	68.9	46.7	21.3	12.2	36.4
10 - 15 "	74.9	34.8	57.1	15.9	-5.0
15 - 20 "	68.1	26.8	53.3	12.2	9.8
20 - 25 "	69.6	18.7	14.9	28.2	14.6
25 - 30 "	21.8	4.0	-3.5	-3.3	-4.4
30 - 35 "	19.4	-0.8	3.7	3.5	0.4
35 miles and over	31.8	20.1	2.1	-5.7	6.0
Railway only					
5 - 10 miles	—	—	—	—	—
10 - 15 "	—	—	—	—	—
15 - 20 "	—	—	—	—	—
20 - 25 "	31.4	7.9	-5.0	-8.6	8.6
25 - 30 "	2.4	-8.1	3.0	7.5	-18.0
30 - 35 "	8.5	-4.3	-20.8	-8.3	5.9
35 miles and over	4.3	-9.3	-1.0	3.6	-9.4
Neither highway nor railway					
5 - 10 miles	—	—	—	—	—
10 - 15 "	26.8	15.2	-1.9	-11.2	5.3
15 - 20 "	20.0	8.9	30.5	-6.1	-0.7
20 - 25 "	14.1	12.1	-4.2	-3.7	-5.4
25 - 30 "	0.8	1.9	-4.7	-5.1	-7.1
30 - 35 "	10.7	9.9	12.6	6.0	-0.3
35 miles and over	-2.6	5.2	-7.8	-10.4	-1.8

After 1930 the highest rates of change occurred in places served exclusively by highways. The differential as between highway and railway,
and highway only, favored the latter, however, just within 25 miles of
central cities. Beyond that distance places with both highway and railway excess maintained higher growth rates. Thus it appears that large-
scale metropolitan expansion based primarily on the motor vehicle began
with 1930, though there were evidences of beginnings in the preceding
decade. Of interest is the fact that as early as 1900-10 satellite places
dependent exclusively on the railway for direct contact with central cities
were losing population. Losses in such places continued down to 1940.
Even the gains in the 1940-50 decade were small. But the highest incidence of population loss occurred between 1900 and 1930 in places without either direct highway or railway access to metropolitan centers.
Losses ceased after 1930 and in 1940-50 substantial gains were recorded.
If the facts were known, it probably would be discovered that growth after
1930 in places with neither highway nor railway access was a consequence
of the development of lateral roads serving the interstices between radial
thoroughfares.

In Table 48 growth rates are reduced to ratios to the average growth
rates for corresponding zones of the thirteen metropolitan areas from which
the sample was drawn. On this basis, it is apparent that satellite places
with both rail and highway contacts maintained, in 1900-10, a near average
rate of growth. They attained their peak rates of increase in 1910 to 1920,
after which decline set in returning them to average growth rates in 1940-
50. Places with only highway access began the 50 years with considerably
less than average growth. Growth rose above average within 10 to 20 miles
of centers in 1920-1930, and since then higher than average rates spread
over all area within 25 miles of centers. Despite the upsurge of growth in
places with neither highway nor railway access after 1930, rates in such
places tended to remain well below the averages for their respective
zones.

There seems little doubt, in view of these data, that the kind of transportation access to the central city has important bearing on the relative
growth of satellite population. It does not follow, of course, that locations
on direct routes must necessarily dominate satellite growth. A more refined classification of location doubtlessly would show that places on
hard-surfaced lateral roads have also grown rapidly. They may grow even
more rapidly in the future. In any event, the inference from this analysis
would seem to be: the more developed is the highway network of a metropolitan area the more rapid will be the growth of its satellite population.

TABLE 48. RATIO OF RATE OF POPULATION CHANGE IN A
SAMPLE OF SATELLITE PLACES TO RATE OF CHANGE OF
ALL POPULATION IN CORRESPONDING DISTANCE ZONE IN
STANDARD METROPOLITAN AREAS WITH CENTRAL CITIES
OF 250,000 OR MORE POPULATION, BY TYPE OF TRANS-
PORTATION ACCESS, DISTANCE ZONE, AND DECADE,
1900 - 1950

Type of transportation access and distance zone	1940-50	1930-40	1920-30	1910-20	1900-10
Highway and railway					
5 - 10 miles	1.0	1.2	1.1	0.7	0.9
10 - 15 "	1.6	1.4	2.0	1.2	0.5
15 - 20 "	0.6	1.0	1.0	1.1	0.9
20 - 25 "	1.6	0.6	1.2	2.0	0.7
25 - 30 "	1.1	1.0	2.3	4.0	3.1
30 - 35 "	1.0	0.9	0.5	2.2	2.6
35 miles and over	2.7	0.8	1.2	3.6	0.8
Highway only [a]					
5 - 10 miles	1.8	3.2	0.4	0.4	0.8
10 - 15 "	2.0	2.7	1.8	0.7	-0.2
15 - 20 "	1.8	1.8	1.3	0.5	0.4
20 - 25 "	2.2	1.4	0.5	1.6	0.8
25 - 30 "	1.0	0.3	-0.2	-0.3	-0.3
30 - 35 "	0.8	-0.1	-0.3	0.4	0.0
35 miles and over	1.9	2.6	0.2	-1.4	0.7
Railway only [a]					
5 - 10 miles	—	—	—	—	—
10 - 15 "	—	—	—	—	—
15 - 20 "	—	—	—	—	—˙
20 - 25 "	1.0	0.6	-0.2	-0.5	0.5
25 - 30 "	0.1	-0.6	0.2	0.7	-1.2
30 - 35 "	0.3	-0.5	-1.9	-1.0	0.5
35 miles and over	0.3	-1.2	-0.1	0.9	-1.1
Neither highway nor railway [a]					
5 - 10 miles	—	—	—	—	—
10 - 15 "	0.7	1.2	-0.1	-0.5	0.2
15 - 20 "	0.5	0.6	0.8	-0.2	0.0
20 - 25 "	0.4	0.9	-0.1	-0.2	-0.3
25 - 30 "	0.0	0.2	-0.3	-0.5	-0.5
30 - 35 "	0.4	1.2	1.2	0.7	0.0
35 miles and over	-0.2	0.7	-0.7	-1.2	-0.2

[a] Minus value indicates that one rate is negative.

CHAPTER VII

MANUFACTURING INDUSTRY AND POPULATION REDISTRIBUTION

In part because of its orientation to an interregional more than to a local market and in part because of its relatively extensive use of land, manufacturing industry tends to scatter over the satellite areas about metropolitan centers. [1] This tendency has been greatly abetted by the electrification of power, the enhanced mobility of labor afforded by the automobile, and the separation of central office functions from producing functions, to mention only a few of the more salient factors that have enlarged the range of choice of sites for the location of manufacturing plants. By contrast, service industry is subject to a much stronger centripetal force. Since it is adapted primarily to local market conditions, the location of service industry is governed to a much greater extent by the need to maximize accessibility within the locality. In other words, service industry seeks locations at points where intra-mural transportation and communication lines converge. Thus, so far as population is attracted to places of employment, the extent to which the labor force of a metropolitan area is engaged in manufacturing employment should be associated with the rate and the direction of population redistribution. More specifically, the higher frequency of employment in manufacturing industry the higher should be the rate of population deconcentration.

The classification of Standard Metropolitan Areas by amount of manufacturing industry is based on the ratio of production workers in manufacturing, as reported in the Census of Manufactures, of 1948, to total population. Areas whose proportion of manufacturing workers exceeded the mean for all areas by more than one-half standard unit are classed as high or manufacturing areas. Those in which the proportions fell short of the mean by more than one-half standard unit are identified as areas of low proportions employed in manufacturing. These may also be characterized as non-manufacturing or service industry areas. The terms high and manufacturing will be used interchangeably, as will also the terms low and non-manufacturing. An intervening class, termed average areas, contains all areas the proportions of manufacturing workers in which deviated from the mean by not more than one-half standard unit. The use of one-half standard unit as the class limit was expedient; a wider spread of the class limits would have yielded too few areas in the high and low, or manufacturing, classes.

It will be noted, in Table 49, that the total number of metropolitan areas comprised in the three classes is less than that dealt with in earlier chapters. The reduction of the number for the purposes of this chapter results largely from the Census Bureau's practice of withholding information for any political unit in which the number of establishments is three or less. Some of the loss also results from the fact that detailed data are not reported for minor civil divisions of less than 10,000 population. This excludes many of the New England Standard Metropolitan Areas, for they are defined in terms of towns rather than counties and towns frequently had less than the minimum population.

The use of 1948 data for the classification by proportion of workers engaged in manufacturing employment is defensible when the question to be answered is: what have been the patterns of population change in metropolitan areas that, in 1948, had varying proportions of manufacturing workers residing in them. This is the question the present chapter seeks to answer. A classification based on the data for a single year is not entirely satisfactory, however, if the primary intention is to measure the correlation of population redistribution and the frequency of manufacturing employment. Metropolitan areas may shift classes from year to year. A perusal of census data will reveal that such shifts do in fact take place. Still, as the following analysis demonstrates, the sorting of areas as of a single year is serviceable in the measurement of that correlation, though the results are not as refined as they might have been.

Central Cities and Satellite Areas

Although metropolitan areas with average proportions of employment in manufacturing industry began the 50-year period with higher growth rates than did those classified as high or manufacturing areas, the two classes maintained comparable rates of change in the decades following 1920. Non-manufacturing areas, according to Table 50, had rates similar to those of the other two classes until 1930, after which date their rates became twice as high as the rates in manufacturing and average areas. The rates of population change in the central cities of the three classes were more sharply differentiated. All groups of central cities increased at

TABLE 49. NUMBER OF STANDARD METROPOLITAN AREAS, BY PROPORTION OF POPULATION EMPLOYED IN MANUFACTURING, SIZE OF CENTRAL CITY, AND DECADE, 1900 - 1950

Proportion of population in manufacturing and size of central city	1940- 50	1930- 40	1920- 30	1910- 20	1900- 10
Total	122	134	132	130	127
High	45_a	46_a	46_a	46_b	46_b
500,000 and over	7^a	7^a	6^a	4^b	3^b
250,000 - 500,000	1	2	2	3	4
100,000 - 250,000	14	14	9	4	2
Under 100,000	23	23	29	35	37
Average	35_c	39_c	38_c	38_c	38_c
500,000 and over	5^c	6^c	5^c	4^c	2^c
250,000 - 500,000	8	8	3	3	5
100,000 - 250,000	6	7	9	10	6
Under 100,000	16	18	21	21	25
Low	42_d	49_e	48	46	43
250,000 and over	3^d	5^e	2	2	2
100,000 - 250,000	11	11	9	3	2
Under 100,000	28	33	37	41	39

[a] Includes three areas with central cities of 1,000,000 or more population (Chicago, Philadelphia, and Detroit).

[b] Includes two areas with central cities of 1,000,000 or more population (Chicago and Philadelphia).

[c] Includes one area with a central city of 1,000,000 or more population (New York).

[d] Includes one area with a central city of 1,000,000 or more population (Los Angeles), and one area with a central city of 500,000-1,000,000 population (Washington, D. C.).

[e] Includes one area with a central city of 1,000,000 or more population (Los Angeles).

decreasing rates, but the central cities of manufacturing areas began and ended the period with the lowest rates. In average areas central city rates of change paralleled rather closely the rates for all central cities as reported in Table 4 (p. 16). The central cities of non-manufacturing areas had the highest growth rates and the smallest decline of growth rates. It was only in this latter class, too, that satellite population increased at progressively higher rates. In both of the other two classes rates reached their highest points in 1920-30, and then declined. Special note should be taken of the fact that the retardation of metropolitan growth during the 1930's was most pronounced in areas with the largest proportions employed in manufacturing industry. Although the effect of the depression years was greatest in central cities, it was also felt in satellite areas. But in the 1940-50 decade growth rates in both central cities and satellite zones of manufacturing areas made the largest recovery.

The principal effect of the adjustment of rates for size differences, as shown in the lower panel of Table 50, is to alter the pattern of change for the so-called non-manufacturing areas. The central cities of areas in that class began the period with the lowest rates of change, rather than the highest, and gained the highest rates after 1930. No retardation of growth in the 1930's is observable in the adjusted rates of areas with relatively small proportions employed in manufacturing. Stated differently, a low proportion of manufacturing employment seems to be associated with stability of growth.

The differences between satellite rates of change in corresponding distance zones of the three classes of areas are similar to those for all satellite areas, as may be seen in Fig. 30. Average areas had the highest rates in all zones within 35 miles of central cities, in 1900-10, and by 1940-50 their zonal rates with a few exceptions had fallen to the lowest position. The least change occurred in the 15-20 and the 20-25 mile zones. On the other hand, non-manufacturing areas had low zonal rates at the outset, particularly in 1910-20, and by 1940-50 their zonal rates were higher than those of either of the two classes. Most of the increase in rate of growth developed between 5 and 20 miles from central cities. In manufacturing areas growth rate increases took place mainly in the 10-15 and 15-20 mile zones. though there is evidence that such a tendency operated in most of the area beyond 20 miles from central cities.

When growth rates are stated as ratios, as in Table 51, the relationship of growth to frequency of manufacturing employment assumes a different aspect. There is no clear relationship between the two variables from 1900 to 1920. Beginning in 1920, however, a direct correlation emerged and continued through the remainder of the period. Deconcentration

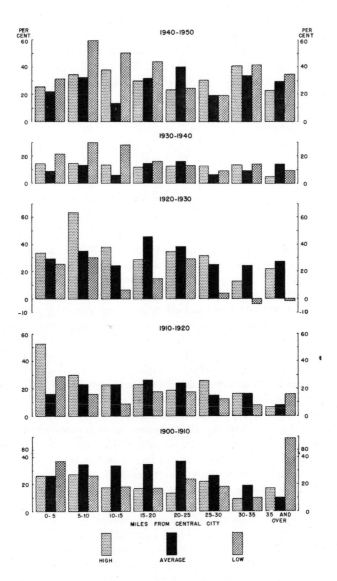

FIGURE 30

PER CENT CHANGE OF SATELLITE POPULATION IN STANDARD METROPOLITAN
AREAS, BY PROPORTION OF POPULATION EMPLOYED IN MANUFACTURING,
DISTANCE ZONE, AND DECADE, 1900-1950

TABLE 51. RATIO OF RATE OF POPULATION CHANGE IN
SATELLITE AREAS TO CENTRAL CITY RATE OF CHANGE
IN STANDARD METROPOLITAN AREA'S, BY PROPORTION
OF POPULATION EMPLOYED IN MANUFACTURING
INDUSTRY, AND DECADE, 1900 - 1950

Proportion of popula- tion in manufacturing	1940- 50	1930- 40	1920- 30	1910- 20	1900- 10
All areas	2.7	2.5	1.4	0.9	0.8
High	3.7	11.4	1.8	0.8	0.7
Average	2.9	2.0	1.5	1.1	1.0
Low	1.7	1.4	0.6	0.5	0.7

progressed most rapidly in manufacturing areas and most slowly in non-manufacturing areas. It is noteworthy that the ratios for average areas were in no decade less than 1.0, and that their satellite rates began to exceed central city rates as early as 1910-20. Again the similarity between ratios in average areas and all areas is apparent. It seems clear that metropolitan areas with average amounts of manufacturing employment are more representative of all metropolitan areas in respect to population redistribution than is any other class of areas observed thus far.

The progressive spread of relatively high rates of growth over the satellite areas of all metropolitan classes is observable in Fig. 31. Although dispersion in this sense began earlier in average areas, it has moved much more rapidly in manufacturing areas. Not until 1930-40, however, were all zones in the satellite portions of high areas growing more rapidly than central cities -- a decade after the growth rates of all zones in average areas exceeded central city rates. But in non-manufacturing areas high relative rates of growth were confined mainly within 20 miles of central cities. Rates in the 30-35 and 35 mile and over zones, in 1940-50, remain as unexplained exceptions.

The deconcentration tendencies in the three classes of metropolitan areas are described in another way in Table 52. The proportion of all increase that accrued to the central cities of manufacturing areas declined from a high of 72 per cent, in 1900-10, to 31 per cent, in 1940-50. Most of the central cities' loss was absorbed in the 5-10 and 10-15 mile zones, though all distance zones gained at the expense of central cities. A less radical change in the distribution of population increase occurred in average areas.

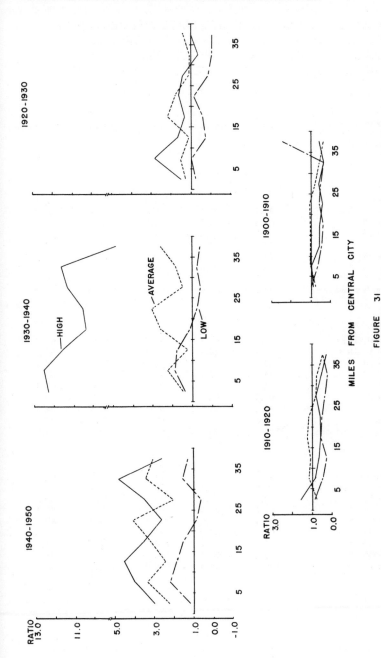

FIGURE 31

RATIO OF RATE OF SATELLITE POPULATION CHANGE TO RATE OF CENTRAL CITY CHANGE IN STANDARD METROPOLITAN AREAS, BY PROPORTION OF POPULATION EMPLOYED IN MANUFACTURING, DISTANCE ZONE, AND DECADE, 1900-1950

TABLE 52. CUMULATIVE PERCENTAGE DISTRIBUTION OF
POPULATION INCREASE IN STANDARD METROPOLITAN
AREAS, BY PROPORTION OF POPULATION EMPLOYED
IN MANUFACTURING, DISTANCE ZONE, AND DECADE,
1900 - 1950

Proportion of population in manufacturing and distance zone	1940-50	1930-40	1920-30	1910-20	1900-10
High					
Central cities	31.2	14.1	54.4	71.5	72.5
0 - 5 miles	39.1	27.0	60.0	78.4	76.8
5 - 10 "	60.6	54.7	77.8	86.2	85.4
10 - 15 "	79.8	74.6	87.9	92.0	91.2
15 - 20 "	87.8	84.5	92.5	95.4	94.6
20 - 25 "	91.9	91.2	96.0	97.2	96.3
25 - 30 "	95.6	96.0	98.2	98.9	98.0
30 - 35 "	97.8	98.1	99.6	99.5	98.4
35 miles and over	100.0	100.0	100.0	100.0	100.0
Average					
Central cities	34.1	44.7	53.6	61.7	63.9
0 - 5 miles	39.2	49.3	58.3	65.4	67.8
5 - 10 "	60.1	67.7	73.1	77.1	78.8
10 - 15 "	73.6	76.1	82.5	87.5	88.9
15 - 20 "	84.2	86.6	90.8	93.0	93.4
20 - 25 "	92.7	93.9	95.5	96.7	96.7
25 - 30 "	95.1	96.1	97.5	98.3	98.6
30 - 35 "	97.6	97.7	98.7	99.4	99.5
35 miles and over	100.0	100.0	100.0	100.0	100.0
Low					
Central cities	43.5	51.6	71.9	71.7	61.3
0 - 5 miles	49.0	58.3	78.1	79.4	69.6
5 - 10 "	73.7	77.6	90.3	87.3	80.8
10 - 15 "	85.6	89.4	92.4	90.3	86.3
15 - 20 "	93.4	95.3	95.5	94.7	89.9
20 - 25 "	96.2	97.9	100.1	97.1	92.4
25 - 30 "	97.1	98.6	100.3	97.9	93.6
30 - 35 "	98.1	99.1	100.2	98.1	93.8
35 miles and over	100.0	100.0	100.0	100.0	100.0

Furthermore, the increased share acquired by satellite area was not so highly concentrated as in manufacturing areas. In non-manufacturing areas the proportion of all increase attracted to central cities increased from 1900 to 1930, and then declined rapidly but not to as low a figure as that of either of the other classes. As with manufacturing areas the major part of the gain in satellite areas was taken up in the 5-10 and 10-15 mile zones. The changes in zones beyond 20 miles from central cities were comparatively small.

The high rates of population deconcentration in manufacturing areas become more understandable when it is observed, in Table 53, that such areas had the greatest concentration of population of any class of areas. Population in low or non-manufacturing areas, on the other hand, has been least concentrated. Evidently the rate of deconcentration is a function of the extent of concentration, as well as of other factors.

All classes of areas passed through a phase of increasing concentration. That phase lasted until 1920 in manufacturing and in average areas, and until 1930 in non-manufacturing areas. But if, instead of the proportion of the population in central cities, the proportion within 10 miles of central cities is taken as the measure of concentration, then average areas ended their concentration phase in 1910. Although non-manufacturing areas experienced both concentration and deconcentration phases, they ended the 50-year period with a more concentrated population than they had at the beginning.

Periods of population concentration were in general marked by declining rates of redistribution. This is shown to be true of all classes of metropolitan areas in Fig. 32. The changes in rates of redistribution from 1900-10 to 1910-20 were of small consequence, however, in manufacturing and in average areas. Contrasting with these changes is the rapid decline in rate of redistribution which occurred in non-manufacturing areas from 1900 to 1930. As the trends swung from concentration to deconcentration rates of redistribution accelerated, attaining their maximum in manufacturing areas between 1940 and 1950.

Size and Type of Satellite Place

The growth rates of almost all sizes of incorporated places in high and in average areas tended to decline, though, as may be seen in Table 54, the decline frequently occurred after 1930 following a period of rate increases. In areas with low proportions of population employed in manufacturing rates of change in incorporated places declined from 1900 to 1930 and then increased through the last two decades. Unincorporated population, on the

TABLE 53.　CUMULATIVE PERCENTAGE DISTRIBUTION OF
POPULATION IN STANDARD METROPOLITAN AREAS, BY
PROPORTION OF POPULATION EMPLOYED IN MANU-
FACTURING, DISTANCE ZONE, AND CENSUS YEAR,
1900 - 1950

Proportion of population in manufacturing and distance zone	1950	1940	1930	1920	1910	1900
High						
Central cities	58.1	62.8	65.2	68.1	66.7	64.6
0 - 5 miles	63.8	68.1	70.1	72.8	70.8	68.8
5 - 10 "	76.2	79.0	80.1	80.6	78.7	76.8
10 - 15 "	86.4	87.6	88.1	88.0	86.8	85.6
15 - 20 "	91.5	92.2	92.5	92.5	91.7	90.9
20 - 25 "	94.7	95.3	95.4	95.3	94.7	94.3
25 - 30 "	97.1	97.4	97.4	97.2	96.7	96.4
30 - 35 "	98.2	98.3	98.3	98.2	97.8	97.6
35 miles and over	100.0	100.0	100.0	100.0	100.0	100.0
Average						
Central cities	56.6	60.4	61.3	63.2	63.1	62.5
0 - 5 miles	60.8	64.4	65.6	67.3	67.5	67.1
5 - 10 "	73.5	75.7	77.0	77.8	78.0	77.6
10 - 15 "	83.9	85.6	86.8	87.7	87.8	87.4
15 - 20 "	90.4	91.4	92.2	92.3	92.1	91.7
20 - 25 "	94.8	95.1	95.5	95.4	95.2	94.7
25 - 30 "	97.0	97.3	97.6	97.5	97.4	97.0
30 - 35 "	98.5	98.6	98.8	98.8	98.7	98.4
35 miles and over	100.0	100.0	100.0	100.0	100.0	100.0
Low						
Central cities	53.4	56.9	60.6	60.2	57.0	53.1
0 - 5 miles	59.3	62.9	66.4	66.8	63.7	60.3
5 - 10 "	76.3	77.3	78.2	77.3	76.5	74.3
10 - 15 "	85.4	85.4	85.7	85.1	85.0	84.4
15 - 20 "	92.1	91.7	92.1	90.9	91.2	91.3
20 - 25 "	95.8	95.7	95.8	95.0	94.6	95.0
25 - 30 "	97.2	97.2	97.3	96.6	96.4	97.1
30 - 35 "	98.1	98.0	98.1	97.2	97.0	97.8
35 miles and over	100.0	100.0	100.0	100.0	100.0	100.0

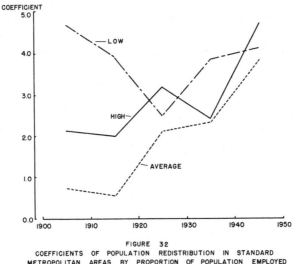

FIGURE 32
COEFFICIENTS OF POPULATION REDISTRIBUTION IN STANDARD
METROPOLITAN AREAS, BY PROPORTION OF POPULATION EMPLOYED
IN MANUFACTURING, 1900-1950

other hand, increased at progressively higher rates in succeeding decades
in most zones of each metropolitan area class. The largest changes between 1900 and 1950 occurred in the high or manufacturing areas.

These changes are made more intelligible in Table 55. The ratios
of incorporated places of 10,000 or more population which are located
within 20 miles of central cities increased in all classes of areas. In
distance zones beyond 20 miles of centers the prevalent tendency was
toward decline, especially in non-manufacturing areas. As a matter of
fact, all sizes of incorporated places 20 or more miles from the centers
of non-manufacturing areas had declining ratios. Incorporated places of
less than 10,000 population in all distance zones of manufacturing and
average areas had increasing relative growth rates. The largest changes
occurred in unincorporated areas.

Although in general the ratios of all sizes and types of places in
manufacturing areas exceeded those in average areas after 1920, the
1930-40 decade is exceptional in this respect. Accelerated growth, due
largely to an acutely depressed central city growth, occurred in even
the largest satellite places. The small places and unincorporated areas,
however, received the greatest relative gains.

Table 54. Per Cent Change of Satellite Population in Standard Metropolitan Areas, by Size and Type of Place, Distance Zone, Proportion of Population Employed in Manufacturing, and Decade, 1900-1950

Size and type of place and distance zone	High					Average					Low				
	1940-1950	1930-1940	1920-1930	1910-1920	1900-1910	1940-1950	1930-1940	1920-1930	1910-1920	1900-1910	1940-1950	1930-1940	1920-1930	1910-1920	1900-1910
50,000 and over															
0-10 miles	35.4	8.9	8.4	23.5	24.4	11.0	3.2	14.5	16.8	43.6	30.3	18.4	-16.0	---	22.0
10-20 miles	8.3	6.8	23.7	---	---	42.2	-0.6	11.3	19.3	35.5	48.0	15.6	155.5	---	25.9
20-30 miles	16.0	8.1	81.3	---	---	---	---	---	---	---	---	---	---	---	78.6
30 miles and over	---	---	---	---	---	---	---	---	---	---	---	---	---	---	---
10,000 - 50,000															
0-10 miles	14.3	5.7	49.7	31.5	27.4	-1.4	2.3	25.7	18.2	30.4	28.3	12.1	9.9	11.7	---
10-20 miles	23.8	3.9	30.4	46.3	26.8	30.5	8.8	42.9	37.1	59.3	69.0	28.9	7.6	9.4	---
20-30 miles	3.4	6.3	42.8	67.6	41.5	9.1	5.8	19.2	27.0	42.2	19.4	4.5	13.9	26.8	---
30 miles and over	7.9	1.7	25.8	15.2	18.3	36.8	0.0	6.2	25.9	27.2	22.6	4.5	-5.1	33.8	---
2,500 - 10,000															
0-10 miles	27.8	7.6	58.4	100.4	44.2	30.4	10.6	45.5	21.5	48.1	33.9	10.9	15.0	13.8	42.7
10-20 miles	42.2	10.4	56.2	26.9	43.7	35.2	13.2	65.0	40.1	47.1	62.8	22.6	8.4	19.8	7.4
20-30 miles	17.9	6.9	36.8	19.9	29.0	25.5	6.9	31.0	20.3	47.4	0.0	8.4	6.2	-12.8	50.9
30 miles and over	21.8	4.2	20.9	14.7	40.2	21.1	6.2	39.0	15.2	31.6	21.3	1.7	-6.0	22.3	99.2
Under 2,500															
0-10 miles	34.6	19.4	108.5	47.7	40.7	38.7	19.5	72.2	37.0	67.3	46.8	23.6	39.9	10.4	54.9
10-20 miles	34.5	14.0	43.8	28.5	18.3	34.1	15.5	55.4	31.7	36.8	31.8	8.4	7.9	19.4	23.0
20-30 miles	30.0	16.3	39.3	20.6	25.3	27.5	9.0	22.6	22.6	41.3	12.3	9.4	0.0	8.9	30.9
30 miles and over	26.8	6.6	22.4	7.2	16.7	24.5	7.9	18.0	20.4	27.4	4.5	9.2	-0.3	0.0	45.1
Unincorporated area															
0-10 miles	39.1	21.5	49.1	22.5	23.4	62.4	22.1	45.2	22.6	18.4	71.2	40.1	45.7	26.5	27.1
10-20 miles	45.0	18.8	26.7	32.7	9.1	9.3	18.8	27.3	12.3	19.7	41.7	25.4	-2.4	11.1	16.8
20-30 miles	43.4	18.0	16.1	3.4	7.0	50.4	20.4	43.4	15.8	22.5	28.8	13.7	27.1	19.4	12.0
30 miles and over	70.4	14.6	10.0	5.9	7.3	34.6	17.2	25.0	8.3	6.3	52.1	14.0	-0.8	14.8	70.3

Table 55. Ratio of Rate of Change of Satellite Population to Central City Rate of Change in Standard Metropolitan Areas, by Size and Type of Place, Distance Zone, Proportion of Population Employed in Manufacturing, and Decade, 1900-1950

Size and type of place and distance zone	High					Average					Low				
	1940-1950	1930-1940	1920-1930	1910-1920	1900-1910	1940-1950	1930-1940	1920-1930	1910-1920	1900-1910	1940-1950	1930-1940	1920-1930	1910-1920	1900-1910
50,000 and over															
0-10 miles	4.1	8.1	0.4	0.7	0.8	1.1	0.6	0.7	0.9	1.3	1.2	1.2	-0.5	---	---
10-20 miles	1.0	6.2	1.1	---	---	4.3	0.0	0.5	1.0	1.1	1.8	1.0	5.0	---	---
20-30 miles	1.9	7.4	3.7	---	---	---	---	---	---	---	---	---	---	---	---
30 miles and over	---	---	---	---	---	---	---	---	---	---	---	---	---	---	---
10,000 - 50,000															
0-10 miles	1.7	5.2	2.3	0.9	0.9	-0.1	0.4	1.2	0.9	0.9	1.1	0.8	0.3	0.4	0.6
10-20 miles	2.8	3.5	1.4	1.4	0.9	3.1	1.7	2.0	1.9	1.8	2.6	1.9	0.2	0.3	0.7
20-30 miles	0.4	5.7	1.9	2.0	1.4	0.9	1.1	0.9	1.4	1.3	0.7	0.3	0.4	0.8	2.1
30 miles and over	0.9	1.5	1.2	0.5	0.6	3.8	0.0	0.3	1.3	0.8	0.9	0.3	-0.2	1.1	---
2,500 - 10,000															
0-10 miles	3.2	6.9	2.7	3.0	1.5	3.1	2.0	2.1	1.1	1.5	1.3	0.7	0.5	0.4	1.1
10-20 miles	4.9	9.5	2.6	0.8	1.5	3.6	2.5	3.0	2.0	1.4	2.4	1.5	0.3	0.6	0.2
20-30 miles	2.1	6.3	1.7	0.6	1.0	2.6	1.3	1.1	1.0	1.4	0.0	0.5	0.2	-0.4	1.4
30 miles and over	2.6	3.8	0.9	0.4	1.4	2.2	1.2	1.8	0.8	1.0	0.8	0.1	-0.2	0.7	2.6
Under 2,500															
0-10 miles	4.0	17.6	4.9	1.4	1.4	4.0	3.7	3.4	1.9	2.0	1.8	1.5	1.3	0.3	1.5
10-20 miles	4.0	12.7	2.0	0.9	0.6	3.5	2.9	2.6	1.6	1.1	1.2	0.5	0.3	0.6	0.6
20-30 miles	3.5	14.8	1.8	0.6	0.9	2.8	1.7	1.1	1.4	1.3	0.5	0.6	0.0	0.3	0.8
30 miles and over	3.0	6.0	1.0	0.2	0.6	2.5	1.5	0.8	1.0	0.8	0.2	0.6	0.0	0.0	1.2
Unincorporated area															
0-10 miles	4.6	19.5	2.2	0.7	0.8	6.4	4.2	2.1	1.2	0.6	2.7	2.6	1.5	0.8	0.7
10-20 miles	5.3	17.1	1.2	1.0	0.3	1.0	3.5	1.3	0.6	0.6	1.6	1.6	-0.1	0.4	0.4
20-30 miles	5.1	16.4	0.7	0.1	0.2	5.2	3.8	2.0	0.8	0.7	1.1	0.9	-0.9	0.6	0.3
30 miles and over	8.2	13.3	0.4	0.2	0.2	3.6	3.2	1.2	0.4	0.2	2.0	0.9	0.0	0.5	1.9

Table 56. Per Cent Distribution of Satellite Population in Standard Metropolitan Areas, by Census Year, Size and Type of Place, Proportion of Population Employed in Manufacturing, and Distance Zone, 1900-1950

Census year and size and type of place	High				Average				Low			
	Miles from central city				Miles from central city				Miles from central city			
	0-10 miles	10-20 miles	20-30 miles	30 miles and over	0-10 miles	10-20 miles	20-30 miles	30 miles and over	0-10 miles	10-20 miles	20-30 miles	30 miles and over
1950												
Total	100.0	100.0	100.0	100.0	100.0	100.0	100.0	100.0	100.0	100.0	100.0	100.0
50,000 and over	13.1	7.3	20.1	0.0	23.5	37.4	0.0	0.0	8.5	14.2	0.0	0.0
10,000 - 50,000	20.8	20.8	11.0	27.2	16.4	21.2	24.9	13.6	19.3	9.6	15.3	18.2
2,500 - 10,000	11.6	15.9	17.7	10.4	14.5	11.4	16.5	20.7	12.8	13.0	9.6	12.8
Under 2,500	4.6	9.2	8.8	11.4	3.8	5.3	7.6	6.5	4.5	6.6	6.2	9.2
Unincorporated area	49.9	46.8	42.4	51.0	41.8	24.7	51.0	59.2	54.9	56.6	68.9	59.8
1940												
Total	100.0	100.0	100.0	100.0	100.0	100.0	100.0	100.0	100.0	100.0	100.0	100.0
50,000 and over	17.2	9.3	21.7	0.0	27.3	33.9	0.0	0.0	9.9	14.0	0.0	0.0
10,000 - 50,000	21.7	23.0	13.1	33.7	21.7	21.0	30.1	13.0	22.8	8.4	15.7	20.2
2,500 - 10,000	11.3	14.6	18.1	11.5	14.4	10.9	17.3	22.4	14.5	11.7	11.8	14.1
Under 2,500	5.2	10.4	8.8	12.9	3.6	5.1	7.9	6.9	4.6	7.3	6.8	12.0
Unincorporated area	44.6	42.7	38.3	41.9	33.0	29.1	44.7	57.7	48.2	58.6	65.7	53.7
1930												
Total	100.0	100.0	100.0	100.0	100.0	100.0	100.0	100.0	100.0	100.0	100.0	100.0
50,000 and over	6.3	5.2	9.8	0.0	29.1	35.1	0.0	0.0	7.5	9.8	0.0	0.0
10,000 - 50,000	26.8	21.2	24.2	35.6	20.8	20.8	28.6	14.2	22.8	7.9	14.6	21.1
2,500 - 10,000	14.4	17.0	11.3	15.0	14.0	11.2	19.3	22.3	11.6	11.5	10.8	11.2
Under 2,500	10.6	12.4	11.8	14.3	3.4	5.2	8.8	8.6	5.0	8.6	7.5	15.7
Unincorporated area	41.9	44.2	36.9	40.1	32.7	27.7	43.3	54.9	48.1	62.2	67.2	52.0
1920												
Total	100.0	100.0	100.0	100.0	100.0	100.0	100.0	100.0	100.0	100.0	100.0	100.0
50,000 and over	8.7	0.0	0.0	0.0	32.3	34.2	0.0	0.0	4.9	6.3	0.0	0.0
10,000 - 50,000	14.1	21.7	28.3	33.5	16.4	17.8	26.3	10.2	19.9	2.1	8.3	13.5
2,500 - 10,000	21.3	14.4	14.5	9.2	13.3	11.7	21.1	20.5	22.4	8.0	8.8	15.8
Under 2,500	10.7	14.8	14.1	13.9	5.0	6.9	10.1	10.3	6.5	14.3	7.1	13.7
Unincorporated area	45.2	49.1	43.1	43.4	33.0	29.4	42.2	59.0	46.3	69.3	74.8	57.0
1910												
Total	100.0	100.0	100.0	100.0	100.0	100.0	100.0	100.0	100.0	100.0	100.0	100.0
50,000 and over	6.1	0.0	0.0	0.0	30.6	33.3	0.0	0.0	0.0	0.0	0.0	0.0
10,000 - 50,000	8.7	12.0	9.7	25.5	15.8	14.2	20.4	9.0	18.0	2.3	9.7	5.7
2,500 - 10,000	13.2	17.6	19.4	11.2	12.4	10.8	19.6	16.9	19.5	5.0	10.0	16.8
Under 2,500	9.0	13.7	15.1	14.4	5.5	7.9	14.0	11.4	7.4	14.2	12.4	16.8
Unincorporated area	63.0	56.7	55.8	48.9	35.7	33.8	46.0	62.7	55.1	78.5	67.9	58.3
1900												
Total	100.0	100.0	100.0	100.0	100.0	100.0	100.0	100.0	100.0	100.0	100.0	100.0
50,000 and over	6.3	0.0	0.0	0.0	21.5	23.6	0.0	0.0	0.0	0.0	0.0	0.0
10,000 - 50,000	8.7	11.1	7.9	24.7	18.4	16.4	8.6	8.3	19.3	2.2	6.7	5.3
2,500 - 10,000	11.7	14.0	17.4	9.2	10.4	7.7	20.5	14.8	8.2	3.8	5.3	11.6
Under 2,500	8.2	13.5	14.0	14.1	5.7	7.7	14.3	12.5	8.8	10.3	11.0	17.0
Unincorporated area	65.1	61.4	60.7	52.0	44.0	44.6	56.6	64.4	63.7	83.7	77.0	70.8

The percentage distribution of population by size and type of satel-place within each zone, shown in Table 56, indicates that average areas have had the greatest concentrations in large satellites and the smallest proportions in unincorporated area. Non-manufacturing areas have had the largest proportions of their zonal populations in unincorporated area. In all classes of areas the proportions in unincorporated areas declined to 1930 and then increased once more. Conversely, the proportions in large satellites increased to 1930 and declined thereafter. This pattern of change occurred in all distance zones.

CHAPTER VIII

INDUSTRIAL RELOCATION AND POPULATION REDISTRIBUTION

It has been shown that deconcentration has been most characteristic of metropolitan areas with the largest proportions of manufacturing workers. That was anticipated on the assumption that manufacturing establishments are more inclined to locate outside of central cities than are other kinds of industries. But it remains to be determined whether the high rates of deconcentration are a function of the centrifugal movement of industry or are characteristic of manufacturing areas independently of the direction taken by industrial relocations. The first of these alternatives is treated in this chapter. A comparison of the findings here with those of Chapter VII will provide at least a partial answer to the second.

By industrial relocation is meant changes in the percentage distribution of place of employment of production workers in manufacturing[1] as between central city and satellite area. Where the central city proportion of the metropolitan area's total number of workers in manufacturing increased through four of the five decades between 1900 and 1950 the trend was toward industrial concentration and the area is placed in a class with that designation. This definition of industrial concentration is altered for areas that are included in the study for only a part of the period. In that event it is required that the central city's proportion should show an increase in every decade. Industrial deconcentration occurred when the central city's proportion of all workers in manufacturing declined through four of the five decades, or if the area is included in the study for but a part of the period, through all decades. A third class is comprised of metropolitan areas in which the changing proportion of manufacturing workers contained in central cities followed no clear trend. The number of areas in each class is shown in Table 57. Perhaps it is unnecessary to point out that industrial relocation is used in a relative sense. Changes in proportions may be produced either by actual plant relocations or by a more rapid expansion of employment in one part of an area than in another.

TABLE 57. NUMBER OF STANDARD METROPOLITAN AREAS, BY DIRECTION OF INDUSTRIAL RELOCATION, SIZE OF CENTRAL CITY, AND DECADE, 1900 - 1950

Direction of industrial relocation and size of central city	1940-50	1930-40	1920-30	1910-20	1900-10
Total	122	134	132	130	127
Concentrating	13	13	13	13	13
100,000 and over	6[a]	6[a]	4	3	2
Under 100,000	7	7	9	10	11
No clear trend	53[b]	60[c]	59[c]	57[d]	54[d]
250,000 and over	6	7	4	4	4
100,000 - 250,000	11	14	9	7	5
Under 100,000	36	39	46	46	45
Deconcentrating	56[e]	61[e]	60[f]	60[f]	60[f]
500,000 and over	11	11	8	6	3
250,000 - 500,000	6	9	5	6	9
100,000 - 250,000	15	13	15	7	3
Under 100,000	24	28	32	41	45

[a] Includes one area with a central city of 250,000-500,000 population (Rochester).

[b] Includes two areas with central cities of 1,000,000 or more population (Philadelphia and Detroit), and one with a central city of 500,000-1,000,000 population (Washington, D. C.).

[c] Includes two areas with central cities of 1,000,000 or more population (Philadelphia and Detroit), and one with a central city of 500,000-1,000,000 population (St. Louis).

[d] Includes one area with a central city of 1,000,000 or more population (Philadelphia), and one with a central city of 500,000-1,000,000 population (St. Louis).

[e] Includes three areas with central cities of 1,000,000 or more population (New York, Chicago, and Los Angeles).

[f] Includes one area with a central city of 1,000,000 or more population (Chicago).

TABLE 58. PER CENT CHANGE OF POPULATION IN STANDARD METROPOLITAN AREAS, BY TYPE OF PLACE, DIRECTION OF INDUSTRIAL RELOCATION, AND DECADE, 1900-1950

Type of place and direction of industrial relocation	1940-50	1930-40	1920-30	1910-20	1900-10
Actual					
Total					
Concentrating	18.5	6.7	18.0	25.8	36.4
No clear trend	23.5	8.9	27.0	26.1	23.3
Deconcentrating	19.4	8.5	26.5	24.3	32.5
Central cities					
Concentrating	15.1	4.3	22.0	34.2	45.2
No clear trend	15.9	5.2	25.4	31.2	27.9
Deconcentrating	10.5	5.7	22.1	24.2	33.0
Satellite areas					
Concentrating	23.3	10.2	12.4	15.9	27.9
No clear trend	35.0	14.8	29.7	18.5	17.2
Deconcentrating	33.1	13.2	35.2	24.4	31.5
Adjusted[a]					
Total					
Concentrating	7.2	2.9	7.4	10.3	15.3
No clear trend	24.3	9.5	27.6	27.5	23.4
Deconcentrating	19.5	11.2	26.5	27.2	32.5
Central cities					
Concentrating	5.8	1.9	8.1	12.9	16.8
No clear trend	15.1	4.9	23.4	31.1	27.1
Deconcentrating	11.2	9.8	23.1	29.4	35.2
Satellite areas					
Concentrating	9.3	4.4	6.4	7.3	13.4
No clear trend	38.4	15.3	34.7	22.2	18.6
Deconcentrating	32.4	13.6	33.3	22.8	27.4

[a] Adjusted for size of central city. Size distribution of all areas used as the standard.

In either case the effect is to reduce the relative importance as a manufacturing site of one part and to increase the importance of the other part.

Central City and Satellite Area

Standard Metropolitan Areas in which industrial concentration was the prevailing trend, though they had the highest rates of change in 1900-10, had the lowest rates of change from 1920 to 1950, as Table 58 indicates. Areas in which there was no clear trend of industrial relocation came into ascendancy in 1910-20 and continued to grow more rapidly than the other classes through the remaining decades. The differences between rates of change in that class and rates of change in areas of industrial deconcentration, however, were very small in the years from 1910 to 1950. Rates of change of central city populations parallel rather closely those of total populations. Departures from similarity of pattern occurred in 1910-20 and 1940-50 in which central city rates of deconcentrating areas fell well below those in the other classes of areas. The satellite populations of deconcentrating metropolitan areas increased most rapidly from 1900 to 1930. Thereafter the highest rates of satellite growth occurred in areas of the no clear trend class. The trends of change are more revealing of the influence of industrial movement than are the rates at any point in time. In concentrating areas the rates of satellite growth declined for 40 years and then increased abruptly in the last decade. The trend in areas with no clear direction evident in industrial relocation was for satellite rates to double during the five decades. And in deconcentrating areas rates of change of satellite population tended to remain at a high level, though they fell away from it in 1910-20 and 1930-40. It would appear that the deconcentrating areas have been more effected by the ebb and flow of migration than have areas in which there was no trend of industrial deconcentration.

The adjustment of growth rates to a standard size of area distribution, the results of which are shown in the lower panel of Table 58, depresses the rates of concentrating areas and expands the rates in areas with no clear trend of industrial movement, especially in their satellite territories. The ascendancy of satellite growth in the no clear trend class began a decade earlier when adjusted rates are used. Barring these slight modifications, the differences in growth tendencies seem not to have been a function of variations in size distribution.

Population changes in satellite areas are shown by distance zones in Fig. 33. The pattern of differential changes among distance zones in concentrating areas shifted radically between 1900 and 1950. In 1900-10 growth was fairly even in most zones. But in succeeding decades growth

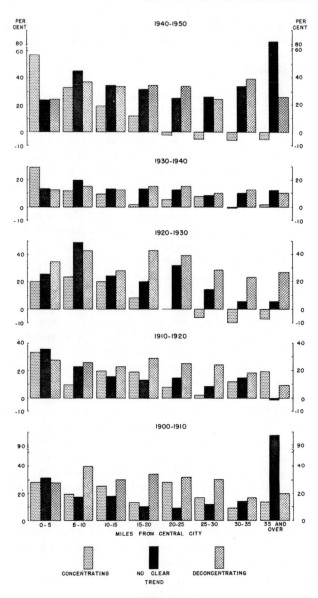

FIGURE 33
PER CENT CHANGE OF SATELLITE POPULATION IN STANDARD METROPOLITAN
AREAS, BY DIRECTION OF INDUSTRIAL RELOCATION, DISTANCE ZONE, AND
DECADE, 1900-1950

concentrated more and more in the inner zones. Rates increased in the 0-5 and 5-10 mile zones, and declined in all other zones. And beyond 20 miles from central cities population losses were prevalent after 1920. In areas with no clear trend all zones beyond 5 miles from central cities had higher rates in 1940-50 than in 1900-10, though in many of them most of the change occurred after 1940. If the 35 mile and over zone is excluded from consideration, growth was more concentrated in the no clear trend areas than in areas of industrial deconcentration. That is, the zones of most rapid growth were further from central cities in the latter than in the former in almost every decade. Whereas high rates in zones beyond 10 miles from centers came late to areas with no clear trend, they must have operated in deconcentrating areas from the beginning.

The more rapid dispersion of population in areas of industrial deconcentration is shown in Table 59. In no decade, as measured by actual rates, did the satellite population of such areas fail to grow as rapidly as central cities. Dispersion did not affect concentrating areas until after 1930. The sudden increase in 1930-40 was more a consequence of low central city rates than of high satellite rates, as reference to Table 58 will indicate. This cannot be said, however, of the high 1930-40 ratio in areas with no clear trend of industrial relocation. Clearly in that one decade dispersion was greatest in areas with no clear trend.

TABLE 59. RATIO OF RATE OF POPULATION CHANGE IN
SATELLITE AREAS TO CENTRAL CITY RATE OF
CHANGE IN STANDARD METROPOLITAN AREAS,
BY DIRECTION OF INDUSTRIAL RELOCATION,
AND DECADE, 1900 - 1950

Direction of indus-trial relocation	1940-50	1930-40	1920-30	1910-20	1900-10
All areas	2.7	2.5	1.4	0.9	0.8
Concentrating	1.5	2.4	0.6	0.5	0.6
No clear trend	2.2	2.8	1.2	0.6	0.6
Deconcentrating	3.2	2.3	1.6	1.0	1.0

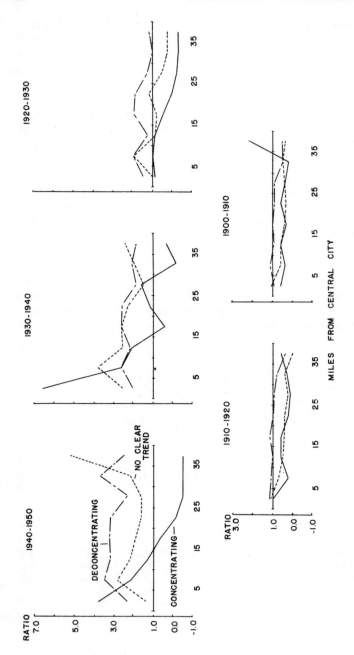

FIGURE 34

RATIO OF RATE OF SATELLITE POPULATION CHANGE TO RATE OF CENTRAL CITY CHANGE IN STANDARD METROPOLITAN AREAS, BY DIRECTION OF INDUSTRIAL RELOCATION, DISTANCE ZONE, AND DECADE, 1900-1950

The reduction of zonal rates to ratios eliminates many of the irregularities observed in Fig. 33. In concentrating areas increases in relative rates of change, shown in Fig. 34, extended over all zones within 20 miles of centers, though only within a 15-mile radius of centers did satellite rates rise above central city rates. In zones beyond 20 miles decline was the rule. Industrial concentration, in other words, exerted a strong centripetal pull on satellite population.

Dispersion accelerated rapidly in 1930-40 in areas within which there was no clear trend of industrial movement. In the next decade population deconcentration subsided in zones 0 to 25 miles from centers, while in outer zones the rates continued their rise. In areas of industrial deconcentration consistent increases occurred in all zones. The centrifugal effect of industrial deconcentration on population growth began early and proceeded without interruption.

These patterns of change are repeated in the cumulative percentage distributions of the amounts of population change of Table 60. The delayed beginnings of dispersion followed by an extraordinary impetus in that direction within areas of industrial concentration is marked by the decline of the central cities' share of population increase from 71 per cent, in 1920-30, to 39 per cent, in 1930-40. During the same period the proportion of increase attracted to satellite areas within 10 miles of central cities doubled, changing from 22 per cent to 45 per cent.

In areas of the no clear trend class the scatter of population increments was a more even process. But as in areas of industrial concentration central cities regained some of their losses in 1940-50. The major increases in the distribution of population increments occurred in the 5-10 and 10-15 mile zones; together these zones received 18 per cent in 1900-10, and 39 per cent in 1940-50.

As has been observed in other connections, the most consistent trend of change in the distribution of population gains took place in areas of industrial deconcentration. Beginning with a relatively high proportion of gain, amounting to 66 per cent in 1900-10, the central cities' share declined without interruption to 33 per cent in 1940-50. That loss was compensated by substantial gains in satellite areas 5 to 20 miles from central cities.

It seems quite probable, after an inspection of Table 61, that the high rates of satellite growth in areas of industrial deconcentration were due partly to the greater degree of population concentration in those areas. The central cities of deconcentrating areas held a larger proportion of their total area populations than did the central cities of the other classes in every census year down to 1950. This was not true, however, of the

TABLE 60. CUMULATIVE PERCENTAGE DISTRIBUTION OF
POPULATION INCREASE IN STANDARD METROPOLITAN
AREAS, BY DIRECTION OF INDUSTRIAL RELOCATION,
DISTANCE ZONE, AND DECADE, 1900 - 1950

Direction of industrial relocation and distance zone	1940-50	1930-40	1920-30	1910-20	1900-10
Concentrating					
Central cities	48.2	39.1	71.3	72.0	61.1
0 - 5 miles	68.7	62.8	77.4	78.8	66.8
5 - 10 "	91.4	84.6	92.7	83.6	75.6
10 - 15 "	100.4	95.6	102.0	90.3	82.7
15 - 20 "	102.8	96.4	104.0	94.0	84.9
20 - 25 "	102.5	98.0	104.0	94.9	87.1
25 - 30 "	102.0	99.3	103.3	95.1	88.3
30 - 35 "	101.7	99.2	102.8	95.5	88.6
35 miles and over	100.0	100.0	100.0	100.0	100.0
No clear trend					
Central cities	41.0	36.7	59.0	71.7	68.4
0 - 5 miles	47.2	45.6	64.8	79.8	76.4
5 - 10 "	71.0	72.6	83.4	88.6	84.9
10 - 15 "	86.1	86.4	92.0	94.9	94.1
15 - 20 "	92.0	93.2	95.5	97.6	96.7
20 - 25 "	95.4	97.2	98.9	99.0	98.0
25 - 30 "	96.8	98.4	99.7	99.5	98.9
30 - 35 "	97.9	99.2	99.9	100.0	99.5
35 miles and over	100.0	100.0	100.0	100.0	100.0
Deconcentrating					
Central cities	33.1	42.4	54.9	65.5	66.2
0 - 5 miles	38.2	48.1	59.9	70.1	69.8
5 - 10 "	59.7	66.2	74.2	80.0	80.7
10 - 15 "	74.8	77.9	82.8	87.6	88.3
15 - 20 "	85.4	87.6	90.1	92.8	92.9
20 - 25 "	92.0	93.6	94.9	96.2	96.0
25 - 30 "	95.0	96.3	97.2	98.3	98.1
30 - 35 "	97.5	97.9	98.2	99.2	98.7
35 miles and over	100.0	100.0	100.0	100.0	100.0

spaces within 10 mile radii of metropolitan centers. And that, of course, is because population deconcentration began earlier in areas of industrial deconcentration.

Expressed as coefficients of redistribution, shown in Fig. 35, the rates of distribution changes show three fairly distinct patterns. In concentrating areas the rate of redistribution declined precipitously from 1900 to 1940, and then increased once more. It is noteworthy that in even the period in which the relative rate of satellite growth increased sharply -- 1930-40, the rate of redistribution continued its decline. In contrast to concentrating areas, the rates of redistribution in areas of deconcentration have followed a trend of increase. A third pattern, if it may be called that, occurred in areas with no clear trend of industrial relocation. In those areas redistribution rates fluctuated widely with only a suggestion of a long-run tendency to increase.

Size and Type of Satellite Place

While all sizes and types of satellite places in concentrating areas had relatively high rates of change, in 1900-10, as shown in Table 62, the rates of all places and in all zones declined rapidly during the following 40 years. Population losses developed after 1920 in places located 20 or more miles from central cities, some of the largest among which occurred in unincorporated areas. Thus all satellite places shared in the low rates of concentrating areas. But rates of change in incorporated places of less than 2,500 population and of unincorporated area within 10 miles of centers remained comparatively high. This together with losses in outer zones is in keeping with the expected effects of industrial concentration.

The highest rates of change occurred in deconcentrating areas after 1910. Rates declined, however, in all incorporated places, particularly in those located within 30 miles of central cities. Industrial deconcentration appears to have stimulated satellite population growth only in unincorporated areas. Rates of change of unincorporated population increased in all zones.

The high rates of satellite population growth in metropolitan areas with no clear trend of industrial relocation were due largely to rapid and increasing rates of growth in unincorporated areas and in the smallest class of incorporated places. Elsewhere trends of declining rates prevailed.

Measures of relative growth, presented in Table 63, were low in all sizes and types of satellite places in concentrating areas. A tendency

TABLE 61. CUMULATIVE PERCENTAGE DISTRIBUTION OF
POPULATION IN STANDARD METROPOLITAN AREAS, BY
DIRECTION OF INDUSTRIAL RELOCATION, DISTANCE
ZONE, AND CENSUS YEAR, 1900 - 1950

Direction of industrial relocation and distance zone	1950	1940	1930	1920	1910	1900
Concentrating						
Central cities	57.3	58.9	60.3	58.3	54.4	49.2
0 - 5 miles	66.1	65.6	65.8	63.7	59.8	56.6
5 - 10 "	80.8	78.8	78.5	75.9	74.1	72.8
10 - 15 "	89.5	87.5	87.0	84.3	83.0	83.0
15 - 20 "	93.4	91.7	91.4	89.1	88.0	89.0
20 - 25 "	95.1	93.8	93.5	91.6	90.8	91.9
25 - 30 "	96.1	95.1	94.8	93.3	92.8	94.4
30 - 35 "	96.6	95.7	95.5	94.2	93.9	95.7
35 miles and over	100.0	100.0	100.0	100.0	100.0	100.0
No clear trend						
Central cities	56.8	60.5	62.0	62.6	60.0	57.2
0 - 5 miles	63.1	66.8	68.2	68.9	66.1	63.3
5 - 10 "	77.8	79.3	80.3	79.1	76.8	74.6
10 - 15 "	89.0	89.7	89.9	89.0	87.8	86.4
15 - 20 "	93.8	94.2	94.4	93.9	93.6	92.7
20 - 25 "	97.0	97.4	97.4	96.9	96.4	96.0
25 - 30 "	98.3	98.6	98.7	98.4	98.2	98.0
30 - 35 "	99.1	99.4	99.4	99.3	99.1	99.0
35 miles and over	100.0	100.0	100.0	100.0	100.0	100.0
Deconcentrating						
Central cities	56.4	60.9	63.1	66.1	65.6	65.2
0 - 5 miles	60.8	65.1	67.2	70.1	69.6	69.3
5 - 10 "	73.8	76.4	77.6	79.0	78.7	78.2
10 - 15 "	83.4	85.0	85.9	87.0	86.7	86.5
15 - 20 "	90.0	90.9	91.4	91.6	91.1	90.9
20 - 25 "	94.2	94.6	94.8	94.9	94.4	94.1
25 - 30 "	96.7	97.0	97.1	97.1	96.6	96.4
30 - 35 "	98.1	98.2	98.2	98.2	97.8	97.7
35 miles and over	100.0	100.0	100.0	100.0	100.0	100.0

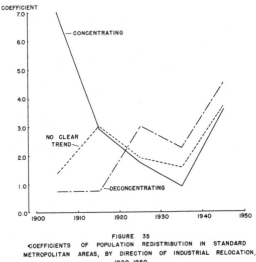

FIGURE 35
COEFFICIENTS OF POPULATION REDISTRIBUTION IN STANDARD
METROPOLITAN AREAS, BY DIRECTION OF INDUSTRIAL RELOCATION,
1900-1950

for ratios to increase is evident in most places of less than 10,000 population located within 20 miles of central cities. But the increases were
small and were limited to the years between 1910 and 1940. Much larger
increases in the relative growth rates of satellite places occurred in areas
of industrial deconcentration. Accelerating growth took place in all
classes of places with less than 10,000 population regardless of location.
There were increases, too, in incorporated places of 10,000-50,000 population located in the 10-20 and the 30 and over mile zones. Metropolitan
areas in which there was no clear direction to the relocation of industry
had increasing ratios in satellites of 2,500 to 50,000 population within
20 miles of centers and in smaller places in all distance zones. Unlike
the deconcentrating areas, in which the increase of ratios was more or
less continuous through the five decades, increase in the no clear trend
areas reached its height in 1930-40.

Differential growth within concentrating areas has shifted the pattern
of distribution not only as between zones but also as between types of
satellite places. Table 64 indicates that in the 0-10 mile zone unincorporated area gained a steadily larger proportion of the population at the
expense of most classes of incorporated places. In all other zones unincorporated areas had declining proportions, while incorporated places
acquired increased proportions. Within deconcentrating areas unincorporated population in all zones declined proportionally until 1930 and

Table 62. Per Cent Change of Satellite Population in Standard Metropolitan Areas,
by Size and Type of Place, Distance Zone, Direction of Industrial Relocation and Decade, 1900-1950

Size and type of place and distance zone	Concentrating					No clear trend					Deconcentrating				
	1940-1950	1930-1940	1920-1930	1910-1920	1900-1910	1940-1950	1930-1940	1920-1930	1910-1920	1900-1910	1940-1950	1930-1940	1920-1930	1910-1920	1900-1910
50,000 and over															
0-10 miles	---	---	---	---	---	10.9	0.5	4.2	11.0	25.5	10.9	0.7	16.0	20.0[a]	46.7[a]
10-20 miles	---	---	---	---	---	7.6	-5.2	5.5	21.8	---	10.0	0.2	13.7[a]	19.0[a]	35.5[a]
20-30 miles	---	---	---	---	---	10.6[a]	2.6[a]	---	---	---	21.8[a]	10.3[a]	81.3[a]	---	---
30 miles and over	---	---	---	---	---	---	---	---	---	---	---	---	---	---	---
10,000 - 50,000															
0-10 miles	4.7[a]	-1.3	12.1	11.6	15.8	21.9	4.4	20.2	-2.4	9.0	9.1	6.8	41.7	30.2	41.8
10-20 miles	10.5[a]	2.4	66.5[a]	43.2	---	17.9	3.2	18.9	31.6	38.9	35.9	10.3	42.2	45.0	52.4
20-30 miles	16.8	---	---	---	---	9.9	4.4	58.1	32.5	---	9.1	5.8	23.3	41.9	46.6
30 miles and over	0.4	3.7[a]	-5.1	33.9[a]	---	6.5	0.6	6.5	19.7	13.9	24.4	1.6	23.8	17.2	21.4
2,500 - 10,000															
0-10 miles	12.9	4.3	8.4	10.1	16.6	23.1	5.7	46.6	55.7	35.3	35.6	12.6	40.6	39.4	51.5
10-20 miles	18.5	8.0	11.0	26.0	46.2	43.5	13.6	36.1	18.5	30.4	43.7	14.0	66.5	39.9	47.8
20-30 miles	-2.7	12.0	-2.5	5.7	37.0	12.6	5.0	20.2	-2.8	24.0	21.5	7.4	36.6	24.0	48.0
30 miles and over	-9.6	-5.9	-6.4	29.4	99.3	12.1	18.8	2.0	-3.3	70.4	26.2	5.5	35.6	15.5	31.0
Under 2,500															
0-10 miles	23.0	25.8	39.9	25.9	64.5	34.3	14.8	20.2	39.6	52.2	46.6	25.5	77.6	34.9	55.1
10-20 miles	5.4	4.6	9.2	19.2	20.4	30.5	12.3	18.9	22.8	20.7	40.5	15.3	57.2	31.9	29.1
20-30 miles	4.9	5.5	-1.9	7.0	28.4	19.8	7.5	58.1	18.5	20.5	29.7	13.8	36.4	24.9	39.3
30 miles and over	-9.5	2.9	-7.4	20.6	46.1	19.5	7.7	6.5	10.9	17.7	28.0	9.5	22.5	7.5	24.1
Unincorporated area															
0-10 miles	57.8	25.0	26.3	16.0	109.5	52.0	31.3	45.5	25.9	18.3	63.4	28.5	47.2	23.2	25.3
10-20 miles	21.1	7.8	7.0	16.2	16.2	38.4	18.1	22.7	7.7	8.4	50.9	25.3	24.6	14.3	20.7
20-30 miles	14.1	3.7	-3.5	5.3	19.3	31.5	13.8	24.3	7.5	4.1	49.2	20.9	37.0	15.1	19.8
30 miles and over	-9.6	2.3	-12.0	7.9	82.1	86.3	14.0	2.8	3.5	6.2	36.8	17.6	22.1	10.2	12.0

[a] Based on less than 5 incorporated places.

Table 63. Ratio of Rate of Change of Satellite Population to Central City Rate of Change in Standard Metropolitan Areas, by Size and Type of Place, Distance Zone, Direction of Industrial Relocation, and Decade, 1900-1950

Size and type of place and distance zone	Concentrating					No clear trend					Deconcentrating				
	1940-1950	1930-1940	1920-1930	1910-1920	1900-1910	1940-1950	1930-1940	1920-1930	1910-1920	1900-1910	1940-1950	1930-1940	1920-1930	1910-1920	1900-1910
50,000 and over															
0-10 miles	--	--	--	--	--	0.7	0.1	0.2	0.4	0.9	1.0	0.1	0.7	0.8	1.4
10-20 miles	--	--	--	--	--	0.5	-1.0	0.2	0.7	--	1.0	0.0	0.6	0.8	1.1
20-30 miles	--	--	--	--	--	0.7	0.5	--	--	--	2.1	1.8	3.7	--	--
30 miles and over	--	--	--	--	--	--	--	--	--	--	--	--	--	--	--
10,000 - 50,000															
0-10 miles	0.3	-0.3	0.6	0.3	0.3	1.4	0.8	0.8	-0.1	0.3	0.9	1.2	1.9	1.2	1.3
10-20 miles	0.7	0.6	3.0	1.3	--	1.1	0.6	0.7	1.0	1.4	3.4	1.8	1.9	1.9	1.6
20-30 miles	1.1	--	--	--	--	0.6	0.8	2.3	1.7	--	0.9	1.0	1.1	1.7	1.4
30 miles and over	0.0	0.9	-0.2	1.0	--	0.4	0.1	0.3	0.6	0.5	2.3	0.3	1.1	0.7	0.6
2,500 - 10,000															
0-10 miles	0.9	1.0	0.4	0.3	0.4	1.5	1.1	1.8	1.8	1.3	3.4	2.2	1.8	1.6	1.6
10-20 miles	1.2	1.9	0.5	0.8	1.0	2.7	2.6	1.4	0.6	1.1	4.2	2.5	3.0	1.6	1.4
20-30 miles	-0.2	2.8	-0.1	0.2	0.8	0.8	1.0	0.8	-0.1	0.9	2.0	1.3	1.7	1.0	1.5
30 miles and over	-0.6	-1.4	-0.3	0.9	2.2	0.8	3.6	0.1	-0.1	2.5	2.5	1.0	1.6	0.6	0.9
Under 2,500															
0-10 miles	1.5	6.0	1.8	0.8	1.4	2.2	2.8	0.8	1.3	1.9	4.4	4.5	3.5	1.4	1.7
10-20 miles	0.4	1.1	0.4	0.6	0.5	1.9	2.4	0.7	0.7	0.7	3.9	2.7	2.6	1.3	0.9
20-30 miles	0.3	1.3	-0.1	0.2	0.6	1.2	1.4	2.3	0.6	0.7	2.8	2.4	1.6	1.0	1.2
30 miles and over	-0.6	0.7	-0.3	0.6	1.0	1.2	1.5	0.3	0.3	0.6	2.7	1.7	1.0	0.3	0.7
Unincorporated area															
0-10 miles	3.8	5.8	1.2	0.5	2.4	3.3	6.0	1.8	0.8	0.7	6.0	5.0	2.1	1.0	0.8
10-20 miles	1.4	1.8	0.3	0.5	0.4	2.4	3.5	0.9	0.2	0.3	4.8	4.4	1.1	0.6	0.6
20-30 miles	-0.9	0.9	-0.2	0.2	0.4	2.0	2.7	1.0	0.2	0.1	4.7	3.7	1.7	0.6	0.0
30 miles and over	-0.6	0.5	-0.5	0.2	1.8	5.4	2.7	0.1	0.1	0.2	3.5	3.1	1.0	0.4	0.4

Table 64. Per Cent Distribution of Satellite Population in Standard Metropolitan Areas, by Census Year, Size and Type of Place, Direction of Industrial Relocation, and Distance Zone, 1900-1950

Census year and size and type of place	Concentrating				No clear trend				Deconcentrating			
	Miles from central city				Miles from central city				Miles from central city			
	0-10 miles	10-20 miles	20-30 miles	30 miles and over	0-10 miles	10-20 miles	20-30 miles	30 miles and over	0-10 miles	10-20 miles	20-30 miles	30 miles and over
1950												
Total	100.0	100.0	100.0	100.0	100.0	100.0	100.0	100.0	100.0	100.0	100.0	100.0
50,000 and over	0.0	0.0	0.0	0.0	8.6	5.3	8.9	0.0	18.7	23.4	7.1	0.0
10,000 - 50,000	14.5	19.7	13.6	23.5	14.8	13.3	3.4	11.4	21.2	21.0	22.4	22.2
2,500 - 10,000	9.4	7.2	21.7	19.3	13.0	11.7	12.3	7.8	13.4	14.4	16.3	16.9
Under 2,500	5.6	13.3	21.7	15.9	5.9	8.6	6.8	12.3	3.4	6.1	7.6	8.1
Unincorporated area	70.5	59.8	43.0	41.3	57.7	61.1	68.6	68.5	43.3	35.1	46.6	52.8
1940												
Total	100.0	100.0	100.0	100.0	100.0	100.0	100.0	100.0	100.0	100.0	100.0	100.0
50,000 and over	0.0	0.0	0.0	0.0	10.7	6.6	10.0	0.0	22.5	28.6	7.6	0.0
10,000 - 50,000	19.4	20.8	11.1	21.7	16.7	15.0	3.8	16.6	25.9	20.8	26.6	23.4
2,500 - 10,000	11.7	7.1	21.2	19.7	14.5	10.9	13.7	10.8	13.2	13.5	17.5	17.6
Under 2,500	6.4	14.6	19.8	16.3	6.0	8.8	7.2	15.8	3.1	5.8	7.7	8.3
Unincorporated area	62.5	57.5	47.9	42.3	52.1	58.7	65.3	56.8	35.3	31.3	40.6	50.7
1930												
Total	100.0	100.0	100.0	100.0	100.0	100.0	100.0	100.0	100.0	100.0	100.0	100.0
50,000 and over	0.0	0.0	0.0	0.0	14.7	6.9	9.4	16.8	25.0	29.6	7.8	0.0
10,000 - 50,000	22.8	21.8	20.1	21.1	16.7	16.1	5.0	16.8	25.0	21.2	26.7	25.4
2,500 - 10,000	11.9	6.3	13.1	21.2	14.8	13.0	13.1	8.1	13.5	12.6	18.9	17.0
Under 2,500	6.7	15.6	19.8	15.8	6.1	9.0	8.8	19.8	3.1	6.4	7.8	9.7
Unincorporated area	58.6	56.3	60.1	41.9	47.7	55.0	63.7	55.3	33.4	30.2	38.8	47.9
1920												
Total	100.0	100.0	100.0	100.0	100.0	100.0	100.0	100.0	100.0	100.0	100.0	100.0
50,000 and over	0.0	0.0	0.0	0.0	12.5	7.9	0.0	0.0	21.8	26.2	3.7	0.0
10,000 - 50,000	24.9	12.7	20.0	20.3	16.4	12.6	10.2	16.7	22.8	19.1	27.6	20.9
2,500 - 10,000	10.5	8.9	19.6	21.7	15.3	11.1	13.9	6.7	15.6	12.9	18.2	16.3
Under 2,500	7.7	17.3	19.6	14.4	7.8	10.3	10.5	18.4	5.1	8.7	10.0	10.5
Unincorporated area	56.9	61.1	60.4	43.6	48.0	58.1	65.4	58.2	34.7	33.1	40.5	52.3
1910												
Total	100.0	100.0	100.0	100.0	100.0	100.0	100.0	100.0	100.0	100.0	100.0	100.0
50,000 and over	0.0	0.4	0.0	0.0	14.0	4.4	0.0	0.0	20.6	24.7	0.0	0.0
10,000 - 50,000	25.1	6.4	16.7	8.6	11.2	12.3	8.2	15.3	17.6	15.1	24.0	19.1
2,500 - 10,000	8.1	10.6	22.5	25.3	15.2	8.9	14.2	7.6	14.9	12.2	17.1	13.1
Under 2,500	8.6	17.3	60.8	16.5	8.7	10.7	12.8	17.6	6.2	10.7	13.5	11.6
Unincorporated area	58.2	65.7	60.8	49.6	50.9	63.7	64.8	59.5	40.6	37.3	45.4	56.2
1900												
Total	100.0	100.0	100.0	100.0	100.0	100.0	100.0	100.0	100.0	100.0	100.0	100.0
50,000 and over	42.6	0.0	0.0	0.0	10.2	0.0	0.0	0.0	15.3	19.1	0.0	0.0
10,000 - 50,000	5.3	12.5	8.1	18.1	13.2	12.9	18.3	8.9	14.6	12.7	12.2	17.4
2,500 - 10,000	8.8	14.3	27.4	23.6	8.3	7.4	5.7	17.8	12.4	10.5	17.1	12.8
Under 2,500					8.5	9.7	11.5	70.2	6.4	10.3	13.7	11.8
Unincorporated area	43.3	73.2	64.5	58.3	59.8	70.0	70.2	67.6	51.3	47.4	57.0	58.0

afterwards recovered some of its loss. Incorporated population, particularly in the larger places, expanded from 1900 to 1930 and then contracted. In every census year after 1900 the satellite population of deconcentrating areas has occupied incorporated places to a much greater extent than in the other classes of metropolitan areas. The trends of changing distribution in areas of no clear industrial relocation have been similar to those in deconcentrating areas. But the former has had a considerably greater concentration of its satellite population in small incorporated places and in unincorporated area.

In conclusion, the dispersion of metropolitan population is closely associated with industrial deconcentration, though it is not entirely dependent on the outward movement of manufacturing industry. Actually, dispersion moved more rapidly, at least after 1920, in areas with high proportions of their populations engaged in manufacturing industry (Table 51) than in areas of deconcentration (Table 59). Parenthetically, manufacturing areas are almost evenly distributed over the three industrial relocation classes, as may be determined from Appendix Table 1. Hence, it appears that there are factors associated with large proportion of manufacturing employment that encourage the centrifugal movement of population over and above that produced by industrial deconcentration itself.

CHAPTER IX

REGIONAL LOCATION AND POPULATION REDISTRIBUTION

The effect of regional location on many population and urban phenomena has been often demonstrated. Hence, it is to be expected that such a variation will appear in distribution tendencies within metropolitan areas. But what makes for regional differentials has not been determined. That is, whether there is any residual effect that may be attributed to regional location remaining after the characteristics of the units under study are standarized or controlled has not been ascertained. So far as population redistribution in metropolitan areas is concerned, it seems unlikely that regional variations can be anything other than the composite effects of variables such as those treated in Chapters III to VIII. Unfortunately, the number of metropolitan units available for study is too small to permit the simultaneous control of all those factors. This chapter, then, will analyze crude regional differences refined only for differences in size of central city.

The number of metropolitan areas in each of the three major regions -- North, South, and West -- is shown in Table 65. The North includes all states north of the Mason-Dixon line and of an arbitrary extension of that line to the western boundary of Kansas. All states south of the line comprise the South. The West, then, is made up of Rocky Mountain and Pacific Coastal states.[1] A disporportionate number of the metropolitan areas excluded from the study are located in the West. In consequence, the number of areas in that region available for study is almost too small for purposes of generalization. Their size distribution, however, compares favorably with that of the North.

Central Cities and Satellite Areas

Metropolitan areas in the West have maintained the highest actual growth rates in every decade since 1900. The lowest rates, as is to be seen in Table 66, occurred in the North in every decade since 1910. Very

TABLE 65. NUMBER OF STANDARD METROPOLITAN AREAS, BY
REGION, SIZE OF CENTRAL CITY, AND DECADE, 1900 - 1950

Region and size of central city	1940-50	1930-40	1920-30	1910-20	1900-10
Total	143	157	155	153	148
North	90	91	91	91	91
1,000,000 and over	4	4	4	3	3
500,000 - 1,000,000	7	8	6	5	2
250,000 - 500,000	6	7	5	5	8
100,000 - 250,000	30	28	23	17	13
Under 100,000	43	44	53	61	65
South	43	54	54	53	49
500,000 - 1,000,000	2	1	1	1	1
250,000 - 500,000	5	8	2	2	2
100,000 - 250,000	8	11	12	6	2
Under 100,000	28	34	39	44	44
West	10	12	10	9	8
1,000,000 and over	1	1	–	–	–
500,000 - 1,000,000	1	1	1	–	–
250,000 - 500,000	–	–	–	1	1
100,000 - 250,000	3	2	2	1	–
Under 100,000	5	8	7	7	7

much the same variation by region applies to central city rates, though
central cities in Southern metropolitan areas grew most rapidly in 1910-20
and 1920-30. The very sharp decline of the central city rate in Northern
areas during 1930-40 should be noted: the rate fell to one-seventh of
what it had been in the preceding decade, while in neither of the other
regions did central cities fall to as low as one-third of their former levels.
The highest rates of satellite population change also occurred in metropolitan areas in the West. Those declined from an exceptionally high
figure of 62 per cent, in 1900-10, to a low of 25 per cent, in 1930-40, and
in the last decade the satellite rate in Western areas increased abruptly
to 73 per cent. In the South satellite rates of change increased slowly
until 1940, exceeding the satellite rate in Northern areas for the first
time in 1930-40. After 1940 the rate in Southern areas almost doubled.
Although satellite population in the North grew at the lowest rates following 1930, the change of rate that took place between 1930-40 and 1940-
50 was comparable to that in Western Areas.

TABLE 66. PER CENT CHANGE OF POPULATION IN STANDARD
METROPOLITAN AREAS, BY TYPE OF PLACE, REGION, AND
DECADE, 1900-1950

Type of place and region	1940-50	1930-40	1920-30	1910-20	1900-10
Actual					
Total					
North	13.5	4.9	23.4	23.8	29.6
South	31.6	16.7	30.0	27.1	25.5
West	51.4	19.0	32.1	29.1	45.4
Central cities					
North	7.2	2.5	18.6	24.2	31.3
South	24.6	13.0	33.9	34.6	32.4
West	29.9	13.5	25.6	25.0	33.7
Satellite areas					
North	23.0	8.7	32.1	22.9	26.8
South	43.4	24.0	23.1	15.9	16.5
West	72.6	25.0	39.7	34.4	61.9
Adjusted[a]					
Total					
North	13.3	4.7	22.0	26.7	28.9
South	22.8	15.6	20.1	15.2	18.3
West	46.8	18.3	17.7	11.9	23.0
Central cities					
North	7.3	2.2	17.6	25.5	31.6
South	13.4	15.5	18.9	21.1	18.3
West	27.6	15.0	13.3	11.8	18.6
Satellite areas					
North	22.5	8.8	29.8	28.6	24.4
South	38.5	15.8	22.3	6.4	12.5
West	66.9	22.1	22.7	12.1	29.2

[a]Adjusted for size of central city. Size distribution of all areas
used as the standard.

Apparently some of the variation of metropolitan change with regional location, observed in the actual rates, was due to irregularities in the size distribution of metropolitan areas among the regions. For when the comparisons are standardized for size of area distribution, as in the lower panel of Table 66, certain alterations of the observed relationships occurs. Particularly noteworthy is the fact that metropolitan areas in the North maintained the highest adjusted rates until 1930, instead of 1910 as the actual rates indicate, after which their growth rates receded to the lowest position. It is also of interest that metropolitan areas in the South and West sustained relatively slight reduction of growth in the depression decade of 1930-40. In other respects the patterns found in the adjusted rates are similar to those revealed in the actual rates.

Fig. 36 indicates that the high rates of satellite growth in metropolitan areas of the West were shared by most distance zones. In only a few instances did zonal rates fall below those in the North or South. Western areas were also distinguished by a rapid diffusion of metropolitan influence as suggested by the large increases in rates of change within zones beyond 10 miles from central cities. Evidence of an outward movement of high growth rates is likewise present in the data for Northern areas. But in the South the rising rates of satellite growth were brought about largely by increases in zones within 20 miles of central cities. At greater distances declining rates were the rule.

It is interesting to note that a centrifugal tendency in the redistribution of population within Western areas has operated since the beginning of the century. In no decade did actual satellite rates fail to exceed central city rates by at least 40 per cent, as may be observed in Table 67. But while in Northern areas satellite growth just kept pace with central

TABLE 67. RATIO OF RATE OF CHANGE OF SATELLITE POPULATION TO CENTRAL CITY RATE OF CHANGE IN STANDARD METROPOLITAN AREAS, BY REGION, AND DECADE, 1900 - 1950

Region	1940-50	1930-40	1920-30	1910-20	1900-10
All areas	2.7	2.5	1.4	0.9	0.8
North	3.2	3.5	1.7	1.0	0.9
South	1.8	1.8	0.7	0.5	0.5
West	2.4	1.8	1.6	1.4	1.8

city growth from 1900 to 1920, it surged far above central city growth in following decades. After 1920 the highest rates of dispersion occurred in Northern rather than in Western metropolitan areas. In the South the growth of satellite population lagged well behind central city growth until 1930. In 1930-40 a sudden acceleration in the relative growth of satellite population occurred. In that decade the ratio for the South equalled the ratio for the West. No further increase followed, however.

The ratios by distance zones, shown in Fig. 37, reveal that the satellite territory in areas of the West over which growth rates exceeded central city rates extended to 30 miles from central cities in 1900-10. The area was enlarged to a 35 mile radius in 1910-20, and to the entire satellite area in 1920-30. A more dramatic change occurred in Northern metropolitan areas. In 1900-10 only the 0-5 mile zones had a growth rate as high as that of central cities. That radius was enlarged by 5 miles in the next decade, and was extended to 35 miles in 1920-30. In 1930-40 all distance zones in Northern areas had higher ratios than comparable zones in Western areas. The tardy development of satellite growth in Southern areas is clearly indicated. As late as 1920-30 only in one zone did satellite growth surpass central city growth. Substantial gains were made in the following 10-year interval; satellite ratios rose above unity over all zones within 25 miles of centers. That radius was reduced to 20 miles, however, in 1940-50.

The differences of growth rate as between central cities and satellite areas are reflected again in the distributions of decennial population increases. These are shown in Table 68. The share of all increase received by central cities of metropolitan areas in the North declined from two-thirds, in 1900-10, to one-third, in 1940-50. The proportions attracted to all zones beyond 5 miles from centers doubled during the 50-year period. Hence while an area with a 15 mile radius contained 90 per cent of the total increase in 1900-10, that proportion, in 1940-50, was spread over an area with a radius of almost 25 miles. In metropolitan areas of the South central cities increased their share of growth from 1900-10 to 1910-20. The proportion declined thereafter from 77 per cent, in 1910-20, to 49 per cent, in 1940-50. Most of the decline in central cities was acquired by the 0-5 and the 5-10 mile zones. In fact, the proportion that accumulated within a 15-mile radius increased from 92 per cent at the beginning of the period under study to 95 per cent, in 1940-50. Central cities of metropolitan areas in the West also attracted larger shares of the increases in 1910-20 than they received in 1900-10. At the same time, however, all distance zones with the exception of the 5-10 and the 35 and over mile zones increased their shares of growth. Virtually all of the increases occurred

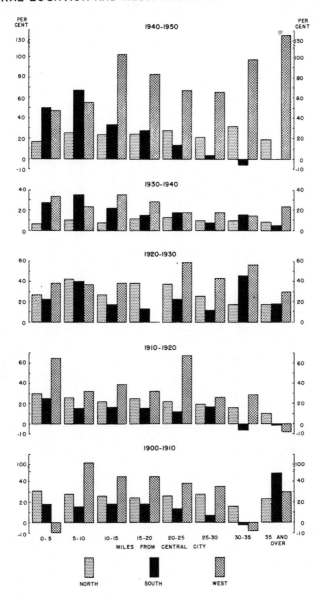

FIGURE 36.
PER CENT CHANGE OF SATELLITE POPULATION IN STANDARD METROPOLITAN
AREAS, BY REGION, DISTANCE ZONE, AND DECADE, 1900 - 1950

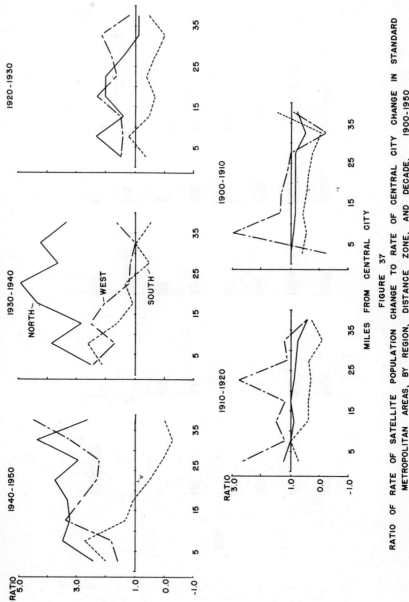

FIGURE 37

RATIO OF RATE OF SATELLITE POPULATION CHANGE TO RATE OF CENTRAL CITY CHANGE IN STANDARD METROPOLITAN AREAS, BY REGION, DISTANCE ZONE, AND DECADE, 1900-1950

TABLE 68. CUMULATIVE PERCENTAGE DISTRIBUTION OF
POPULATION INCREASE IN STANDARD METROPOLITAN
AREAS, BY REGION, DISTANCE ZONE, AND DECADE,
1900 - 1950

Region and distance zone	1940-50	1930-40	1920-30	1910-20	1900-10
North					
Central cities	32.6	31.6	51.0	65.0	66.1
0 - 5 miles	41.2	40.1	58.4	72.9	72.7
5 - 10 "	62.1	61.8	75.5	82.9	82.2
10 - 15 "	77.0	74.0	85.0	90.3	90.0
15 - 20 "	85.8	84.4	91.8	94.5	93.6
20 - 25 "	92.1	91.8	96.1	96.9	96.1
25 - 30 "	95.2	95.2	98.0	98.4	97.8
30 - 35 "	97.7	97.4	98.8	99.2	98.5
35 miles and over	100.0	100.0	100.0	100.0	100.0
South					
Central cities	48.7	51.5	72.5	76.7	71.7
0 - 5 miles	58.8	60.9	76.8	82.0	76.5
5 - 10 "	86.1	82.2	89.9	88.4	84.3
10 - 15 "	95.2	92.5	95.0	94.1	92.0
15 - 20 "	98.9	96.6	97.2	97.7	96.7
20 - 25 "	99.9	99.1	99.0	98.9	98.2
25 - 30 "	100.0	99.6	99.6	99.8	98.8
30 - 35 "	100.0	99.8	99.6	99.7	98.7
35 miles and over	100.0	100.0	100.0	100.0	100.0
West					
Central cities	28.9	37.4	42.5	48.4	42.6
0 - 5 miles	31.1	41.6	44.8	51.9	43.4
5 - 10 "	52.4	63.7	69.1	76.7	83.2
10 - 15 "	71.9	80.4	78.9	85.8	90.9
15 - 20 "	85.3	91.6	86.4	90.2	94.5
20 - 25 "	91.6	95.8	95.0	96.8	96.7
25 - 30 "	94.1	97.6	97.3	98.6	98.3
30 - 35 "	97.6	98.5	98.2	99.3	98.2
35 miles and over	100.0	100.0	100.0	100.0	100.0

at the expense of the 5-10 mile zone which had received 41 per cent of the population increment in 1900-10. Dispersion continued to 1950. The proportion contained by a 15-mile radius, in 1900-10, was spread over an area with a 25-mile radius in 1940-50.

The distributions of the total populations changed much more slowly. In Northern metropolitan areas, as Table 69 indicates, population was increasingly concentrated between 1900 and 1920. Deconcentration followed 1920 and continued through the next 30 years. The 5-10 mile zones absorbed most of the losses from central cities. Southern metropolitan areas entered the 20th century with the lowest degree of population concentration and by 1950 they had the most highly concentrated populations. Their period of increasing concentration ended in 1930, however; but while the subsequent deconcentration was comparatively rapid, it did not reach far into satellite areas. All zones beyond 10 miles from central cities experienced declining proportions of total populations. The association of rapid growth with concentration noted in an earlier chapter does not apply to metropolitan areas in the West. Deconcentration has been continuous in the West since 1900. The proportions in all zones within 35 miles of centers increased more or less steadily after 1910. In every census year since 1910 Western metropolitan areas have had the most widely scattered populations.

Rates of redistribution, shown graphically in Fig. 38, have tended to increase in all regions. The rates of both the North and the West varied inversely with those of the South. That is to say, low rates in Northern and Western areas coincide with high rates in Southern areas, and to a lesser extent high rates in the North and West coincide with low rates in the South. These variations do not correspond to phases of concentration and deconcentration: rates fluctuated rather widely regardless of the direction taken by population redistribution. Thus the inverse correlation of Southern with Northern and Western redistribution rates poses an interesting question for speculation.

Size and Type of Satellite Place

Regional differences likewise appeared in the growth trends in satellite places of various sizes and types. Table 70 reveals that in Northern areas all incorporated satellites had declining rates of change from 1900 to 1940. After 1940 rates increased, though in few instances did they return to levels that obtained prior to 1930-40. The largest declines occurred in incorporated places located within 10 miles of central cities.

TABLE 69. CUMULATIVE PERCENTAGE DISTRIBUTION OF
POPULATION IN STANDARD METROPOLITAN AREAS,
BY REGION, DISTANCE ZONE, AND CENSUS YEAR,
1900 - 1950

Region and distance zone	1950	1940	1930	1920	1910	1900
North						
Central cities	57.2	60.5	61.8	64.3	63.7	62.5
0 - 5 miles	64.1	67.2	68.4	70.7	70.7	68.8
5 - 10 "	76.5	78.4	79.4	80.2	79.6	78.7
10 - 15 "	86.0	87.2	87.9	88.5	88.1	87.5
15 - 20 "	91.4	92.1	92.6	92.7	92.3	91.9
20 - 25 "	94.9	95.3	95.5	95.4	95.1	94.8
25 - 30 "	97.0	97.2	97.4	97.2	97.0	96.7
30 - 35 "	98.3	98.3	98.4	98.3	98.1	98.0
35 miles and over	100.0	100.0	100.0	100.0	100.0	100.0
South						
Central cities	59.3	62.6	66.2	64.2	60.2	56.4
0 - 5 miles	66.6	69.0	72.0	70.3	66.2	63.1
5 - 10 "	83.0	81.9	82.6	80.1	77.9	76.1
10 - 15 "	91.9	90.8	90.6	89.1	87.8	87.0
15 - 20 "	96.1	95.1	95.4	94.9	94.3	93.8
20 - 25 "	98.2	97.6	97.8	97.4	97.1	96.9
25 - 30 "	99.3	99.0	99.1	99.0	98.8	98.9
30 - 35 "	99.5	99.3	99.4	99.3	99.2	99.3
35 miles and over	100.0	100.0	100.0	100.0	100.0	100.0
West						
Central cities	42.6	49.7	52.4	53.4	56.3	58.5
0 - 5 miles	45.0	52.1	54.9	55.3	57.9	62.3
5 - 10 "	65.6	72.3	73.7	76.6	81.0	80.5
10 - 15 "	78.8	82.2	83.0	85.0	88.0	88.4
15 - 20 "	88.9	90.6	90.7	89.2	92.1	92.1
20 - 25 "	94.2	95.4	95.3	95.8	95.0	94.7
25 - 30 "	96.3	97.4	97.4	97.5	97.0	96.9
30 - 35 "	97.9	98.6	98.7	98.1	97.7	97.2
35 miles and over	100.0	100.0	100.0	100.0	100.0	100.0

Table 70. Per Cent Change of Satellite Population in Standard Metropolitan Areas, by Size and Type of Satellite Place, Distance Zone, Region, and Decade, 1900-1950

Size and type of place and distance zone	North					South					West				
	1940-1950	1930-1940	1920-1930	1910-1920	1900-1910	1940-1950	1930-1940	1920-1930	1910-1920	1900-1910	1940-1950	1930-1940	1920-1930	1910-1920	1900-1910
50,000 and over															
0-10 miles	-1.3	-1.7	6.4	12.2	25.1	57.7[a]	----	-16.0[a]	----	----	26.5	9.3	34.5	44.0[a]	124.3[a]
10-20 miles	4.3	-32.8	12.6	19.2	35.5[a]	----	----	----	----	----	48.0[a]	15.7	----	----	----
20-30 miles	21.8[a]	10.3[a]	81.3[a]	----	----	----	----	----	----	----	10.6[a]	2.6[a]	----	----	----
30 miles and over	----	----	----	----	----	----	----	----	----	----	----	----	----	----	----
10,000 - 50,000															
0-10 miles	2.6	2.4	32.6	25.9	30.8	45.6	11.1	18.8	7.1[a]	34.8[a]	61.4	31.8	21.6	32.9	115.0
10-20 miles	19.1	4.9	31.6	36.3	43.8	8.1	3.2	80.3[a]	6.5[a]	10.8[a]	107.9[a]	31.4	19.3	----	----
20-30 miles	5.1	4.7	29.0	35.7	32.9	-9.5	5.8	20.7	27.3	56.0[a]	49.0	10.8	-23.9[a]	109.7[a]	----
30 miles and over	18.3	1.3	17.8	18.6	20.6	----	----	----	----	----	42.6	5.3	----	----	----
2,500 - 10,000															
0-10 miles	19.1	5.1	40.5	46.4	47.8	66.0	22.7	35.5	-5.9	16.6	95.3	30.2	39.6	12.9	19.1
10-20 miles	33.8	-20.3	56.1	30.9	42.7	46.1	4.8	8.8	27.2	47.3	89.0	32.3	86.5	53.7	-13.1
20-30 miles	18.5	6.0	34.6	17.1	42.4	-43.7	10.5	28.4	21.3	8.5	72.2	11.3	66.1	-7.1	42.0
30 miles and over	14.9	3.9	24.4	18.5	42.9	17.9	2.8	12.7	3.1	----	67.0	17.7	62.9	-30.1	----
Under 2,500															
0-10 miles	33.5	17.8	88.0	42.1	57.4	51.8	26.1	51.5	12.5	24.5	87.8	17.0	25.0	16.4	54.4
10-20 miles	28.7	12.0	43.2	28.1	23.8	39.1	12.8	24.3	26.4	25.3	77.7	35.4	43.5	32.1	74.3
20-30 miles	24.7	10.3	27.3	22.1	35.3	7.9	11.2	18.5	25.5	12.6	121.1	29.7	3.5	48.0	44.1
30 miles and over	17.7	5.5	14.2	8.1	25.7	-11.7	0.4	-4.9	20.3	65.4	61.1	32.3	39.5	31.2	20.7
Unincorporated area															
0-10 miles	49.8	19.6	45.0	25.6	22.4	63.6	36.1	35.5	21.5	13.9	76.3	42.8	47.8	22.5	40.2
10-20 miles	33.8	102.6	28.7	11.5	13.0	31.3	22.5	10.7	13.6	15.7	109.7	36.4	31.9	30.2	44.9
20-30 miles	40.0	17.5	30.9	12.0	16.7	20.6	15.6	16.0	9.0	6.9	90.0	26.5	53.7	41.0	33.8
30 miles and over	30.8	16.2	15.0	8.8	13.5	-3.2	8.1	12.5	3.7	28.4	182.7	20.0	26.3	13.1	27.3

[a] Based on less than 5 incorporated places.

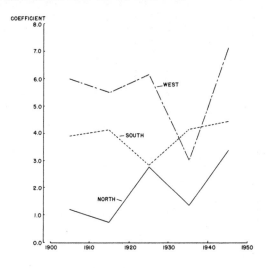

FIGURE 38.
COEFFICIENTS OF POPULATION REDISTRIBUTION IN STANDARD
METROPOLITAN AREAS, BY REGION, 1900-1950

Thus most of the increases in the rates of satellite growth observed in Table 66 and Fig. 36 were a function of accelerating growth in unincorporated areas.

In the South, on the other hand, most incorporated places within 20 miles of metropolitan centers experienced increasing rates of growth, while those 20 or more miles distant had declining rates of growth. Substantial increases also occurred in unincorporated rates in zones within 30 miles of centers. Unincorporated population in the outermost zone changed with a declining rate which became a loss of population in the last decade. A centripetal tendency in the growth of population in Southern metropolitan regions is clearly manifested in these data.

A third pattern of satellite change developed in the West. Satellites of 50,000 or more population located within 10 miles of central cities sustained declining rates of change. But large satellites 10 or more miles from centers and all incorporated population of less than 10,000 population regardless of location increased their populations at progressively higher rates. Unincorporated rates followed a similar trend in all distance zones. In all classes of satellite places the largest increases occurred in the most distant zones.

The ratios of satellite rates to central city rates, shown in Table 71, describe a somewhat different pattern of change in Northern metropolitan

Table 71. Ratio of Rate of Change of Satellite Population to Central City Rate of Change in Standard Metropolitan Areas, by Size and Type of Satellite Place, Distance Zone, Region, and Decade, 1900-1950

Size and type of place and distance zone	North					South					West				
	1940-1950	1930-1940	1920-1930	1910-1920	1900-1910	1940-1950	1930-1940	1920-1930	1910-1920	1900-1910	1940-1950	1930-1940	1920-1930	1910-1920	1900-1910
50,000 and over															
0-10 miles	-0.2	-0.7	0.3	0.5	0.8	2.3	---	-0.5	---	---	0.9	0.7	1.3	1.8	3.7
10-20 miles	0.6	-13.1	0.7	0.8	1.1	---	---	---	---	---	1.6	1.2	---	---	---
20-30 miles	3.0	4.1	4.4	---	---	---	---	---	---	---	0.4	0.2	---	---	---
30 miles and over	---	---	---	---	---	---	---	---	---	---	---	---	---	---	---
10,000 - 50,000															
0-10 miles	0.4	1.0	1.8	1.1	1.0	1.9	0.9	0.6	0.2	1.1	2.1	2.4	0.8	1.3	3.4
10-20 miles	2.7	2.0	1.7	1.5	1.4	0.3	0.2	2.4	0.2	0.3	3.6	2.3	0.8	---	---
20-30 miles	0.7	1.9	1.6	1.5	1.1	-0.4	0.4	0.6	0.8	1.7	1.6	0.8	-0.9	4.4	---
30 miles and over	2.5	0.5	1.0	0.8	0.7	---	---	---	---	---	1.4	0.4	---	---	---
2,500 - 10,000															
0-10 miles	2.7	2.0	2.2	1.9	1.5	2.7	1.7	1.0	-0.2	0.5	3.2	2.2	1.5	0.5	0.6
10-20 miles	4.7	-8.1	3.0	1.3	1.4	1.9	0.4	0.3	0.8	1.5	3.0	2.4	3.4	2.1	-0.4
20-30 miles	2.6	2.4	1.9	.7	1.4	-1.8	0.8	0.8	0.6	0.3	2.4	0.8	2.6	-0.3	1.2
30 miles and over	2.1	1.6	1.3	.8	1.4	0.7	0.2	0.4	0.1	---	2.2	1.3	2.5	-1.2	---
Under 2,500															
0-10 miles	4.7	7.1	4.7	1.7	1.9	2.1	2.0	1.5	0.4	0.8	2.9	1.3	1.0	0.7	1.6
10-20 miles	4.0	4.8	2.3	1.2	0.8	1.6	1.0	0.7	0.8	0.8	2.6	2.6	1.7	1.3	2.2
20-30 miles	3.4	4.1	1.5	0.9	1.1	0.3	0.9	0.5	0.7	0.4	4.1	2.2	0.1	1.9	1.3
30 miles and over	2.5	2.2	0.8	0.3	0.8	-0.5	0.0	-0.1	0.6	2.0	2.0	2.4	1.5	1.2	0.6
Unincorporated area															
0-10 miles	6.9	7.8	2.4	1.1	0.7	2.6	2.8	1.0	0.6	0.4	2.6	3.2	1.9	0.9	1.2
10-20 miles	4.7	41.0	1.5	0.5	0.4	1.3	1.7	0.3	0.4	0.5	3.7	2.7	1.2	1.2	1.3
20-30 miles	5.6	7.0	1.7	0.5	0.5	0.8	1.2	0.5	0.3	0.2	3.0	2.0	2.1	1.6	1.0
30 miles and over	4.3	6.5	0.8	0.4	0.4	0.1	0.6	0.4	0.1	0.9	6.1	1.5	1.0	0.5	0.8

areas. On this basis declines occurred in all satellites of 50,000 or more population and in satellites of 10,000-50,000 population located in the 0-10 and 20-30 mile zones. All other sizes and types of satellite places in all distance zones had increasing relative rates of growth. The delayed penetration of dispersion into unincorporated areas is noteworthy: not until 1920-30 did unincorporated rates rise significantly above central city rates.

The conversion of rates to ratios does not alter the pattern of change in Southern metropolitan areas observed in Table 70. Despite the high growth rates attained by satellite places in the South, their ratios are, with two exceptions, consistently below those in the North. The two exceptions are places of 10,000-50,000 and of 50,000 or more population located within 10 miles of centers. Similarly in the West the changes in relative rates correspond to the changes in absolute rates. In other words, ratios increased in all size classes and distance zones except in places of 50,000 or more population within the 0-10 mile zone.

As a consequence of differential rates of change in the satellite areas in Northern metropolitan areas, the proportions of the populations within each zone that occupied incorporated places of 2,500 or more population increased to 1920 and then declined to 1950. The proportion in unincorporated area and in the smallest class of incorporated places declined to 1930 and increased in succeeding census years. In no zone did unincorporated population ever exceed 57 per cent. By contrast, unincorporated population in Southern areas was never lower than 68 per cent and in 1900 it comprised 99 per cent of the 30 mile and over zone. As in Northern areas, unincorporated population within 20 miles of Southern metropolitan centers declined to 1930 and increased thereafter. The decline was continuous, however, 30 or more miles from centers. The proportions in incorporated places tended to follow an opposite and complementary trend. In the West the proportion of unincorporated population within 10 miles of central cities has generally been less than that in places of 50,000 or more population, and the proportions in satellites of less than 2,500 population have been negligible. Distributions in zones beyond 10 miles from Southern centers as well as the changes in those distributions have been comparable to those in other parts of the country.

Table 72. Per Cent Distribution of Satellite Population in Standard Metropolitan Areas, by Census Year, Size and Type of Place, Region, and Distance Zone, 1900-1950

Census year and size and type of place	North				South				West			
	\- Miles from central city \-				\- Miles from central city \-				\- Miles from central city \-			
	0-10 miles	10-20 miles	20-30 miles	30 miles and over	0-10 miles	10-20 miles	20-30 miles	30 miles and over	0-10 miles	10-20 miles	20-30 miles	30 miles and over
1950												
Total	100.0	100.0	100.0	100.0	100.0	100.0	100.0	100.0	100.0	100.0	100.0	100.0
50,000 and over	17.8	20.2	7.4	0.0	2.6	0.0	0.0	0.0	35.6	16.2	11.6	0.0
10,000 - 50,000	21.3	21.0	20.7	23.0	8.9	7.8	11.1	0.0	19.7	21.0	18.1	14.3
2,500 - 10,000	12.1	13.3	17.7	15.8	7.9	7.5	5.2	8.8	9.2	14.9	12.7	16.4
Under 2,500	3.9	7.4	8.6	10.1	4.2	7.6	8.5	3.5	0.8	2.6	3.1	6.9
Unincorporated area	44.9	38.1	45.6	51.1	76.4	77.1	75.2	87.7	34.7	45.3	54.5	62.4
1940												
Total	100.0	100.0	100.0	100.0	100.0	100.0	100.0	100.0	100.0	100.0	100.0	100.0
50,000 and over	22.1	23.8	7.6	0.0	2.7	0.0	0.0	0.0	43.1	21.0	17.4	0.0
10,000 - 50,000	25.3	21.8	24.5	24.0	9.9	9.3	13.4	0.0	18.8	19.4	20.3	21.6
2,500 - 10,000	12.4	12.2	18.7	17.1	7.6	6.7	10.0	7.4	7.3	15.2	12.3	21.3
Under 2,500	3.6	7.1	8.6	10.6	4.4	7.2	8.6	3.8	0.6	2.8	2.3	9.3
Unincorporated area	36.6	35.1	40.6	48.3	75.4	76.8	66.0	88.8	30.2	41.6	47.7	47.8
1930												
Total	100.0	100.0	100.0	100.0	100.0	100.0	100.0	100.0	100.0	100.0	100.0	100.0
50,000 and over	23.6	37.3	7.5	0.0	0.0	0.0	0.0	0.0	48.7	17.2	19.9	0.0
10,000 - 50,000	25.3	22.6	24.4	25.5	11.5	8.9	12.6	4.0	15.1	20.1	18.0	24.2
2,500 - 10,000	12.1	12.2	19.8	17.1	9.4	6.9	8.2	0.0	8.3	15.9	13.8	15.3
Under 2,500	3.6	7.4	8.9	12.1	4.9	8.1	8.1	3.9	1.1	3.5	4.7	13.6
Unincorporated area	35.4	20.5	39.4	45.3	74.2	76.1	71.1	92.1	26.8	43.3	43.6	46.9
1920												
Total	100.0	100.0	100.0	100.0	100.0	100.0	100.0	100.0	100.0	100.0	100.0	100.0
50,000 and over	18.8	22.6	3.3	0.0	4.3	4.6	12.2	0.0	62.5	6.6	13.6	0.0
10,000 - 50,000	26.9	21.1	26.9	22.6	7.3	5.4	4.4	---	6.6	7.2	8.7	16.5
2,500 - 10,000	13.8	12.4	17.6	16.2	8.8	8.5	4.4	4.0	5.4	21.8	11.8	22.4
Under 2,500	5.2	9.0	11.3	12.5	4.2	8.5	9.4	4.1	2.5	11.8	3.6	61.1
Unincorporated area	35.3	34.9	40.9	48.7	75.4	81.5	74.0	91.9	23.0	59.2	74.1	61.1
1910												
Total	100.0	100.0	100.0	100.0	100.0	100.0	100.0	100.0	100.0	100.0	100.0	100.0
50,000 and over	20.8	19.6	24.2	19.9	11.7	1.3	8.1	0.0	44.0	0.0	0.0	0.0
10,000 - 50,000	20.3	19.1	18.9	14.9	5.2	6.0	6.1	4.3	18.7	0.0	21.6	3.6
2,500 - 10,000	14.3	11.1	14.4	13.7	5.8	8.2	9.8	3.1	4.2	21.6	4.3	10.0
Under 2,500	5.9	10.6	0.0	0.0	0.0	0.0	0.0	0.0	2.7	14.1	15.1	26.5
Unincorporated area	38.7	39.6	42.5	51.5	77.3	84.5	76.0	92.6	30.4	64.3	65.7	63.5
1900												
Total	100.0	100.0	100.0	100.0	100.0	100.0	100.0	100.0	100.0	100.0	100.0	100.0
50,000 and over	16.5	13.1	0.0	0.0	8.2	1.4	5.8	0.0	35.6	0.0	0.0	0.0
10,000 - 50,000	20.8	17.3	12.6	15.8	4.6	5.3	6.4	0.0	15.8	0.0	0.0	0.0
2,500 - 10,000	10.0	10.0	19.2	13.2	4.5	5.7	6.5	1.2	1.9	6.9	17.5	10.0
Under 2,500	6.1	10.5	15.2	14.3					2.6	11.0	11.9	26.5
												24.8

CHAPTER X

SUMMARY

All Metropolitan Areas

Population growth declined in all metropolitan areas between 1900 and 1950. A larger decline occurred in Standard than in Extended Metropolitan Areas. With the declining rates of change occurred a shift of growth from central cities to satellite areas; that is, the decreasing rates of increase were functions mainly of the slowing growth of central cities, for growth rates in satellite areas increased over the 50-year period. As a consequence of certain historical factors the trend lines were not smooth curves, however.

When growth rates are plotted by distance zones the result for Extended Metropolitan Areas is a fairly uniform gradient, i.e., rates decline with distance from central city. No such gradient appears in the data for Standard Metropolitan Areas. It is to be inferred, therefore, that the definition of the Standard Metropolitan Area is selective of the most rapidly growing parts of satellite areas. In other words that concept of metropolitan area encompasses the parts of outlying area that are most immediately responsive to developments in the central city.

The scope of metropolitan influence, as measured both by the ratios of metropolitan area growth rates to total United States rates and by the ratios of zonal rates to central city rates, was progressively extended in the decades since 1900-10. Approximately 25 to 30 miles were added to the radius of metropolitan influence.

Redistribution of population moved toward concentration from 1900 to 1920, and toward dispersion from 1920 to 1950. A conclusion from this as well as from observation of changes in growth rates in central cities and in distance zones, is that metropolitan development in the first half of the 20th century involved, first, a rapid growth of centers at the expense of satellite areas, and, subsequently, a centrifugal movement to satellite areas to the detriment of growth in central cities. It is probable that the maturation of centers is a requisite to the expansion of settlement in satellite areas.

Indirect support of these inferences is found in the changes of growth rates in different sizes and types of satellite places. Incorporated places of 25,000 or more, most of which are located within 10 miles of central cities, had declining rates of growth from 1900 to 1950. Declining rates appeared in smaller incorporated satellites in later decades. Beginning in 1920 growth rates in unincorporated areas accelerated rapidly. Thus nearly all of the increased growth of total satellite population after 1920 took place in unincorporated area.

Size of Central City

The absence of a clear relationship of metropolitan growth with size of central city is due partly to the facts that growth of central cities varied inversely with size while the growth of satellite areas varied directly with size of central city. In general, the rates of change in central cities declined during the 50 years, the greatest declines having occurred in the largest and in the smallest size classes. Satellite rates followed a trend of increase in all but the 1,000,000 and over size class. Although growth rates correlate negatively with density, the coefficients are not large enough to have explanatory value.

The larger the size of the central city the more extensive has been the part of the satellite area over which growth rates have exceeded the average growth of the total population of the nation. This is also true of the satellite rates as compared to central city rates. The relationship between size of central city and dispersion is evident again in the spread of decennial population increments.

Growth rates in different sizes and types of satellite places varied more or less directly with size of central city. The relationship was least equivocal where small incorporated places and unincorporated areas were concerned. Rates of change in incorporated places of 25,000 or more population declined, and in unincorporated areas the trend was toward increase. The highest rates of change in incorporated population occurred in zones between 10 and 20 miles from central cities. Ratios of satellite rates to central city rates were more closely related to size of central city than were the rates themselves.

Average Annual Growth Rate of Central City

Satellite as well as total populations have grown most slowly in areas whose central cities have had the lowest annual rate of growth, and most rapidly where central cities have increased at the highest rates. Relative growth rates, however, reveal an inverse relationship with average annual rate of central city growth. Ratios for distance zones in areas with slowly growing central cities have been consistently at or above unity. On the other hand, the 1930-40 decade was the first in which the ratio for any distance zone in areas with rapidly growing central cities exceeded unity. The dispersion of population increments was greater as measured both by the distance of the spread and the amounts involved where the average annual rate of central city growth was lowest. Deconcentration began earliest in areas with lowest rates of central city growth and latest in areas of highest rates of growth in central cities. Control of size of central city introduces no qualifications of these observations. The differentials among metropolitan areas distinguished by average annual rate of central city growth also occurred in the growth trends of various sizes and types of satellite places.

Deconcentration was directed mainly toward small incorporated places and unincorporated area. Further, satellite growth has been an inverse function of central city growth.

Distance between Central Cities

Growth rates varied directly with distance between central cities. That relationship was characteristic of all distance zones after 1910. Until 1920 the differences between relative growth rates of satellite areas were negligible. Following 1920 the highest ratios developed in areas the central cities of which were within 50 miles of other central cities. The more isolated areas had the lowest ratios of satellite growth. The outlying zones of areas 50 to 100 miles from other areas, however, had higher ratios than did similar zones in areas within 50 miles of other areas, in both 1910-20 and 1940-50. The less the distance between central cities the smaller was the proportion of all increase gained by central cities and the larger was the share received by satellite area. Nevertheless, the percentage distributions of population indicate that deconcentration began a decade earlier (1920) in areas 50-100 miles removed from other areas than in those located within 50 miles of other areas.

Some of the irregularities observed in the relationship between redistribution tendencies and proximity of central cities to one another were due to unequal weighting by size of central city. When the rates are standardized for size of central city, deconcentration is found to have been inversely related to distance between central cities. The change in the relative growth rates of satellite places conform to that relationship.

Selected Geographic Features

The lowest rates of change in all decades occurred in areas at river locations, and the highest rates were experienced in metropolitan areas at other than water locations. While that was true also of central city rates, it did not apply to satellite rates. Areas with central cities located on sea or lake coasts maintained the highest satellite rates in every decade but 1930-40. Relative growth rates have been highest, particularly in zones beyond 15 miles from centers, in coastal areas, and lowest in areas at other than water locations.

The dispersion of growth in coastal locations has proceeded without interruption from 1900 to 1950. In the other location classes dispersion was more limited and was occasionally reversed. Despite continuous deconcentration in areas at coastal locations, the central cities of such areas, in every census year until 1950, contained a larger proportion of their area populations than did central cities at other locations. Although the concentration phase of population redistribution in areas at other than water locations ended in 1930, in 1950 those areas had the most highly concentrated populations. Differences in size of central city were not responsible for the variations in population redistribution among the three location classes.

In areas at river locations deconcentration progressed most rapidly on the central city side, though after 1930 rivers appear to have lost much of their barrier effect on population redistribution.

All satellite places of less than 50,000 population in areas at coastal locations increased their relative growth rates. But in the other location classes increases were confined to the small places within 20 miles of centers.

Until 1930 growth was most rapid in satellite places served by both highways and railways. After 1930 the importance of the railway for intra-area transportation diminished, for the highest rates passed to places located on highways only. Low rates of growth and frequent population losses occurred in areas with only railway and with neither railway nor highway access to central cities.

Proportion of Population Employed in Manufacturing

The populations of metropolitan areas with low proportions employed in manufacturing in 1948 have grown most rapidly, while those with the largest proportions so employed have grown at the lowest rates. Average areas had the highest satellite rates in 1900-10, manufacturing areas gained most rapidly in 1910-20 and 1920-30, and in the last two decades the satellite populations of non-manufacturing areas grew at the fastest rates. The relative growth rates of satellite population in manufacturing areas exceeded those of other classes after 1920; the lowest ratios occurred in non-manufacturing areas. Ratios increased, however, in all distance zones of all classes of areas. Decennial increments were distributed more widely in succeeding decades, particularly in manufacturing areas. Areas with high proportions employed in manufacturing had the most concentrated populations in every census year, but the amount of deconcentration after 1920 also exceeded that in other classes of areas. The least concentration of population obtained in non-manufacturing areas. With one or two exceptions the observed association of redistribution with the proportion of population employed in manufacturing was repeated in each size class

Industrial Relocation

Rates of population change were low in metropolitan areas in which industry has been deconcentrating and high in areas where there has been no clear trend of industrial relocation. The differences, however, were small. Central city rates varied as did rates for the total populations. Satellite rates were highest in areas of industrial deconcentration from 1900 to 1930, and after that the highest rates occurred in areas of no clear industrial relocation trend. In areas of concentration satellite rates declined to 1940 and then increased in the last decade. Growth has been widely dispersed in deconcentrating areas since 1900. On the other hand, growth has concentrated increasingly in concentrating areas. As was expected, the highest ratios of satellite growth to central city growth occurred in deconcentrating areas, while the lowest ratios were found in areas of industrial concentration. The differences in the tendencies to dispersion are reflected also in the changing distributions of population increments. The most concentrated as well as the most rapidly deconcentrating population was that of areas of industrial dispersion. Areas in which industry has been moving centripetally had a more concentrated population at the end than at the beginning of the 50-year period. No significant deviations from these generalizations appeared when size of central city was controlled.

All sizes and types of satellite places experienced declining rates of change in areas of industrial concentration, especially in zones 10 or more miles from centers. Industrial deconcentration accelerated satellite growth only in unincorporated area. The satellite population of deconcentrating areas has been more concentrated in incorporated places than has that of either of the other industrial relocation classes.

Regional Location

The most rapidly growing metropolitan areas, since 1900, have been those in the West, while the lowest rates of growth occurred in Northern areas. But while the relative growth of satellite areas was highest in the West, from 1900 to 1920, the North has led in that respect since 1920. Ratios of satellite growth to central city growth have been consistently low in the South.

Whereas decennial increments to metropolitan populations were spread more and more widely in Northern and Western areas, they were concentrated increasingly in the 0-5 and 5-10 mile zones in Southern areas.

In every census year since 1910 metropolitan areas in the West have had the most widely scattered population. Deconcentration has been the dominating trend in population redistribution within Western areas since the beginning of the century. That trend began in Northern areas in 1920 and in Southern areas in 1930.

Regional differences in redistribution tendencies remain when size of central city is controlled. They appear also in the data on rates of change in all sizes and types of satellite places.

A Comparison of Variables

It has been observed that all variables studied are associated with differences in population redistribution within metropolitan areas. Table 73 provides a partial summary of the findings. The characteristics related to the highest ratios of satellite growth to central city growth are contrasted with the characteristics associated with the lowest ratios of satellite to central city growth. Although the differences between high and low ratios vary from decade to decade, in all but five instances the former exceeds the latter by 50 per cent or more.

In no one metropolitan area are combined all of the characteristics that make for high ratios of satellite growth. And in only two metropolitan areas -- Amarillo and Jackson, Miss. -- do all factors related to low ratios of satellite growth coincide.[1] An approximation of the effect of such a coincidence, however, may be gained by observing the ratios in individual areas in which are combined five or more of the seven high ratio factors or a like number of low ratio factors. Table 74 lists the metropolitan areas that have the given number of characteristics. It is

TABLE 73. RATIO OF RATE OF CHANGE OF SATELLITE POPULATION TO CENTRAL CITY RATE OF CHANGE IN STANDARD METROPOLITAN AREAS, BY RATIO LEVEL, CHARACTERISTIC, AND DECADE, 1900 - 1950

Ratio level and characteristics of metropolitan areas	1940-50	1930-40	1920-30	1910-20	1900-10
High ratio					
Central city with 500,000-1,000,000 population	4.1	10.1	2.9	1.1	1.6
Low average annual rate of central city growth	3.5	10.0	2.3	1.1	1.2
Central city within 50 miles of other central cities	2.7	3.8	1.8	0.8	0.9
Central city at sea or lake coast location	3.5	2.3	1.8	1.1	1.1
High proportion employed in manufacturing	3.7	11.4	1.8	0.8	0.7
Industry deconcentrating	3.2	2.3	1.6	1.0	1.0
North	3.2	3.5	1.7	1.0	0.7
Low ratio					
Central city with less than 100,000 population	1.3	1.7	0.6	0.4	0.4
High average annual rate of central city growth	1.8	2.2	0.7	0.4	0.2
Central city 100 or more miles of other central cities	1.8	1.9	0.6	0.8	0.7
Central city at other than water location	1.7	2.3	0.7	0.4	0.3
Low proportion employed in manufacturing	1.7	1.4	0.6	0.5	0.7
Industry concentrating	1.5	2.4	0.6	0.5	0.6
South	1.8	1.8	0.7	0.5	0.5

TABLE 74. RATIOS OF RATE OF CHANGE IN SATELLITE
POPULATION TO CENTRAL CITY RATE OF CHANGE IN
STANDARD METROPOLITAN AREAS WITH FIVE OR
MORE LOW RATIO FACTORS, BY DECADE,
1900-1950

Ratio level and metro-politan area	1940- 50	1930- 40	1920- 30	1910- 20	1900- 10
High ratio					
Baltimore	6.9	3.7[b]	5.4	--[a]	2.5
Boston	2.7	--	5.5	2.3	1.2
Buffalo	47.3	25.9	2.8	1.3	1.3
Chicago	4.7	16.6	2.4	1.9	1.5
Cleveland	9.9	5.2	8.9	2.3	0.7[c]
Galveston	13.7	5.1	1.5	0.9	--
Milwaukee	3.6	13.8	3.3	1.7	1.1
Philadelphia	3.6	69.3	4.7	1.3	1.0
Pittsburgh	11.1[d]	14.3[e]	2.7	2.5	3.3
Reading	--[f]	--	9.5	0.6	0.4
San Francisco	3.5[h]	--	1.7	1.9	3.6
Wheeling	--[g]	--	1.6	1.2	5.2
York	3.1	3.2	0.9	0.9	0.3
Low ratio					
Amarillo	0.7	0.1	0.6	0.3	0.6
Corpus Christi		0.4	0.6		
Fresno	1.1	1.8	0.6	0.8	1.0
Jackson, Miss.	--[i]	0.8	0.1	--[j]	0.0
Lubbock		0.1	0.4	2.9	
Phoenix	1.4	0.5	1.1		
Shreveport	--[k]	0.3	0.5	0.5	0.1
Sioux Falls	0.3	--[l]	0.1	0.1	0.4

[a] Central city rate 31.4; satellite rate -27.0.
[b] Central city rate -1.3; satellite rate 3.4.
[c] Central city rate -2.1; satellite rate 19.0.
[d] Central city rate -1.1; satellite rate 11.5.
[e] Central city rate -0.5; satellite rate 8.9.
[f] Central city rate 0.0; satellite rate 16.0.
[g] Central city rate -3.7; satellite rate -2.6.
[h] Central city rate -0.9; satellite rate 5.8.
[i] Central city rate 58.2; satellite rate -12.8.
[j] Central city rate 7.3; satellite rate -19.2.
[k] Central city rate 29.6; satellite rate -5.2.
[l] Central city rate 21.0; satellite rate -3.7.

immediately apparent that in all metropolitan areas possessing five or more
more high ratio factors, except for York, the ratios are in three or more
decades well above those shown for high ratio areas in Table 73. In most
of those rapid dispersion to satellite areas began after 1920. On the
other hand, ratios for the low ratio areas are considerably below in most
instances the ratios shown for the corresponding level in Table 73. The
Fresno and Phoenix metropolitan areas alone show any tendency toward
the development of population drift to satellite areas.

APPENDIX

Appendix table 1. Characteristics of Metropolitan Areas

Metropolitan area	Size of central city					Growth rate Ave. annual 1900-1950	Distance between central cities (Miles)	Geographic feature	Proportion of population employed in manufacturing	Direction of industrial relocation	Regional location
	1940-1950 [a]	1930-1940 [a]	1920-1930 [a]	1910-1920 [a]	1900-1910 [a]						
Akron	4	3	4	5	5	High	Within 50	Other	High	Deconcentrating	North
Albany - Schnectady	4 [b]	4	4	4	5	Low	50 - 100	River	Average	Deconcentrating	North
Albuquerque	5	5	5	5	5	High	100 or more	Other	Low	Deconcentrating	West
Allentown - Bethlehem	4	4	4	5	5	Med.	Within 50	River	High	No clear trend	North
Altoona	5	5	5	5	5	Low	Within 50	Other	Low	------	North
Amarillo	5	5	5	5	5	High	100 or more	Other	Low	Concentrating	South
Asheville	5	5	5	5	5	Med.	50 - 100	Other	Average	Deconcentrating	South
Atlanta	3	3	4	4	5	Med.	50 - 100	Other	Average	Deconcentrating	South
Atlantic City	5	5	5	5	5	Med.	50 - 100	Coast	Low	No clear trend	North
Augusta	5	5	5	5	5	Low	50 - 100	Other	Low	Deconcentrating	South
Austin	5	5	5	5	5	High	50 - 100	Other	Low	No clear trend	South
Baltimore	2	2	2	2	2	Low	Within 50	Coast	High	Deconcentrating	South
Baton Rouge	-	5	5	5	5	High	50 - 100	River	Low	No clear trend	South
Bay City	5	5	5	5	5	Low	Within 50	Coast	Average	No clear trend	North
Beaumont - Port Arthur	-	4	5	5	5	High	50 - 100	River	Average	No clear trend	South
Binghamton	5	5	5	5	5	Low	50 - 100	River	High	Deconcentrating	North
Birmingham	3	3	4	4	5	High	50 - 100	Other	Average	No clear trend	South
Boston	2	2	2	2	2	Low	Within 50	Coast	-	-	North
Bridgeport	4	4	4	4	5	Med.	Within 50	Coast	-	-	North
Brockton	5	5	5	5	5	Low	Within 50	Other	-	-	North
Buffalo	2	2	2	3	3	Low	50 - 100	Coast	High	Deconcentrating	North
Canton	4	4	5	5	5	Med.	Within 50	Other	High	Concentrating	North
Cedar Rapids	5	5	5	5	5	Med.	Within 50	Other	Average	Concentrating	North
Charleston, S.C.	5	5	5	5	5	Low	50 - 100	Coast	Low	Deconcentrating	South
Charleston, W.V.	5	5	5	5	5	High	Within 50	River	Low	-	North
Charlotte	4	4	5	5	5	High	50 - 100	Other	Average	Deconcentrating	South
Chattanooga	-	4	5	5	5	High	100 or more	River	High	No clear trend	South
Chicago	1	1	1	1	1	Low	50 - 100	Coast	High	Deconcentrating	North
Cincinnati	3	3	3	3	3	Low	Within 50	River	Average	Deconcentrating	North
Cleveland	2	2	2	2	3	Med.	Within 50	Coast	High	Deconcentrating	North
Columbia	5	5	5	5	5	High	50 - 100	Other	Low	Deconcentrating	South
Columbus, Ga.	5	5	5	5	5	High	50 - 100	Other	Average	Deconcentrating	South
Columbus, O.	3	3	4	4	4	Med.	Within 50	Other	Low	Deconcentrating	North
Corpus Christi	-	5	-	-	-	High	100 or more	Coast	Low	-	South

Appendix table 1 (cont'd). Characteristics of Metropolitan Areas

Metropolitan area	Size of central city					Growth rate Ave. annual 1900-1950	Distance between central cities (Miles)	Geographic feature	Proportion of population employed in manufacturing	Direction of industrial relocation	Regional location
	1940-1950	1930-1940	1920-1930	1910-1920	1900-1910						
Dallas	-	3	4	5	5	High	Within 50	Other	Low	Concentrating	South
Davenport - Rock Island Moline	5	5	5	5	5	Low	50 - 100	River	High	No clear trend	North
Dayton	4	4	4	4	5	Med.	Within 50	Other	High	No clear trend	North
Decatur	5	5	5	5	5	Med.	Within 50	Other	Average	No clear trend	North
Denver	1	1	-	1	-	--	--	Other	--	--	--
Des Moines	4	4	4	5	5	Med.	50 - 100	Other	Low	Concentrating	North
Detroit	1	1	1	3	3	High	50 - 100	Coast	High	No clear trend	North
Duluth - Superior	4	4	5	5	5	Med.	100 or more	Coast	Low	Concentrating	North
Durham	5	5	5	5	5	High	Within 50	Other	High	Concentrating	South
El Paso	-	-	-	-	-	--	--	--	--	--	--
Erie	4	4	5	5	5	Med.	50 - 100	Coast	High	Deconcentrating	North
Evansville	5	5	5	5	5	Low	100 or more	River	High	Concentrating	North
Fall River	4	4	4	4	4	Low	Within 50	Coast	--	--	North
Flint	4	4	5	5	5	High	Within 50	Other	High	Concentrating	North
Fort Wayne	4	4	4	5	5	High	50 - 100	Other	Average	No clear trend	North
Fort Worth	4	4	4	5	5	High	Within 50	Other	Low	No clear trend	South
Fresno	5	5	5	5	5	High	100 or more	Other	Low	--	West
Gadsden	5	5	5	5	5	High	50 - 100	Coast	High	Concentrating	South
Galveston	5	4	4	4	5	Low	Within 50	Other	Low	Deconcentrating	South
Grand Rapids	4	4	4	4	5	Low	50 - 100	Other	High	Deconcentrating	North
Green Bay	5	5	5	5	5	Med.	100 or more	Coast	Average	No clear trend	North
Greensboro - High Point	5	5	5	5	5	High	50 - 100	Other	High	Deconcentrating	South
Greenville	5	5	5	5	5	High	50 - 100	Other	High	No clear trend	South
Hamilton - Middletown	5	5	5	5	5	Med.	Within 50	Other	High	Deconcentrating	North
Harrisburg	5	4	5	5	5	Low	Within 50	River	Average	Deconcentrating	North
Hartford	4	4	4	5	5	Med.	Within 50	River	--	--	North
Houston	3	3	4	5	5	High	Within 50	Coast	Low	Deconcentrating	South
Huntington - Ashland	5	5	5	5	5	High	50 - 100	River	Average	Concentrating	North
Indianapolis	3	3	3	4	4	Med.	50 - 100	Other	Average	Deconcentrating	North
Jackson, Mich.	5	5	5	5	5	Low	Within 50	Other	Average	Deconcentrating	North
Jackson, Miss.	5	5	5	5	5	High	100 or more	Other	Low	Concentrating	South
Jacksonville	-	-	-	-	-	--	--	--	--	--	South
Johnstown	5	5	5	-	5	Low	Within 50	Other	Low	Concentrating	North
Kalamazoo	5	5	5	5	5	Med.	Within 50	Other	High	Deconcentrating	North

Appendix table 1 (cont'd). Characteristics of Metropolitan Areas

Metropolitan area	Size of central city					Growth rate Ave. annual 1900-1950	Distance between central cities (Miles)	Geographic feature	Proportion of population employed in manufacturing	Direction of industrial relocation	Regional location
	1940-1950[a]	1930-1940[a]	1920-1930[a]	1910-1920[a]	1900-1910[a]						
Kansas City	2	2	3	3	3	Med.	Within 50	River	High	Deconcentrating	North
Kenosha	5	5	5	5	5	High	Within 50	Coast	High	No clear trend	North
Knoxville	-	4	5	5	5	Med.	50 - 100	Other	Average	Deconcentrating	South
Lancaster	5	5	5	5	5	Low	Within 50	Other	High	No clear trend	North
Lansing	5	5	5	5	5	High	Within 50	Other	High	No clear trend	North
Laredo	-	5	5	5	5	Med.	100 or more	Coast	-	----	South
Lawrence	5	5	5	5	5	Med.	Within 50	River	-	----	North
Lexington	5	5	5	5	5	Low	50 - 100	Other	Low	No clear trend	South
Lima	5	5	5	5	5	Med.	50 - 100	Other	Average	Concentrating	North
Lincoln	5	5	5	5	5	Med.	50 - 100	Other	Low	Concentrating	North
Little Rock	5	5	5	5	5	Med.	100 or more	River	Low	No clear trend	South
Lorain - Elyria	5	5	5	5	-	Med.	Within 50	Coast	Average	No clear trend	North
Los Angeles	1	1	-	-	-	High	50 - 100	Coast	High	Deconcentrating	West
Louisville	3	3	4	4	4	Low	50 - 100	River	Average	Deconcentrating	South
Lowell	4	4	4	5	-	Low	Within 50	River	-	----	North
Lubbock	-	5	5	5	-	High	100 or more	Other	-	----	South
Macon	5	5	5	5	5	Med.	50 - 100	Other	Average	Deconcentrating	South
Madison	5	5	5	5	5	High	50 - 100	Other	Low	Concentrating	North
Manchester	5	5	5	5	4	Low	Within 50	River	-	No clear trend	North
Memphis	3	3	4	4	4	Med.	100 or more	River	Average	No clear trend	North
Miami	-	-	-	-	-	----	100 or more		-	----	
Milwaukee	2	2	3	3	3	Med.	Within 50	Coast	High	Deconcentrating	North
Minneapolis - St. Paul	2	2	2	2	3	Med.	100 or more	River	Average	Deconcentrating	North
Mobile	5	5	5	5	5	Med.	100 or more	Coast	Average	No clear trend	South
Montgomery	5	5	5	5	5	Med.	50 - 100	Other	Low	No clear trend	South
Muncie	5	5	5	5	5	High	50 - 100	Other	High	Deconcentrating	North
Nashville	4	4	4	4	4	Med.	100 or more	River	Average	Concentrating	South
New Bedford	4	4	5	5	5	Low	Within 50	Coast	-	----	North
New Britain - Bristol	5	5	5	5	5	High	Within 50	Other	-	----	North
New Haven	4	4	4	4	4	Low	Within 50	Coast	-	----	North
New Orleans	-	3	3	3	3	Low	50 - 100	Coast	Low	No clear trend	South
New York	1	1	1	1	1	Med.	50 - 100	Coast	Average	Deconcentrating	North
Norfolk - Portsmouth	4	4	5	5	5	High	50 - 100	Coast	Low	No clear trend	South
Ogden	5	5	5	5	5	Med.	Within 50	Other	Low	Deconcentrating	West

Appendix table 1 (cont'd). Characteristics of Metropolitan Areas

Metropolitan area	Size of central city					Growth rate Ave. annual 1900-1950	Distance between central cities (Miles)	Geographic feature	Proportion of population employed in manufacturing	Direction of industrial relocation	Regional location
	1940-[a] 1950	1930-[a] 1940	1920-[a] 1930	1910-[a] 1920	1900-[a] 1910						
Oklahoma City	4	4	4	5	-	High	50 - 100	Other	Low	Deconcentrating	South
Omaha	4	4	4	4	4	Med.	50 - 100	River	Low	Concentrating	North
Orlando	-	-	-	-	-	--	---	---	--	---	--
Peoria	4	4	5	5	5	Low	50 - 100	River	Average	Deconcentrating	North
Philadelphia	1	1	1	1	1	Low	Within 50	River	High	No clear trend	North
Phoenix	5	5	-	-	-	High	100 or more	Other	Low	Deconcentrating	West
Pittsburgh	2	2	2	2	3	Low	Within 50	River	Average	Deconcentrating	North
Pittsfield	5	5	5	5	5	Med.	Within 50	Other	--	No clear trend	North
Portland, Me.	5	5	5	-	-	Low	50 - 100	Coast	--	No clear trend	North
Portland, Oregon	-	-	-	-	-	--	---	---	--	---	--
Providence	3	3	4	4	4	Low	Within 50	Coast	Average	Concentrating	North
Pueblo	-	5	-	-	-	Low	100 or more	Other	Average	---	West
Racine	5	5	5	5	5	Med.	Within 50	Coast	High	No clear trend	North
Raleigh	5	4	4	5	5	High	Within 50	Other	High	No clear trend	South
Reading	4	4	4	4	5	Low	Within 50	River	High	Deconcentrating	North
Richmond	4	4	4	4	5	Med.	50 - 100	River	Average	No clear trend	South
Roanoke	5	5	5	5	5	High	50 - 100	Other	Average	---	South
Rochester	3	3	3	4	4	Low	50 - 100	Coast	High	No clear trend	North
Rockford	5	5	5	5	5	Med.	50 - 100	Other	High	Deconcentrating	West
Sacramento	4	5	5	5	5	High	Within 50	River	Low	Deconcentrating	West
Saginaw	5	5	5	5	5	Med.	Within 50	Coast	High	No clear trend	North
St. Joseph	5	5	5	5	4	Low	Within 50	River	Average	Concentrating	North
St. Louis	-	2	2	2	2	Low	50 - 100	River	Average	No clear trend	North
Salt Lake City	4	4	4	5	-	Med.	Within 50	Other	Low	Deconcentrating	West
San Angelo	5	5	5	5	5	High	100 or more	Other	--	---	South
San Antonio	-	4	4	4	-	High	50 - 100	Other	Low	No clear trend	South
San Bernardino	-	-	-	-	-	--	---	---	--	---	--
San Diego	-	-	-	-	-	--	---	---	--	---	--
San Francisco - Oakland	2	2	2	3	3	Med.	Within 50	Coast	Average	Deconcentrating	West
San Jose	5	5	5	5	5	High	Within 50	Other	Average	---	West
Savannah	5	5	5	5	5	Med.	50 - 100	Coast	Average	Deconcentrating	South
Scranton	4	4	4	4	-	Low	50 - 100	Other	Low	Deconcentrating	North
Seattle	-	-	-	-	-	--	---	---	--	---	--
Shreveport	5	5	5	5	5	High	100 or more	Other	Low	Deconcentrating	South
Sioux City	5	5	5	5	5	Med.	50 - 111	River	Low	Concentrating	North
Sioux Falls	5	5	5	5	5	High	100 or more	Other	Low	Concentrating	West

Appendix table 1 (cont'd). Characteristics of Metropolitan Areas

Metropolitan area	Size of central city					Growth rate Ave. annual 1900-1950	Distance between central cities (Miles)	Geographic feature	Proportion of population employed in manufacturing	Direction of industrial relocation	Regional location
	1940-1950[a]	1930-1940	1920-1930	1910-1920	1900-1910[a]						
South Bend	4	4	5	5	5	Med.	50 - 100	Other	High	No clear trend	North
Spokane	4	4	4	4	-	Low	100 or more	Other	Low	No clear trend	West
Springfield, Ill.	5	5	5	5	5	Med.	Within 50	Other	Low	Deconcentrating	North
Springfield, Mo.	5	5	5	5	5	Med.	100 or more	Other	Low	No clear trend	North
Springfield, O.	5	5	5	5	5	Low	Within 50	Other	High	----	North
Springfield - Holyoke	4	4	4	4	4	Low	Within 50	River	--	No clear trend	North
Stamford - Norwalk	4	5	5	5	5	High	Within 50	Coast	--	----	North
Stockton	5	5	5	5	5	High	Within 50	River	Low	Deconcentrating	West
Syracuse	4	4	4	4	4	Low	Within 50	Other	High	No clear trend	North
Tacoma	-	-	-	-	-	--	---	---	--	----	--
Tampa - St. Petersburg	-	-	-	-	-	--	---	---	--	----	--
Terre-Haute	5	5	5	5	5	Low	50 - 100	River	Average	No clear trend	North
Toledo	3	3	4	4	4	Med.	50 - 100	Coast	Average	No clear trend	North
Topeka	5	5	5	5	5	Med.	50 - 100	Other	Low	Deconcentrating	North
Trenton	4	4	5	5	5	Low	Within 50	River	High	Deconcentrating	North
Tulsa	4	4	5	5	5	High	50 - 100	Other	Low	Concentrating	South
Utica - Rome	4	5	5	5	5	Low	Within 50	Other	High	Deconcentrating	North
Waco	-	5	5	5	5	Med.	50 - 100	Other	Low	No clear trend	South
Washington	2	3	3	3	3	Med.	Within 50	River	Low	No clear trend	South
Waterbury	5	5	5	5	5	Med.	Within 50	Other	High	----	North
Waterloo	5	5	5	5	5	High	Within 50	Other	High	Concentrating	North
Wheeling - Steubenville	5	5	5	5	5	Low	Within 50	River	High	Deconcentrating	North
Wichita	4	4	4	5	5	High	100 or more	Other	Low	No clear trend	North
Wichita Falls	5	5	5	5	5	High	100 or more	Other	Low	No clear trend	North
Wilkes Barre - Hazelton	5	5	5	5	5	Low	Within 50	River	Low	No clear trend	South
Wilmington	4	4	4	5	5	Low	Within 50	River	High	Deconcentrating	South
Winston Salem	5	5	5	5	5	High	50 - 100	Other	High	Deconcentrating	South
Worcester	4	4	4	4	4	Low	Within 50	Other	--	No clear trend	North
York	5	5	5	5	5	Low	Within 50	Other	High	Deconcentrating	North
Youngstown	4	4	5	5	5	Med	Within 50	Other	High	No clear trend	North

[a] 1. 1,000,000 and over
2. 500,000 - 1,000,000
3. 250,000 - 500,000
4. 100,000 - 250,000
5. Under 100,000

[b] Area not in study

Appendix table 2. Population in Standard and Extended Metropolitan Areas at the Beginning and at the End of Each Decade, by Distance Zones, 1900-1950

Type of metropolitan area and distance zone	1950	1940	1940	1930	1930	1920	1920	1910	1910	1900
Standard Metropolitan Areas										
Total	74,752,984	62,433,458	66,280,931	61,376,780	58,980,287	47,234,553	47,120,246	37,842,271	37,558,718	29,025,992
Central cities	41,786,414	37,381,460	39,869,502	37,923,688	36,616,115	30,161,635	29,955,285	23,793,535	23,441,484	17,819,542
All satellite area	32,966,570	25,051,998	26,411,429	23,453,092	22,364,172	17,072,918	17,164,961	14,048,736	14,117,234	11,206,450
0-5 miles	4,834,191	3,911,407	4,157,597	3,764,929	3,680,737	2,914,255	2,966,248	2,293,245	2,349,276	1,836,809
5-10 miles	10,470,630	7,683,032	8,143,176	7,081,167	6,707,428	4,751,580	4,885,371	3,957,916	3,992,008	3,084,990
10-15 miles	7,339,531	5,550,705	5,831,959	5,224,188	4,990,278	3,978,812	3,948,248	3,283,363	3,309,473	2,648,812
15-20 miles	4,277,616	3,218,413	3,456,905	3,047,519	2,803,503	2,112,136	2,113,413	1,734,494	1,711,043	1,392,778
20-25 miles	2,610,197	1,998,310	2,071,679	1,824,863	1,802,416	1,335,055	1,273,736	1,053,780	1,041,052	838,695
25-30 miles	1,430,334	1,160,987	1,198,473	1,096,221	1,025,840	827,762	828,844	696,234	696,550	563,232
30-35 miles	831,193	607,446	617,661	557,011	513,896	439,067	435,701	378,073	366,661	321,009
35 miles and over	1,172,878	921,718	933,979	857,194	840,074	714,251	713,400	651,631	651,171	520,125
Extended Metropolitan Areas										
Total	91,122,250	77,437,212	82,307,268	76,615,719	74,222,515	61,802,003	61,670,397	51,802,434	51,289,678	42,080,553
Central cities	41,786,414	37,381,460	39,869,502	37,923,688	36,616,115	30,161,635	29,955,285	23,793,535	23,441,484	17,819,542
All satellite area	49,335,836	40,055,752	42,437,766	38,692,031	37,606,400	31,640,368	31,715,112	28,008,899	27,848,194	24,261,011
0-5 miles	4,884,181	3,943,641	4,193,325	3,795,353	3,711,162	2,933,521	2,983,264	2,305,724	2,360,980	1,846,940
5-10 miles	10,875,929	8,010,261	8,483,398	7,394,600	7,020,950	5,034,220	5,169,354	4,218,397	4,255,209	3,325,956
10-15 miles	8,611,710	6,628,280	6,948,762	6,268,821	6,042,476	4,969,936	4,946,561	4,230,105	4,230,693	3,531,682
15-20 miles	6,777,444	5,441,637	5,789,931	5,253,110	5,014,591	4,176,670	4,166,592	3,712,300	3,661,804	3,237,838
20-25 miles	5,557,407	4,690,548	4,929,361	4,540,644	4,502,060	3,943,385	3,890,566	3,590,040	3,551,191	3,223,354
25-30 miles	4,838,783	4,296,974	4,529,708	4,247,706	4,164,739	3,849,067	3,831,948	3,564,917	3,506,511	3,230,033
30-35 miles	3,771,849	3,370,229	3,627,702	3,433,480	3,397,176	3,174,721	3,163,734	2,970,855	2,930,130	2,765,378
35 miles and over	4,018,533	3,674,182	3,935,579	3,768,317	3,753,246	3,558,848	3,563,093	3,416,561	3,351,676	3,099,830

CHAPTER 1

1. See R. D. McKenzie, *The Metropolitan Community* (New York: The McGraw-Hill Co., 1933), for an extensive treatment of metropolitan development.

2. The term area, or Standard Metropolitan Area, was first used in 1950, and is defined on pp. 7-9 of this report. In prior census years the term employed was Metropolitan District the definition of which changed from census to census. See W. S. Thompson, *The Growth of Metropolitan Districts in the United States: 1900-1940* (Washington, D. C.: U. S. Government Printing Office, 1947) for a statement of the various definitions used.

3. R. D. McKenzie, *op. cit.;* Amos H. Hawley and Donald J. Bogue, "Recent Shifts in Population: The Drift toward the Metropolitan District," *The Review of Economic Statistics,* XXIV (Aug., 1942), 143-48; W. S. Thompson, *op. cit.;* Donald J. Bogue, *Population Growth in Standard Metropolitan Areas, 1900-1950* (Washington, D. C.: U. S. Government Printing Office, 1953).

4. 1950 Census of Population. *Population of Standard Metropolitan Areas: April 1, 1950* (U. S. Bureau of the Census: Washington, D. C., 1950), Series PC-3, pp. 1 and 3.

5. The number of zones is often less than eight in Standard Metropolitan Areas because of the definition which results in many instances in one county areas.

CHAPTER II

1. Centrifugal is used here and elsewhere in this report in a relative sense. None of the data employed throw any light on the sources of population growth in metropolitan areas. Centrifugal, then, means simply that the effect of differential growth is to increase the population in the satellite areas relative to that of central cities, regardless of whether the added population originates from the center of from outside the metropolitan area.

2. For other uses of this measure see National Resources Planning Board, *Industrial Location and National Policy* (Wash., D. C.: U. S. Gov. Printing Office), E. M. Hoover, Jr. "Interstate Redistribution of Population, 1850-1940", *The Journal of Economic History,* Vol. I (Nov., 1941), pp. 199-205.

3. It is interesting to note that the number of incorporated satellite places tends to double successively in each smaller size class, especially in Extended Metropolitan Areas. No doubt the rate of progression is a function of the class interval, yet it seems likely that some geometric pattern might appear regardless of class interval size. There is here a suggestion of a tendency to equilibrium in the number and size distribution of service subcenters such as was proposed by Christaller *(Die Zentralen Orte Suddeutschlands,* Jena, 1933).

CHAPTER IV

1. Appendix Table 1 lists the metropolitan areas in each class.

CHAPTER V

1. Measures of distance were obtained from: C. A. Whitten, *Air-Lines Distances Between Cities in the United States,* U. S. Dept. of Commerce, Coast and Geodetic Survey, Special Publication No. 238. (U. S. Gov't Printing Office: Washington, D. C., 1947).

CHAPTER VI

1. Use was made of the map of "Principal Waterways of the United States" (Army Map Service, Corps of Engineers, Dept. of the Army, 1942) to identify river locations.

2. This is not to over-look air transportation. The major concern here, however, is with surface means of transport.

3. See R. D. McKenzie, *op. cit.,* Chs. X, XI, and XII.

4. These are: Atlanta; Buffalo; Chicago; Columbus, O.; Dallas; Detroit; Indianapolis; Louisville; Milwaukee; Minneapolis; Rochester; St. Louis; and San Francisco.

CHAPTER VII

1. See D. J. Bogue, *The Structure of the Metropolitan Community,* Ch. XIV.

CHAPTER VIII

1. As reported in the *Census of Manufacturers,* 1899, 1909, 1929, 1939, 1948.

CHAPTER IX

1. See Appendix Table 1.

CHAPTER X

1. See Appendix Table 1.

BOOKS PUBLISHED BY

The Free Press